Religious Education and
Freedom of Religion and Belief

Religion, Education and Values

SERIES EDITORS:

Dr Stephen Parker
The Rev'd Canon Professor Leslie J. Francis
Dr Rob Freathy
Dr Mandy Robbins

Volume 2

PETER LANG

Oxford • Bern • Berlin • Bruxelles • Frankfurt am Main • New York • Wien

Religious Education and Freedom of Religion and Belief

Stephen Parker, Rob Freathy and Leslie J. Francis (eds)

PETER LANG

Oxford • Bern • Berlin • Bruxelles • Frankfurt am Main • New York • Wien

Bibliographic information published by Die Deutsche Nationalbibliothek.
Die Deutsche Nationalbibliothek lists this publication in the Deutsche National-
bibliografie; detailed bibliographic data is available on the Internet at
http://dnb.d-nb.de.

A catalogue record for this book is available from the British Library.

Library of Congress Cataloging-in-Publication Data:

Parker, Stephen
 Religious education and freedom of religion and belief / Stephen
Parker, Rob Freathy and Leslie J. Francis.
    p. cm.
 Includes bibliographical references and index.
 ISBN 978-3-0343-0754-3 (alk. paper)
 1. Religious education--Cross-cultural studies. 2. Religious
freedom--Cross-cultural studies. 3. Moral education--Cross-cultural
studies. I. Freathy, Rob. II. Francis, Leslie J. III. Title.
 BV1471.3.P35 2012
 268--dc23

                        2012020555

Cover image © HuHu Lin, www.fotolia.com

ISSN 2235-4638
ISBN 978-3-0343-0754-3

© Peter Lang AG, International Academic Publishers, Bern 2012
Hochfeldstrasse 32, CH-3012 Bern, Switzerland
info@peterlang.com, www.peterlang.com, www.peterlang.net

Printed in Germany

Contents

Foreword

The International Seminar on Religious Education and Values (ISREV, http://www.isrev.org) is the most important international association in the field of Religious Education. It is an association of 233 Religious Education scholars from 36 countries. A major seminar session is organized in a different country every two years, with the seventeenth having taken place in Canada in 2010. ISREV was founded in 1978 by John M. Hull, the distinguished Australian academic (currently Honorary Professor of Practical Theology at The Queen's Foundation, and Emeritus Professor of Religious Education at the University of Birmingham), and John H. Peatling, then of the Character Research Project in Union College, Schenectady, New York. The first meeting had research papers from thirty-two scholars attending from ten countries. The seventeenth meeting, in Ottawa, Canada, had research papers from 110 scholars attending from over thirty countries. ISREV has no religious basis or test itself, and has members specializing, for example, in Protestant and Catholic Christian, Jewish, Muslim, and secular traditions. Educationists and policy makers from across the world are interested in the work of ISREV, with members of the government in host countries regularly attending the seminars. In this time of conflict over religion in almost every country of the world, dialogue is needed more than ever.

Each seminar has a broad theme, and the theme for the Ottawa meeting was Religious Education and freedom of religion and belief. That theme is a clear marker of the deliberate attempt of researchers to influence policy makers, professional practitioners, and learners around the world. This book is one of the results of the seminar, a selection of roughly one in ten of the papers presented – a powerful argument for the contribution of Religious Education to freedom in the modern world. Religion is continuing to find its place in a more open and more diverse society, and Religious Education can help people not only understand religions but also understand how they can work together in a more free political system. The diversity in society is not only a religious diversity, but also a diversity that includes secular humanism and other 'worldviews' or 'stances for living' – that is, other ways of being and becoming outside religions or religious traditions. Freedom of religion and belief means little if the societies claiming such freedom create a pretence of a wholly neutral or independent space from which people can 'peer over the wall' at religious or other ways of being. Ecological campaigners say 'Don't throw anything away: there is no place called "away". With respect to both religion and education, there is, similarly, no place called 'neutral'. Everywhere is somewhere, and chapters in this book investigate the history of the development of Religious Education, in particular countries such as England, Canada, South Africa, and Latvia. This is one of the many joys of ISREV. Researchers from around the world come together with their own understandings and their own contexts in order to listen to and talk with people with other understandings and from other contexts.

The philosopher Martin Buber wrote that dialogue is important, not because we should give up our own positions, but because we should make the imaginative leap to the reality of the other person. As Buber's colleague and biographer said of him, 'the I-Thou relationship [initially described in Buber's *I and Thou*] "teaches us to meet others and to hold our ground when we meet them", ... [which] goes hand in hand with remaining on one's own side of the relationship' (Maurice Friedman in the introduction to Buber, 2002: xiii–xiv; see also Friedman, 1999). A number of the chapters in this book refer to dialogue in Religious Education classrooms, as well as political and academic dialogue. None of this is – or should be – the timid dialogue of pretended neutrality or weak compromise, but the robust dialogue amongst people who have and may retain fundamental differences.

I am delighted, as General Secretary of ISREV, to commend this book to its readers. It is itself a contribution to dialogue amongst researchers and all interested in Religious Education, and an example of dialogue amongst the authors themselves. ISREV lives by the vigour of its dialogue, and if this in turn contributes to freedom of religion and belief, then the value of the research completed by its members, the seminar in Ottawa, and the exemplary material in this volume, will be all the more valuable.

Julian Stern
General Secretary of ISREV

References

Buber, M. (2002). *Between man and man*. London: Routledge.
Friedman, M. (1999). The interhuman and what is common to all: Martin Buber and sociology. *Journal for the Theory of Social Behaviour, 29*(4), 403–417.

STEPHEN PARKER, ROB FREATHY AND LESLIE J. FRANCIS

Introduction

Article 18 of the Universal Declaration of Human Rights (General Assembly of the United Nations, 1948) asserts that:

> Everyone has the right to freedom of thought, conscience and religion; this right included freedom to change his religion or belief, and freedom, either alone or in community with others and in public or private, to manifest his religion or belief in teaching, practice, worship and observance.

This clear statement of the basic human right for freedom of religion and belief provides huge opportunities and significant challenges for Religious Education and for religious educators across the globe. It was discussion of these opportunities and challenges that inspired the seventeenth session of the International Seminar on Religious Education and Values (ISREV), convened at St Paul University, Ottawa, Canada, during July 2010. This volume on *Religious Education and Freedom of Religion and Belief* draws together some of the key work stimulated and nurtured by that meeting of the seminar.

The International Seminar on Religious Education and Values was formed in Birmingham University, England, in 1978 and has continued to meet every other year across Europe and North America. The Seminar now draws together over 223 leading researchers in Religious Education from 36 countries, embracing a variety of religious and secular traditions concerned with many different aspects of Religious Education relevant both to secular schools and to faith communities. Such informed diversity brought a rich range of perspectives to the theme of Religious Education and freedom of religion and belief. In the present volume this diversity is reflected by organizing key contributions within three categories: historical perspectives, theoretical perspectives, and empirical perspectives.

The first section on historical perspectives draws together four detailed and informed discussions of developments in England, Canada, Latvia and Australia. From England, Rob Freathy and Stephen Parker draw on a wide range of previously neglected or unutilized primary documentary sources to illustrate a covert agenda underpinning the significant transitions which took place in Religious Education theory and policy in the late 1960s and 1970s. From Canada, Lorna M. A. Bowman draws on primary and secondary sources to provide an overview of the development of publicly-funded religious schools across Canada and the social and political forces at work, with particular attention to Newfoundland, Ontario and Quebec. From Latvia, Dzintra Iliško charts the transition of Latvian society from a monolithic soviet worldview to a state of religious diversity, and the impact of this transition on Religious Education in schools since 1991. From Australia, Peta Goldburg analyses the continuing significance of the series of Education Acts passed by various Australian States in the late 1800s for current opportunities and challenges facing Religious Education within the nation as a whole. Together, these four chapters provide a powerful reminder of how current connections between Religious Education and freedom of religion and belief are both facilitated and constrained by historical contexts.

The second section on theoretical perspectives draws together six discussions articulated by religious educators from England, South Africa, Canada, Sweden and Germany. From England, Jeff Astley distinguishes a freedom *for* religious belief from a deeper freedom *of* belief in the sense of an 'inner freedom' of human beings to control their religious state of mind, heart and spirit. Also from England, Brian Gates explores the concept of 'conscience' in connection with the personally-centred process of making moral sense within both religious and secular traditions. From South Africa, Petro du Preez presses the case that not just Religious Education but also the whole curriculum should be profoundly moral, human-rights orientated and should create enabling spaces for human beings to express their freedom of religion(s) and belief(s). From Canada, Mario O. D'Souza enquires into the possibility, place and implications of first principles in the context of religious and cultural pluralism. He argues that, although the freedom of religion and belief rise above the terrestrial limits of political society, they are neither independent of such society, nor are the dispositions and convictions of one's religion and belief unrelated to the terrestrial pursuit of the common good. From Sweden, Karin Nordström discusses the paradox of education for freedom when educational interventions themselves restrict freedom. From Germany, Manfred L. Pirner discusses whether religious schools are able to promote the human right of freedom of religion and belief, and contribute to the common good in pluralist societies. Together these six chapters provide a powerful reminder of the complexity of the issues raised by the interface between human rights and issues concerning freedom of religion and belief. Clear thinking and clarity of expression are crucial for the proper engagement of Religious Education in this field.

The third section on empirical perspectives draws together three discussions from South Africa, England, and Australia. From South Africa, René Ferguson investigates how participation by teachers in a learning community, a community of practice, contributes toward improving their professional knowledge base for Religious Education as a focus area for Citizenship Education. From England, Kevin O'Grady also discusses the contribution to research made by a community of practice. He illustrates this contribution by focusing on the experience of secondary-age Religious Education pupils and how they might exercise freedom of belief during lessons. From Australia, Jan Grajczonek reports on part of a qualitative study conducted in the early years within a Catholic primary school. Using Conversation Analysis and Membership Categorization Analysis, she identifies how teachers were construing young children as all belonging to, and sharing, the same religious beliefs. Together these three chapters provide a powerful reminder of how the debate regarding the connection between Religious Education, human rights, and freedom of religion and belief need to be informed not only by historical and theoretical perspectives, but also by giving close attention to the empirical reality as experienced by schools and expressed by pupils.

PART I

Historical Perspectives

ROB FREATHY AND STEPHEN PARKER

1 Freedom from Religious Beliefs: Humanists and Religious Education in England in the 1960s and 1970s

Abstract

On the basis of an analysis of a wide range of previously neglected or unutilized primary documentary sources, this chapter argues that the significant transitions which took place in Religious Education theory and policy in England in the late 1960s and early 1970s were, at least in part, catalyzed by a concerted and organized campaign by the British Humanist Association with the intention of either abolishing Religious Education, establishing a secular alternative (such as moral education) or secularizing the subject's aims and broadening its content to include world religions and secular worldviews. Notable Humanists, such as Harold Blackham, and many liberal Christians and Religious Education academics and professionals, sought together to develop educationally valid and multi-faith forms of 'open' Religious Education and moral education which would be suitable for all pupils and teachers regardless of their religious or secular backgrounds. These arguments are exemplified through a case study of the *Birmingham Agreed Syllabus of Religious Instruction* published in 1975. This was influenced by the then Chairman of the British Humanist Association, Harry Stopes-Roe, and generated much controversy, primarily for its inclusion of secular 'stances for living', of which Communism was the most contentious. The contribution of Humanists to the secularization, or at least extensive liberalization, of the aims of Religious Education has been severely underplayed in the existing historiography.

Introduction

In an article in the *British Journal of Religious Education*, we promoted rigorous historical studies that are grounded in the appropriate historiography, utilize a wide range of original documentary and non-documentary primary sources and contextualize Religious Education in its wider political, social and cultural milieu (Freathy & Parker, 2010). We also advocated using such a methodology to explore the contemporary debate concerning the significant transition which took place in the nature and purpose of Religious Education in England in the late 1960s and early 1970s. For some, this has been characterized as a shift from child-centred, neo-confessional, Christian instruction to phenomenological, *non-confessional*, multi-faith Religious Education (Parsons, 1994: 173–174), whilst for others it represents a shift to a new moderate, liberal, ecumenical and in certain respects secular confessionalism (Barnes & Wright, 2006: 65–66). In our current research, we are focusing particularly upon the *Birmingham Agreed Syllabus for Religious Instruction* published in 1975 (City of Birmingham Education Committee, 1975a).

In England, since the 1944 Education Act, it has been a statutory requirement to provide weekly Religious Instruction (RI) (or Religious Education as it came to be known) and daily Collective Worship in every state-maintained school to all pupils, except those wholly or partly withdrawn by their parents. In fully state-maintained schools, as opposed to those partially funded by faith communities, Religious Education has been defined by Agreed Syllabuses drawn up by local conferences that consist of four committees representing the Anglican Church of England, other denominations, teacher associations and the Local Education Authority (LEA). In contrast to the dominant tradition up until that point, the Birmingham Agreed Syllabus (BAS) sought to provide an 'educational' rationale for Religious Education directed 'towards developing a critical understanding of the religious and moral dimensions of human experience and away from attempting to foster the claims of particular religious standpoints' (City of Birmingham Education Committee, 1975a: 4).

Furthermore, it provided a multi-faith approach from the first year of primary school, which covered six world religions and required pupils to compare and contrast religious and non-religious 'stances for living'. While Humanism was specifically mentioned in the statutory syllabus, Communism was specified as an alternative in the accompanying non-statutory handbook for teachers (City of Birmingham Education Committee, 1975b). Overall, the BAS included requirements for a form of Religious Education that has been referred to as a 'major breakthrough' (Hull, 1984: 29) and as 'the total revolution of subject matter' (Priestley, 2006: 1012).

The existing historiography has contextualized curriculum change in Religious Education in English schools in the 1960s and 1970s with regard to many factors, but too frequently the BAS has been described simply as a product of a particular theological outlook (e.g. Ninian Smart's phenomenological approach to the study of religion combined with John Hick's pluralist theology) or merely as a de-contextualized staging-post in the development of Agreed Syllabuses and/or Religious Education pedagogical theory. To address this, and other historiographical deficiencies, we have sought to provide a detailed case study of the formation and implementation of the BAS – and wider developments and changes in Religious Education – within a broader historical context and with recourse to relevant secondary sources, published and unpublished documentary primary sources and life history interviews (see Parker & Freathy, 2011a, 2011b). This chapter deals with one particularly noticeable feature of the evidence so far, namely, the influence of Humanist individuals, such as Harry Stopes-Roe and Harold J. Blackham, and organizations, such as the British Humanist Association, upon Religious Education theories and policies.

The Birmingham Agreed Syllabus in public and political discourse

Once the drafting of the new BAS had commenced, Harry Stopes-Roe (1924–) (Senior Lecturer in Science Studies in the Extra Mural Department, University of Birmingham) became highly influential in promoting the inclusion of Humanism in the syllabus and monitoring the extent to which it endorsed faith-nurturing aims. Stopes-Roe was Chairman of the British Humanist Association (BHA) and a co-opted member of two of the syllabus' working parties. His co-option was largely due to considerable and persistent lobbying by local Humanists as well as his friendship with John Hick (then H. G. Wood Professor of Theology, University of Birmingham) who was Chairman of the syllabus's Co-ordinating Working Party. It was Stopes-Roe who coined 'stances for living' as an inclusive term used in the syllabus to describe both secular and religious ways of life.

The original version of the BAS was completed in Autumn 1973, but there were objections to its inclusion of non-religious 'stances for living' and questions were raised about whether the single-page syllabus fulfilled the legal requirements of the 1944 Education Act. This protestation helped to generate the publicity which ensured that the BAS brought significant new trends in Religious Education in England 'vividly before the general public for the first time' (Hull, 1984: 29, 83, 85). In the context of a level of paranoia about the influence of political extremism – especially Communism – upon British society in the 1970s, a lengthy correspondence was published in both *The Birmingham Post* and the Birmingham *Evening Mail* about the inclusion of Communism within the curriculum documentation with headlines such as 'Subversion', 'Communist textbook', 'The teaching of communism' and 'Happy Marx' (Copley, 2008: 107). Furthermore, in response to attempts to bring about 'a fundamental public debate on the role of Religious Education', local comparisons were drawn 'with Tennessee's celebrated "monkey trial" in 1925' in which John Scopes, a County High School teacher, was tried for teaching the theory of evolution in violation of a recently passed state law (Ezard, 1974).

On 10 February 1974, *The Observer* – a national newspaper – published an article on its front page titled 'Reds-under-the-crib row' in which Neil Scrimshaw, the Conservative Party spokesperson for education on Birmingham City Council, described the syllabus as 'a complete manual on how to teach Communism under the guise of Religious Education'. A year later, in an article in *The Guardian* (Scrimschaw, 1975), Scrimshaw continued, 'We object first and foremost in principle to an irreligion or an antireligion being presented together with religious faiths. ... It is opening the floodgates to a study of communism in a religious atmosphere. We regard it as a licence both to preach and to teach Communism.' As the controversy continued, there was a debate about the BAS in the House of Lords on 26 March 1975 (Hansard, Vol. 358, Cols. 1171–1175), which gained coverage in *The Times* under the headline 'Communism in Religious Education' (27 March 1975). The debate was opened by Lord Gisborough who asked the Labour Government, first, whether it approved 'of the decision of Birmingham Education Committee that the teaching of Communism should be included in their new religious education syllabus', and second, whether Lord Crowther-Hunt, as Minister of State for Education (1974–1976), '[w]ould agree that Communism has nothing to do with religion, or, if it has, then so has the teaching of the philosophies of Conservatism, Fascism and Socialism' and 'that the teachers' handbook, while containing 150 favourable references, does not mention Labour camps, the KGB and the like' (Cols. 1171–1172). In response, Lord Crowther-Hunt declared that the government 'does not exercise powers over what is taught in the schools' and that 'we do not want to reach a position in which the Secretary of State in any Government, can actually dictate what is taught in the schools' (Col. 1174). All bar one of the other explicit references to the BAS in parliamentary discussions in the 1970s criticized its inclusion of secular 'stances for living', particularly Communism.

Subsequent legal advice recommended extending and clarifying the aims and content of the syllabus, particularly to ensure that non-religious subject matter was used to advance instruction in religion rather than taught for its own sake (Stopes-Roe, 1976: 134; Hull, 1984: 85). In response, a letter in *The Times* from representatives of the BHA, including Harold Blackham, Francis Crick, Hans Eysenck and Harold Pinter, stated, 'If the courts uphold these opinions – or if Birmingham implicitly accepts them by rejecting the syllabus – the case for reform of the religious provisions of the 1944 Education Act will surely be irresistible. Not only the Humanists and religious minorities, who have long denounced it as discriminatory, but many mainstream Christians and the vast majority of teachers and educationists will find this legal barrier to continued development of the subject intolerable' ('Religious education', 28 June 1974). Contrary to their wishes, a revised version of the syllabus was published in May 1975, but the debates continued, for example, at a designated conference at Manchester College, Oxford in March 1976 and in a Special Feature on 'The Birmingham Syllabus & Handbook 1975' in *Learning for Living* (15[4], 1976).

In the *Learning for Living* Special Issue, Stopes-Roe criticized the revisions that were made between the 1973 and 1975 versions of the BAS. He argued that the original syllabus had been fair and balanced with respect to religious and non-religious 'stances for living', but that the final version was 'dominated by religion' (1976: 133). This was evident in regard to two elements: first, 'the material as a whole is slanted in a religious direction', and second, 'particularly for the younger ages, fundamental emotional forces [e.g. wonder, mystery and love] are taken over by religion' (Stopes-Roe, 1976: 135). It was also evident in the contrasting statements regarding the purposes of Religious Education in the 1973 and 1975 versions of the syllabus. The original version stated (Stopes-Roe, 1976: 134) (our italics added):

> The purpose of 'religious education' is not only to enlarge and deepen the understanding of the different *stances for living* to which different people are committed but also in some cases to stimulate within the pupils a personal search for meaning and in others to illuminate a sense of meaning which they already have.

By contrast, the final version stated that the purpose is (our italics added):

> to enlarge and deepen the pupils' understanding of *religion* by studying world religions, and by exploring all those elements in human experience which raise questions about life's ultimate meaning and value. This involves informing pupils in a

descriptive, critical and experiential manner about what *religion* is, and increasing their sensitivity to the areas of experience from which a *religious* view of life may arise. It should stimulate within the pupils, and assist them in the search for, a personal sense of meaning in life, whilst enabling them to understand the beliefs and commitments of others.

Stopes-Roe (1976: 135) argued that the realization of the aim to increase pupils' 'sensitivity to the areas of experience from which a religious view of life may arise' would establish 'religious indoctrination'. His charges were refuted, rather unconvincingly, by John Hick (1976) and John Hull (1976b). The primary issue at stake was whether Religious Education could justifiably prioritize religious aims, methods and/or content and, if not, whether it could continue as a 'compulsory' curriculum subject in its current form.

Stopes-Roe's criticisms of the partiality of the final version of the syllabus were also evident in the BHA's pamphlet *Objective, Fair and Balanced: A New Law for Religion in Education* which was co-authored by Stopes-Roe and published in October 1975. On the assumption that it is improper for fully state-maintained schools in a religiously plural society to bias children for or against religion (British Humanist Association, 1975: 35), the BHA advocated repealing and amending the religious clauses in the 1944 Education Act so as to replace Religious Education with 'Education in Stances for Living'. This new curriculum subject would provide pupils with an opportunity to be educated together in an objective, fair and balanced manner about the religious and non-religious outlooks and systems of belief upon which people build their lives (British Humanist Association, 1975: 32). To facilitate this, the pamphlet presented 'a draft Bill' (British Humanist Association, 1975: 1) ready to be introduced in the next Session of Parliament as a Private Members Bill by Mr Geoffrey Edge (Labour Member of Parliament). In fact, Edge got no further than submitting a written question – answered negatively – to the Secretary of State for Education and Science to ask whether he would remove the compulsory act of Collective Worship in fully state-maintained schools and replace compulsory Religious Instruction with optional teaching of comparative religious and non-religious studies for life (Hansard, House of Commons,

7 November 1975, Vol. 899, Col. 328). It was the third such question to
have been asked in the House of Commons that year about the statutory requirements for Religious Education in the 1944 Education Act (4
February and 6 May 1975). At the time, Hull (1976a: 123) argued that
the religious clauses of the 1944 Education Act were not under serious
political threat, but the possibility of abolition was palpable enough to per-
suade Raymond Johnstone (Director of the Nationwide Festival of Light
movement), the Marchioness of Lothian (Chair of the Order of Christian
Unity), Charles Oxley (Headmaster of Scarisbrick Hall School) and Mary
Whitehouse (Honorary General Secretary of the National Viewers and
Listeners Association) to launch the 'Save Religion in State Schools' campaign on 27 January 1976.

The above account provides evidence that individual Humanists, such
as Harry Stopes-Roe, and the BHA more generally, sought to influence
the development of, and subsequent discourse about, the BAS of 1975.
However, our in-depth study of primary sources shows that the influence
of the BHA was felt in Birmingham at least as early as 1967 when work
on the BAS had not even begun. The Reverend D. J. W. Bradley (a senior
Anglican cleric, member of the LEA's Standing Advisory Council for
Religious Education and Diocesan Director of Education) opined that it
is 'no longer possible automatically to claim for Christianity an exclusively
privileged status in public education without an affront to the liberty
of the citizen'. Moreover, perceiving the reconsideration of the aims of
Religious Education as an opportunity rather than a threat, he continued, 'we Christians need not despair ... We readily recognize that a more
"open" approach to both religious education and the daily act of collective
worship ... is now dictated by progressive thought outside and inside the
Churches' (*The Birmingham Post*, 24 October 1967). In this regard, Bradley
referred explicitly to the BHA's *Religion in Schools: Humanist Proposals
for State-Aided Schools in England and Wales* (1967) (see below) and the
organization's ongoing campaign to reform or repeal the religious clauses
of the 1944 Education Act.

Harold Blackham and the BHA

The BHA had its roots in the Union of Ethical Societies which was founded in 1895 by the American Stanton Coit (1857–1944) (Royle, 1994: 419). Ethicists envisaged 'a universal and synoptic morality which would unite individuals of different creeds' (Wright, 2008: 811). One of their initiatives was the formation of the Moral Instruction League in England in 1897 to promote systematic and secular moral instruction based on social or civic morality rather than duty to God. After the First World War, the League was abolished and the Union of Ethical Societies fell into decline, that is, until 1963 when the BHA was founded through an alliance of the Union of Ethical Societies and the Rationalist Press Association (est. 1899). (The second organization withdrew after legal problems in 1967.) The inaugural meeting of the BHA was held in the House of Commons with A. J. Ayer (Wykeham Professor of Logic, University of Oxford and President of the BHA, 1965–1970) among those present. From its inception, the BHA began campaigning for the elimination of world poverty, the repeal of Sunday Observance Laws, freedom of speech, the removal of privileges given to religious groups, and the reform of the 1944 Education Act.

The BHA's first Executive Director (1963–1968) was Harold J. Blackham (1903–2009). Blackham's family background was in Congregationalism. Both his father and grandfather had been Congregationalist preachers (Copson, 2009, January 27). He had studied English and Ethics at Birmingham University, before spending two years teaching Divinity, History and English at Doncaster Grammar School ('Obituary', 2009b). There, he felt impelled to extend the boundaries of the Divinity syllabus 'to deal with the difficult questions he was wrestling with himself' (Smoker, 2009). Then, having taken up work as a freelance lecturer and writer, he underwent an intellectual crisis in which he rejected 'all forms of supernatural religion', whilst retaining 'an intensely moral view of the world', and exhibiting a determination to work 'ecumenically and equally with religious and non-religious individuals and organizations on the basis of the common values of all people of good will' ('Obituary', 2009b). In 1935, Blackham succeeded Stanton Coit as minister at the Ethical Church in Bayswater and as Chairman of the Union of Ethical Societies (Taylor, 2009: 247). In 1938, he helped to organize a World Union of Freethinkers conference in London which was 'the last manifestation of the old international free-thought movement before the twin onslaught of fascism and communism' ('Obituary', 2009b). In 1945, Blackham launched a quarterly magazine, *The Plain View*, which lasted for 20 years and drew contributions from individuals, such as the first director-general of UNESCO, Julian Huxley, and the classical scholar, Gilbert Murray ('Obituary', 2009b). Having organized another World Union of Freethinkers conference in 1946, with the theme of 'The Challenge of Humanism', Blackham decided that the organization was too old-fashioned for the new needs of society. Instead he worked with other 'Freethinkers' internationally, such as the Dutch philosopher and Humanist leader Jaap van Praag, to develop the International Humanist and Ethical Union which was established in 1952 with Huxley as its first President and Blackham as Secretary-General. Blackham's subsequent writings included books, such as *Six Existentialist Thinkers* (1952), *The Human Tradition* (1953), *Political Discipline in a Free Society* (1961), *Religion in a Modern Society* (1966) and *Humanism* (1968), as well as edited works, such as *Objections to Humanism* (1963) in which Humanists responded to criticisms of the Humanist worldview. By this time, his efforts to bring the Ethical and Rationalist organizations in Britain together had led to the formation of the BHA of which he was the effective founder (Copson, 2009, January 27).

In terms of education, Blackham had a lifelong commitment to moral education and worked with people like Cyril Bibby, Lionel Elvin, Sir Gilbert Flemming and Edward Blishen to make the BHA a significant advocate of moral education and personal development in schools ('Obituary', 2009a). In terms of Religious Education, Blackham (1964: 19) argued that 'religion in state schools' should adopt 'a genuine [open] educational approach that is not a Christian monopoly' and which can 'conciliate non-Christians and gain the support of all genuine educators'. The aims of such a programme would include a commitment to moral development based upon a 'common foundation in social morality and personal relations' (Blackham, 1964: 19). According to Blackham (1964: 20), this would inevitably lead to consideration of the fundamental sets of beliefs, allegiances and values, namely Abrahamic monotheism, Indian metaphysics, politico-cultural absolutes (e.g. Marxism and Fascism) and Humanism, as well as the confrontations and dialogues between them. Blackham (1964: 20) hoped that such an approach would meet the 'real needs of the growing child' and concentrate 'upon the attainment of responsible living and thinking'. If this change did not occur, he threatened 'an increasing demand on the part of Humanists for alternative courses in the secondary schools and the training colleges' (Blackham, 1964: 19). In a later publication, Blackham (1969: 3) also argued that it was unrealistic and unwise to expect 'the nation' to determine the philosophical foundations of moral education in state schools. This could only be derived from the shared tasks and ideals of school communities themselves which must seek to enable pupils 'to think for themselves and to make their own responsible decisions' (Blackham, 1969: 6).

Some of Blackham's proposals were endorsed by the BHA's *Religion in Schools: Humanist Proposals for State-Aided Schools in England and Wales* (1967) which was referred to by Bradley above. It argued that fully state-maintained schools should develop new ways of teaching about Christianity and other religions and ways of life, such as through History, Literature and Social Studies. They should also develop 'methods of moral education not related to religious beliefs, using all aspects of school life as well as the opportunities that the classroom can give' (British Humanist Association, 1967: 14; see Hill, 1967). These recommendations, and the requisite amendments to the 1944 Education Act, could be justified on the basis that:

(i) 'a harmful conflict' may develop between the teaching and practice of the school and home (British Humanist Association, 1967: 3);

(ii) the rights of pupils and teachers to withdraw from Collective Worship and Religious Education were not working (British Humanist Association, 1967: 6); and

(iii) moral education should not be based on widely questioned beliefs and sanctions, but on the common values, influences and experiences of the whole-school community (British Humanist Association, 1967: 8).

Humanists, liberal Christians and religious educators

In contrast to their largely negative public and political reception, the arguments of Humanists found a more sympathetic hearing amongst liberal and ecumenically-minded Christians and Religious Education academics and professionals. In 1965, *Religious and Moral Education: Some Proposals for County Schools by a Group of Christians and Humanists* was published by a group of Christians (including Colin Alves, F. H. Hilliard and Roy Niblett) and BHA members (including Harold Blackham, James Hemming and Paul H. Hirst). The twenty-two authors agreed that pupils in fully state-maintained schools 'need to be taught about the Christian religion as part of their cultural history' and 'have the opportunity to share in an experience of the Christian religion as part of their total education' (Alves et al., 1965: 2). However, Religious Education should adopt a genuinely 'open approach' to help pupils make 'as freely as possible' their own personal commitments (Alves et al., 1965: 2). To avoid the possibility that a rejection of religion may remove any moral foundation, the authors agreed that moral education in secondary schools 'should be explicitly planned to help [pupils] prepare themselves for responsible living' and to consider 'the nature and destiny' of humankind (Alves et al., 1965: 3). In the Sixth Form (sixteen- to eighteen-year-olds), for example, they called for a compulsory course in moral and religious education including 'some study of religions other than Christianity and of [non-religious] ideologies such as communism' (Alves et al., 1965: 4). Lower down the secondary school, they called for provision by teams of teachers with varied beliefs and standpoints, the use of discussion-based methods relating to real-life issues, and an emphasis on common moral values (Alves et al., 1965: 7–10), whilst in primary schools, they advocated classrooms characterized by honesty, sincerity and respectfulness, and the presentation of common moral values in such a way that pupils remain free to develop their own values (Alves et al., 1965: 11–12).

Perhaps it was an indication of the esteem with which he was held and the credible position that Humanism had attained for itself that Blackham was invited to present a paper at the conference on comparative religion held in Shap, in Cumbria, at Easter 1969, which led to the formation of the Shap Working Party on World Religions in Education under the auspices of Ninian Smart, John Hinnells and Geoffrey Parrinder. Blackham (1970: 55–56) supported the comparative study of religion because:

(i) 'education is broadened by including some acquaintance with the diversity of cultures in the world';
(ii) education would be deepened because '[s]tandards are formed only by comparisons'; and
(iii) it provides 'an opportunity for the study of religion as such, as a distinctive type of experience'.

Nevertheless, the purpose of such study was not to provide pupils with 'a faith to live by', but 'to give some insight into different ways of thinking about the world and human life, some sense of the history of ideas, some understanding of distinctively religious experience and claims' (Blackham, 1970: 57). For him, Religious Education as defined by the 1944 Education Act, moral education and comparative religion represented three independent programmes of study, and, in the interests of increased flexibility and professional rather than ecclesiastical control, he called for the repeal of the religious clauses of the 1944 Education Act because they were no longer related to contemporary actualities or educational needs (Blackham, 1970: 57).

In 1967, the Social Morality Council (SMC) (later the Norham Foundation) was co-founded by the BHA for 'joint study and action on moral issues by religious and non-believers' and 'to promote morality in all aspects of the life of the community' (Social Morality Council, 1970: 1). It was comprised of Anglicans, Roman Catholics, members of the Free Churches, Jews, Humanists, educational professionals and members of the wider community (Taylor, 2009). Its President was B. C. Butler (1902–1986) (Roman Catholic Auxiliary Bishop of Westminster) and its Vice-President was the Humanist Lord Ritchie-Calder (1906–1982) (Professor of International Relations, Edinburgh University). Butler believed that the SMC was the latest and most significant manifestation of ecumenism because it sought a '[r]approchement between religious believers and non-believers' which is where 'the cleavage of society is most acute'. Thereby, he hoped 'common ground' could be found 'to face the vast moral issues of our time' (Social Morality Council, 1970: 1). A working party of the SMC published *Moral and Religious Education in County Schools* (1970). It was chaired by Blackham and its membership included Christians, Humanists, Jews and observers from Her Majesty's Inspectorate and the Schools Council Project on Religious Education in Secondary Schools. It called upon fully state-maintained schools to encourage a 'sympathetic understanding of a religious approach to life' and reinforce 'common foundations in moral values' based upon 'underlying solidarity in the nexus of interdependence which is the basis of human existence and the source of inviolable obligation' (Social Morality Council, 1970: 6 and 12). Methodologically, it advocated a whole-school approach to moral education, including regular discussion periods (Social Morality Council, 1970: 7–9), and an open, multi-faith and discussion-based form of Religious Education which enables pupils 'to understand what the Christian faith means in the context of other beliefs sincerely held by men and women of integrity and goodwill who do not find it possible to accept a Christian commitment' and 'to create in [pupils] a more sensitive understanding of their own beliefs and of the different beliefs by which others govern their lives' (Social Morality Council, 1970: 13). It also recommended the replacement of Agreed Syllabus Conferences with national and local advisory councils involving representatives of religious faiths, Humanism, parents, teachers and pupils (Social Morality Council, 1970: 9).

At this point, with these specific recommendations in mind, it is worth returning to the BAS, which was the product of an Agreed Syllabus Conference first formally convened in the same year as the SMC working party report was published. The Agreed Syllabus Conference consisted of the usual committees representing the Church of England, LEA and teacher associations, but expanded the constituency of the fourth committee representing 'other denominations', as specified by the 1944 Education Act, so as to provide representation not just from the non-Anglican Christian churches, but also from Judaism, Islam, Sikhism, Hinduism and Humanism (i.e. Stopes-Roe). As a consequence, the nature of the agreement at the heart of the syllabus' construction shifted from an ecumenical definition of agreed Christian truth to a multi-faith definition of what was considered worthy of study in Religious Education (Hull, 1984: 30–32). By seeking to ensure that Religious Education was 'seen as an educationally valid component of the school curriculum, subject to the same disciplines as other areas of study', and in recognizing that it took place in a local and global context containing 'many with no deep commitment of any kind' (City of Birmingham Education Committee, 1975a: 4), the BAS adopted a secular and multi-faith approach that was in many ways based upon the kind of 'common ground' identified by the Humanists and liberal Christians who participated in the SMC. Like the BAS, the SMC also recognized that, because 'society today is truly plural, in the sense not only that numerous religious communities co-exist in it but also that a large section of it is non-believing', the 'State cannot legislate for a unity in the schools which does not exist outside them' (Social Morality Council, 1970: 6). These were arguments that had been made most vociferously by Humanists since the early 1960s in their efforts to free state-maintained educational institutions from Christian hegemony (Parker & Freathy, 2011b).

Conclusion

The above evidence suggests that the significant transitions which took place in Religious Education theory and policy in England in the late 1960s and early 1970s, such as the formation of the BAS, were catalysed, at least in part, by a concerted and organized campaign by the BHA with the intention of either abolishing Religious Education, establishing a secular alternative (such as moral education) or secularizing the subject's aims and broadening its content to include world religions and secular 'stances for living'. In regard to the latter objective, many liberal Christians and Humanists sought together, on the basis of the 'common ground' they had identified between them, to develop educationally-valid and multi-faith forms of 'open' Religious Education and moral education which would be suitable for all pupils and teachers regardless of their religious or secular backgrounds. It was a vision which cohered with that of many academics and professionals in Religious Education and cognate disciplines in the late 1960s.

The contribution of Humanists, most notably Harold Blackham on the national stage and Harry Stopes-Roe on a local one, to the discourses which led to the secularization, or at least extensive liberalization, of Religious Education theory and policy in England has been severely underplayed in the existing historiography (e.g. Copley, 2008). In terms of pressure group activity, more attention has been given to what David Rose (2003) has called the Christianizers or 'cultural restorationists', such as the participants in the 'Save Religion in State Schools' campaign, for whom the above developments did not represent the defence of the civil liberties of secular and non-Christian citizens, but the overthrow of Christian education and an attack on the Christian identity and morality of Britain. The arguments between the adherents of these contrasting viewpoints provoked the majority of the twenty-six questions and debates that focused on Religious Education in the British Houses of Parliament during the 1970s. In general, the contributors to these discussions repeatedly asserted 'an inextricable association between a traditional [Christian] form of Religious Education and the moral development of young people, the quality of national life, and (in the view of some) the very survival of Britain' (Bell, 1985: 193). Knowledge of the context in which such debates arose is important in understanding later, and more well-known, disputes regarding the Christian content of Religious Education in the 1988 Education Reform Act and subsequent government circulars (Bates, 1996; Copley, 2008).

The neglect of the contribution of Humanists to the discourses which led to the transformation of Religious Education theory and policy in England may also be due to the fact that contemporary discourse on Religious Education was often distracted by secondary issues, such as the inclusion of Communism as a secular 'stance for living' in the non-statutory teachers' handbook which accompanied the BAS. This 'red herring' diverted attention away from the more profound paradigm shift which was occurring within the subject and any serious debate about its underlying causes.

Another, perhaps more significant, factor is that histories of Religious Education have tended to highlight the contribution of a canon of theoretical literature from academics, such as Ninian Smart, John Hick and John Hull, whilst ignoring the wider religious and secular discourses of which their publications were a part. This has a consequence of airbrushing certain stakeholders out of the picture. Although one can imagine reasons why religious educators writing the history of their own subject might look to their own community and its supporters to find those responsible for Religious Education curriculum change, this is unfair on individuals such as Harold Blackham who made a profound, albeit often challenging, contribution to the relevant discourses by enabling 'a Humanist voice to be heard at a time of domination of a Christian religious perspective' (Taylor, 2009: 249). It also skews the historiography somewhat by suggesting that the history of Religious Education can be represented as a logical and uninterrupted sequence of theoretical developments, rather than a 'controversial, convoluted, and ideological' story (Barnes & Wright, 2006: 65–66), in which multiple historical conflicts and contingencies led to curriculum changes that were often only rationalized post hoc.

In terms of the subsequent development of Religious Education and moral education, Blackham went on to become the co-founder of the *Journal of Moral Education* in 1971, which was owned by the SMC and became the leading interdisciplinary journal in the field globally (Gates, 2009: 303); edited the influential National Foundation for Educational Research report titled *Moral and Religious Education in County Primary Schools* (1976) which had 'well-informed and imaginative things to say about children's gains from [Moral Education], Religious Education and collective worship' (Gates, 2009: 303); ensured that the BHA was a member organization of the Religious Education Council of England and Wales when it was founded in 1973; and, in 1983, was Guest Editor for a Special Issue of the *Journal of Moral Education* on 'Moral Education, Religious Education and Ethical Theory', which spawned a series of meetings with LEA Advisors and teachers, resulting in 'A Statement – Relations of [Moral Education] with Religious Education: the Need for Understanding and Cooperation' (*Journal of Moral Education*, *14*(1), 4–8 January 1985). In the mid-1980s, Blackham also became involved with the establishment of a Moral Education Centre at Leicester University and enhanced co-operation with the Moral Education Research and Information Centre at St Martin's College, Lancaster, under the direction of Brian Gates. More broadly, Blackham's legacy includes the International Humanist and Ethical Union, which is now a worldwide union of over 100 organizations in forty nations, and the BHA, of which he became President between 1974 and 1977, and which continues as a national charity supporting and representing the non-religious through its educational and secular civic activities (Taylor, 2009). When he died in 2009, Blackham was widely acknowledged as the '[p]ioneering philosopher behind the British Humanist Association' (Copson, 2009, February 9), the 'driving force of the modern Humanist movement' ('Obituary', 2009b) and the 'architect of the British and international humanist movements' (Copson, 2009, January 27). Thus, in terms of the BAS, which is where our research started, although it was Harry Stopes-Roe who brought the influence of Humanism to bear on the formation of this particular local syllabus, he was following a broader national and international agenda set previously by Harold Blackham. Whether similar influences were brought to bear upon curriculum developments in Religious Education in other national contexts is a matter for further research. It is clear from our evidence, however, that alongside national and international campaigns for the right to freedom *of* religion and belief in education, it is also necessary to take seriously the campaigns of those demanding freedom *from* religious beliefs in education as a prerequisite to exercising their right to 'freedom of thought, conscience and religion' (Universal Declaration of Human Rights, Article 18, United Nations, 2011).

References

Alves, C. et al. (1965). *Religious and moral education: Some proposals for county schools by a group of Christians and humanists.* Leicester: Blackfriars Press.

Barnes, L. P., & Wright, A. (2006). Romanticism, representations of religion and critical religious education. *British Journal of Religious Education, 28*(1), 65–77.

Bates, D. (1996). Christianity, culture and other religions (Part 2): F. H. Hilliard, Ninian Smart and the 1988 Education Reform Act. *British Journal of Religious Education, 18*(2), 85–102.

Bell, A. (1985). Agreed syllabuses of religious education since 1944. In I. Goodson (Ed.), *Social histories of the secondary curriculum* (pp. 177–200). Lewes: Falmer Press.

Blackham, H. J. (1964). A humanist view of religious education. *Learning for Living, 4*(2), 19–20.

Blackham, H. J. (1969). Introduction. In C. Macy (Ed.), *Let's teach them right: Perspectives on religious and moral education* (pp. 1–7). London: Pemberton Books.

Blackham, H. J. (1970). A Humanist Approach to the Teaching of Religion in Schools. In J. R. Hinnells (Ed.), *Comparative religion in education: A collection of studies* (pp. 50–58). Newcastle upon Tyne: Oriel Press.

British Humanist Association. (1975). *Objective, fair and balanced: A new law for religion in education.* London: The Association.

City of Birmingham Education Committee. (1975a). *Agreed syllabus of religious instruction.* Birmingham: City of Birmingham Education Committee.

City of Birmingham Education Committee. (1975b). *Living together: A teachers' handbook of suggestions for religious education.* Birmingham: City of Birmingham Education Committee.

Copley, T. (2008). *Teaching religion: Sixty years of religious education in England and Wales.* Exeter: Exeter University Press.

Copson, A. (2009, January 27). BHA mourns Harold Blackham (1903–2009): 'Architect of the humanist movement'. *British Humanist Association.* Retrieved March 8, 2012, from http://www.humanism.org.uk/news/view/209

Copson, A. (2009, February 9). Harold Blackham: Pioneering philosopher behind the British Humanist Association. *The Guardian.* Retrieved March 8, 2012, from http://www.guardian.co.uk/world/2009/feb/09/obituary-harold-blackman-humanist

Ezard, J. (1974, July 9). Monkey business in the scripture class, *The Guardian.*

Freathy, R. & Parker, S. (2010). The necessity of historical inquiry in educational research: The case of religious education. *British Journal of Religious Education, 32*(3), 229–243.

Gates, B. (2009). Harold Blackham 1903–2009: An obituary, *British Journal of Religious Education, 31*(3), 303–304.

Hick, J. (1976). Education and the Law – a comment, *Learning for Living, 15*(4), 135–136.

Hill, M. (1967). *Moral education in secondary schools: Suggested syllabus (11–16)*. London: British Humanist Association.

Hull, J. (1976a). Editorial, *Learning for Living, 15*(4), 122–124.

Hull, J. (1976b). Religious Indoctrination in the Birmingham agreed syllabus? *Faith and Freedom, 30*, 27–35.

Hull, J. (1984). *Studies in religion and education.* Lewes: Falmer Press.

Obituary: Harold Blackham. (2009a). *New Humanist.* Retrieved March 8, 2012, from http://newhumanist.org.uk/1986

Obituary: Harold Blackham: Driving force of the modern Humanist movement. (2009b, January 28). *The Times.* Retrieved March 8, 2012, from http://www.thetimes.co.uk/tto/opinion/obituaries/article2084292.ece

Parker, S. G., & Freathy, R. J. K. (2011a). Context, complexity and contestation: Birmingham's agreed syllabuses for religious education since the 1970s, *Journal of Beliefs and Values, 32*(2), 247–262.

Parker, S. G., & Freathy, R. J. K. (2011b). Ethnic diversity, Christian hegemony and the emergence of multi-faith religious education in the 1970s. *History of Education,* Retrieved March 8, 2012, from http://www.tandfonline.com/doi/abs/10.1080/0046760X.2011.620013

Parsons, G. (1994). There and back again? Religion and the 1944 and 1988 Education Acts. In G. Parsons (Ed.), *The growth of religious diversity: Britain from 1945: Vol. 2* (pp. 161–198). London: Routledge.

Priestley, J. G. (2006). Agreed syllabuses: Their history and development in England and Wales 1944–2004. In M. de Souza, K. Engebretson, G. Durka, R. Jackson, & A. McGrady (Eds), *International handbook of the religious, moral and spiritual dimensions in education. Part 2* (pp. 1001–1017). Dordrecht: Springer.

Rose, D. (2003). The voice of the cultural restorationists: recent trends in RE policy-making. *Curriculum Journal, 14*(3), 305–326.

Royle, E. (1994). Secularists and rationalists, 1800–1940. In S. Gilley & W. Sheils (Eds), *A history of religion in Britain: Practice and belief from pre-Roman times to the present* (pp. 406–422). Oxford: Blackwell Publishers.

Scrimshaw, Neil (1975, February 25). Teach-in: Lessons in humanism. *The Guardian.*

Short, E. (1969, January 10). *Speech by the Secretary of State for Education & Science. At the opening of Alnwick Church of England Junior School.* National Archives file: DES: Schools Branch (Registered Files). Correspondence on revised education bill and provisions (ED 183.5).

Smoker, B. (2009, April 8). Harold Blackham: Philosopher, and the first head of the British Humanist Association. *The Independent.* Retrieved March 8, 2012, from http://www.independent.co.uk/news/obituaries/harold-blackham-philosopher-and-the-first-head-of-the-british-humanist-association-1665264.html

Social Morality Council. (1970). *Moral and religious education in county schools.* London: Social Morality Council.

Stopes-Roe, H. V. (1976). Education and the law in Birmingham, *Learning for Living,* *15*(4), 133–135.

Taylor, M. J. (2009). Obituary: Harold Blackham (1903–2009), *Journal of Moral Education, 38*(2), 247–250.

United Nations. (2011). Universal Declaration of Human Rights. Retrieved March 8, 2012, from http://www.un.org/en/documents/udhr/

Wright, S. (2008). 'There is something universal in our movement which appeals not only to one country, but to all': international communication and moral education 1892–1914. *History of Education, 37*(6), 807–824.

LORNA M. A. BOWMAN

2 Freedom of Religion and Publicly Funded Religious Schools in Canada

Abstract

Contemporary Canada is a diverse multicultural country. The colonizers were Britain and France. On becoming a dominion colony in 1867, the *British North America Act* (BNA Act: Constitution Act, 1867) enshrined rights of publicly funded religious-sponsored education for Roman Catholics and Protestants. Without the provision of Catholic education in Québec and Ontario, Confederation would not have occurred. The BNA Act made Education the responsibility of each province. Today, many parents from the diverse religious traditions in Canada send their children to independent religious schools. Changing religious and cultural sensibilies in Québec have resulted in the demise of the Catholic schools system, whereas in Ontario it is the only religious system that receives government funding. This chapter falls into the disciplines of Church and Educational History, with particular attention to the relationship between the Church and State. Primary and secondary resources are utilized to provide an overview of publicly funded religious schools across Canada and the social and political forces at work, with particular attention to Newfoundland, Ontario and Québec. The chapter concludes with an analysis of the contemporary religio-cultural context to raise questions about the rights of all religious groups in Canada with regard to the 1867 BNA Act.

Introduction

In 1867, the *British North America Act* (BNA Act) established Canada as a Dominion colony of the United Kingdom of Great Britain and Ireland. Section 93 of the BNA Act, committed education to the provinces as their full responsibility and included specific provisions for the funding of religious teaching reflective of the religio-cultural sensibilities of the British and French as the primary colonizers. Section 93:2 provided specific protection for Roman Catholics in Ontario and Protestants in Québec. This chapter examines the formative historical, religio-cultural and political forces and contexts that have come to characterize the relationship between Church and State in matters of education and religion in Canada. It concludes with a brief analysis of the developments of the twentieth century and the various situations across the country today.

Canada's historical and religio-cultural context

'Canada' is the French rendering of the Iroquois word 'kanata' which means 'dwelling place or land'. As a nation state, Canada occupies most of North America, extending from the Atlantic in the east to the Pacific in the west, and northward into the Arctic Ocean. The southern boundary is its political demarcation with the United States of America. As a land mass, it is the world's second largest country but has a sparse population of thirty-four million people who reside primarily near the southern border with the United States. Historically, migrants have traveled to Canada from the four points of the compass. The United Nations considers Canada the most ethnically diverse nation in the world. Officially bilingual, with French and English as its two official languages, in 1971 Canada became officially multicultural through an act of Parliament. In contrast to the United States which often describes itself as a cultural 'melting pot' Canada speaks of itself as a 'cultural mosaic'.

The present ethnic, religious and cultural diversity of Canada is such that one must speak of the religio-cultural preferences and characteristics of many Canadian ethnic groups. This is particularly true of those who migrated to Canada in the nineteenth and twentieth centuries. It is also true of the Jewish and Dutch migrants after the Second World War, and of those of Asian, African and Muslim diasporas. Publicly funded religious schools in Canada, however, are inextricably tied to Canada's early colonial history and demographic makeup.

From the early 1600s, Canada's primary colonizers were Britain and France. North America's encounter with Europe was characterized by 'the three M's – missions, merchants and military' (Kim, 1996; Sanneh, 1983). These religious, economic and political forces were to determine areas of religious and linguistic influence, the trading and military alliances with the First Nations and Inuit aboriginal peoples, and the treaties that were signed by the European countries – not only between Great Britain and France but also with Portugal and Spain – vis-à-vis their respective territorial rights.

In 1713, France yielded Newfoundland, the Acadian peninsula, Hudson Bay and trade with the Iroquois Nation to Britain. Canada was initially the name of the French colony along the St Lawrence River; the other colonies of New France were Acadia, Louisiana and Newfoundland. In 1759, the British defeated the French on the Plains of Abraham near present-day Québec City; the next year Montréal fell. At the first Treaty of Paris, signed in 1763, France yielded New France to Britain. Following the American Revolution, a second Treaty of Paris was signed in 1783. This treaty led to the resolution of all other British and French interests to the south of the St. Lawrence River and resulted in the fuller establishment of the United States of America, particularly along the Atlantic seaboard.

Immediately following the 1763 treaty, a Royal Proclamation by the British Parliament changed the name of 'Canada' to 'Québec'. Québec was a translation of the Algonquin word for 'strait' or 'narrowing of the river' at the present day location of Québec City. The British then embarked upon a systematic, but ultimately unsuccessful, effort to assimilate its new French subjects through 'British' education. They underestimated the commitment of the French to their language and civil culture as well as their religion. For the French this included education, where it existed, in the French vernacular by the vowed women and men religious and the clergy of the Roman Catholic Church who had come to new France from Europe as missionaries.

The territory of Québec was then divided by Britain into Upper and Lower Canada in 1771. The 1774 *Québec Act* of the British Parliament extended Upper Canada into the Great Lakes and gave it English law and institutions; Lower Canada was allowed to retain French civil law, language and Roman Catholicism. This provision for French Catholics took place fifty-five years before Britain's 1829 *Emancipation Act* that permitted Roman Catholics to vote or sit in the British Parliament and fifty years before the 1844 restoration of the Roman Catholic Church in England. As a consequence the French in Lower Canada were enfranchised civically, culturally and religiously.[1] Historically, this is one of the first cases of *state-sanctioned freedom of religious practice* anywhere in the world. The freedoms provided for Britain's French subjects would be determinative for the future relationship between Church and State in Canada, particularly in matters pertaining to religion and education.

The years following 1774 were marked by ongoing struggle over education and religious schooling in both Upper and Lower Canada (Walker, 1955). In Lower Canada, Britain continued to attempt to implement an educational system geared to English-speaking Protestants. French Catholics not only resisted, refusing to send their children to school, but rebelled. In predominantly Protestant Upper Canada, English-speaking Catholics fought for Catholic schools throughout the province.

---

1   Until today, Québec is the only province in Canada to have a bi-juridical legal system under which civil matters are regulated by French-heritage civil law and criminal law operates according to Canadian common law.

Religious instruction and common education in Canada

The early 1800s saw the birth of common (public) education in North America. Travel between Upper and Lower Canada to the United Sates was common. For all practical purposes, the border was porous and the requirements for immigration nonexistent. In 1830, Robert Baldwin, a member of the Legislature in Upper Canada, advocated for 'a system of education under the control of the Provincial Legislature, with Schools and Colleges in which there should be no preference of sectarian tenants ... equally accessible to ... every religious creed' (cited in Walker, 1955). Canada's immigrant population, both Protestant and Catholic, believed that religion and education went hand in hand. Just as Sir James Kay Shuttleworth had attempted to imbue popular education in Victorian England with middle-class values through religious training, it was believed that education in British North America *had* to instill Christian moral principles through the teaching of the faith. For Protestants, this meant knowledge of the Bible (Tholfsen, 1974). Charles Duncombe, an immigrant from the United States and an elected member of the Legislature, 'thought that Biblical truths could be taught in common without offense to any Christian' (Walker, 1955). In his 1836 *Report on the Subject of Education* he recommended that 'if any religious sect attached to their own peculiarities as to fear the influence of religious instruction exerted by those who differ ... they could institute schools taught by ... their own sect. ... *Our schools must have these* influences; but whether it shall be by the *united* or by the *separate action of religious sects* is a matter of secondary consequence' (emphasis added; cited by Walker, 1955). Duncombe's Report formed the basis for education in Upper Canada [later Ontario] until 1871, becoming the rationale not only for public schools with non-sectarian religious instruction but also for separate religious schools.

In 1840, with an *Act of Union*, Britain created one Legislative Assembly for a *United Province of Canada* with two *regions* – Canada East and Canada West. The 1841 *Common School Act* recognized elementary *separate* schools as part of the public system. 'Any group [Protestant or Catholic] professing

a Religious Faith different from that of the majority of the inhabitants in a
township and dissenting from the "regulations, arrangements or proceed-
ings" of the commissioners, was empowered to set up a separate school,
which could also participate in the provincial funding for the common
schools' (Houston & Prentice, 1988). Minority Protestants in Lower Canada
(now Québec) were supportive of the minority Catholics in Upper Canada
(now Ontario) and in 1863 Catholic education rights were set forth in the
Scott Act (Walker, 1964).

The British North America Act, 1867

With the British North America Act (BNA Act) of 1867, the Province of
Canada [Canada East (Québec) and Canada West (Ontario)] together with
Nova Scotia and New Brunswick formed a larger union of two distinct
cultures – that of the French and the British. The BNA Act made clear
distinction between those areas of life that were to fall under the federal
government and those that were to be the responsibility of the provinces.
Section 93 of the Act on *Education* enshrined educational rights for religious minorities, at the provincial level, including 'Separate or Dissentient
Schools existing at the time of Union' (BNA Act: Constitution Act, 1867:
S. 93:3). Nowhere else in the BNA Act is religion mentioned. In actual
practice, Section 93 referred to separate Protestant schools in Québec and
separate Catholic schools in Ontario. It was envisioned that Québec's public
system would be Catholic and Ontario's Protestant. This reflected the religious spirit of the times. Recognition of religions or worldviews other than
Christianity was not part of the *Zeitgeist*, for example, at Confederation,
in 1867, fewer than two thousand Jews resided in Canada; Jewish children
would have to attend public schools where Christianity was portrayed as
normative (Kutnik, 1989). Needless to say, at the time, no one considered
the rights of the so-called 'heathen' or 'pagan' aboriginal peoples. In contrast to the United States of America, however, this cooperation between

Church and State continues to be a distinct characteristic of Canadian society, particularly in matters pertaining to education.

The Contemporary Situation

Repatriation of the British North America Act, 1867 in 1982

In 1982, Canada repatriated the BNA Act. Ninety-five years after the con-federation of the first four provinces, Canada was no longer a Dominion colony. Québec chose not to participate in the deliberations nor to sign the new constitution. The new *Constitution Act, 1982* included the BNA Act as *Constitution Act, 1867* as well as the *Canadian Charter of Rights and Freedoms*. The first of the Charter's fundamental freedoms is 'free-dom of conscience and religion'; freedom from religious discrimination is also stipulated (Constitution Act, 1982: S. 1:2a and 15:1).[2] Section 93 of *Constitution, 1867* continues to temper provincial control of educa-tion by protecting denominational rights enshrined in law on Union with Canada at the date when each province negotiated its educational terms of reference.[3] *Constitution, 1867* also makes it *possible* but not obligatory for provincial authorities to subsidize minority religious or independent

---

2   In 1996, the Constitution Acts 1867 to 1982 were consolidated with footnotes that document both the process by which each province negotiated its federation with Canada and the other amendments up to 1982 (Constitution Act, 1867, 1996, fn. 6). Of particular interest is Section 93, pertaining to Education. Each of Canada's ten provinces has inherent and often different constitutional governing responsibilities and authority that are distinct from those of the federal government. The three ter-ritories fall directly under the federal government with differing but limited powers delegated to each.

3   See http://www.oneschoolsystem.org/denominational-rights.html (retrieved March 13, 2012) for a summary of Section 93 as negotiated at confederation for Ontario, Manitoba 1870, Section 22; Saskatchewan, 1905, Section 17; Alberta, 1905, Section 17; and Newfoundland, 1949.

schools other than those specified under Section 93. Thus, schools such as Jewish schools in Québec and Hutterite schools in Manitoba are subsidized by their respective ministries of education. As we move well into the third millennium, fully or partially funded separate Roman Catholic schools are found in Alberta, Saskatchewan and Ontario. Partial funding for independent schools, including minority religious schools that follow the designated provincial curricula, is found in British Columbia, Alberta, Saskatchewan, Manitoba and Québec.[4] Since the completion of the funding of Catholic schools in Ontario in 1985, the province has come to call it the Catholic public system rather than the Catholic separate school system. Although Ontario is the only province with a fully funded Roman Catholic (separate) system, the province provides no funding of any kind to independent or religious schools (Johnston & Swift, 2000). In recent years, changing religious sensibilities in Canada as well as cultural, political and economic conditions have resulted in dramatic Constitutional amendments pertaining to the funding of public religious schooling in Newfoundland and Québec. The Catholic school system in Ontario also wonders about its future.

Province of Newfoundland and Labrador

Newfoundland[5] (Newfoundland and Labrador), 1.6 per cent of today's Canada's national population of whom 37 per cent is Catholic (Census

---

4   For a full overview of the issues see the *Canadian Encyclopedia 2010* regarding the Ontario Schools Question, New Brunswick Schools Question, North-West Schools Question and Separate School (http://www.thecanadianencyclopedia.com/). This chapter does not address the situations in the territories but is part of the writer's ongoing research.

5   The *British North America Act, 1949* referred to the province simply as Newfoundland which is home to 90% of the population. In recent years it has become known provincially as 'Newfoundland and Labrador', making the name inclusive of its continental territory. This is of particular importance to the economy because of Labrador's rich natural resources.

2001: Statistics Canada, 2001), entered Confederation in 1949. Since Confederation with the rest of Canada, the population has grown from approximately 350,000 to 505,000 in 2006 (Statistics Canada, 2006). As England's oldest colony, dating to the early 1600s, approximately 50 per cent of the population was historically Irish Catholics. Fagan (2004), a Newfoundlander, Catholic educator and historian, has traced the history of religion and education in the former colony. From 1836, Catholic schools received funding equitably with Protestant schools, initially those of the Church of England. (See http://faculty.marianopolis.edu/c.belanger/nfldhistory for information on the history of education in Newfoundland.) With the *BNA Act, 1949* it was believed that Newfoundland's Union with Canada had entrenched the established denominational system. For its size, Newfoundland is small demographically. In fact, no roads united the ports or small coastal villages located around the island until 1967 when Canada celebrated its Centennial. Building the Trans Canada Highway across the newest province, with linkages to the ports, provided greater access to and from the province. Previously, travel from port to port or to the capital, St. John's, or the mainland, required travel by sea. Religiously, this meant that many of the small port communities were (and remain) uni-denominational.

At the time of Confederation in 1949, in lieu of Section 93 on Education of the BNA Act, Newfoundland negotiated Term 17. Term 17 guaranteed funding to Roman Catholic, Anglican, Pentecostal, United Church of Canada and Salvation Army schools as well as freedom to unite denominational schools. That some of these denominations ran schools is at first surprising to those with no knowledge of the geography and development of Newfoundland and Labrador. The Salvation Army, for example, had been founded in Newfoundland in 1885 and became, for a period of time, the largest Protestant denomination in the province. This was, in great measure, because of its work as a church and educator across the island, particularly in the ports (Piper, 2000). The referendum leading to Newfoundland entering Confederation in 1949 was fully supported by the Catholic population, the largest religious denomination, and in return they fought for Term 17 guaranteeing their Catholic schools (Fagan, 2004).

In the 1970s, the major Protestant denominations in Newfoundland formed a single consolidated school board. Growing secularity in the 1990s, together with the high cost of the independent denominational schools, and most especially the demise of the fishery, caused the Newfoundland provincial government to initiate federal changes to Term 17. Two provincial referenda, held in 1995 and 1997, led to two Constitutional amendments which, in 1998, eliminated denominational school rights throughout Newfoundland and Labrador. Many Catholics, still the largest religious denomination and the one with the most developed school system for the purpose of education in faith, felt betrayed. In 2000, the Catholic population launched an appeal to the Supreme Court of Newfoundland. It was denied. In 2002, the Supreme Court of Canada refused to hear their case. Today, the Legislature of Newfoundland and Labrador has exclusive control over education. It must, however, provide courses 'not specific to a religious denomination' and 'religious observances shall be permitted in a school where requested by parents' (Newfoundland Act, 1949: 17:2, 17.3, amended 1998).

Province of Québec

Québec is the second largest province in Canada. It includes 23 per cent of Canada's population of whom 83 per cent are Catholic (Census 2006 and 2001: Statistics Canada, 2001, 2006). It no longer has public denominational school systems (Bowman, 2007). Growing secularity in Québec in the 1960s replaced the direct influence of the Roman Catholic Church with a growing commitment to its French cultural heritage. In 1976, Québec passed Bill 101, *The Charter of the French Language*, restricting all admission to English schools to children who had at least one parent who had attended an English-language elementary school *in Québec*. Since 1976 all immigrants to the province have been required to access French language schools no matter their home country or place of origin elsewhere in Canada. In 1997, linguistic rather than denominational boards were established by the Legislature by means of an amendment to the *British North America Act, 1867* 'so that Québec [could] recover its full capacity to act in matters of education' (Bill 109: Constitution Amendment, 1997). This may be seen as a new interpretation of the BNA Act, 1867 but it was also in keeping with the original spirit of the Act that made education the full responsibility of each of the provinces. *Constitution Amendment, 1997* states simply '93A. Paragraphs (1) to (4) of section 93 do not apply to Québec.' Needless to say, these are the statements of the BNA Act, 1867 pertaining to the provision of denominational and dissentient schools for Ontario and Québec.[6]

Initially, with the change, Québec parents could choose moral, Catholic or Protestant religious education classes for their children. Unlike Newfoundland's religious services' provision, however, this was not a constitutional right but a part of the province's *Ethics and Religious Culture* programme (Québec Ministry of Education, 2007). Eventually, a common curriculum on values and the world's religions was introduced across the province. This curriculum must also be taught in *all* public and private schools if they are to be accredited by the Québec Ministry of Education. The required teaching of this prescribed curriculum continues to be challenged by the province's Catholic schools who are one of the beneficiaries of Québec's longtime practice of partially funding religious and independent schools that follow the provincial curriculum.

Province of Ontario

Ontario, Canada's largest province, represents 39 per cent of the population of whom 37 per cent are Catholic. Its provision for religious schooling stands in strong contrast to the rest of Canada and is, perhaps, the most controversial. Although the provincial government fully funds Catholic schools, private and independent religious schools receive no financial support of any kind. Toronto, the capital and seat of provincial government, is Canada's largest and most ethnically diverse city. Here, Roman

---

6   Since Québec had not participated in the 1982 repatriation of the BNA Act, 1867, it was necessary that the amendment be made to the 1867 BNA Act.

Catholics remain a major political force as they do across the province (Catholic Hierarchy, 2005).

In 1985, Ontario passed Bill 30 that completed the funding of Roman Catholic schools from elementary through secondary education. This funding renewed earlier grievances among other religious groupings, including those that were Jewish and Christian Dutch Reformed. In 1945 and 1967, the Canadian Jewish Congress expressed concern over the provision of Christian religious instruction in public schools (Canadian Jewish Congress, 1945, 1967). In 1978, Hebrew schools sought admission to the public system in their own right. In 1979, following the advice of the Mackay Report on *Religious information and moral development*, Ontario Courts ruled mandatory religious instruction inadmissible in public schools (Mackay et al., 1969; United Nations, 1999). This, in effect, served to bar any religious group from seeking to establish a new public or separate school in the public or separate systems comparable to the Catholic schools.

In light of the 1982 *Charter of Rights and Freedoms*, the funding of Catholic schools was again challenged by parental representatives of both Jewish and Christian Reformed independent schools. In 1985, the challenge was referred initially to the Ontario Court of Appeal and then, in 1987, to the Supreme Court of Canada. Canada's Supreme Court 'upheld the constitutionality of the legislation' but acknowledged the *privileged status of Ontario Catholics* and opined such funding might be discriminatory and violate the Charter (emphasis added, United Nations, 1999: S. 2.8). A follow-up appeal to the Supreme Court in 1996 resulted in the subtle finding that the 'funding of Catholic Schools could not give rise to an infringement of the Charter because the province of Ontario was constitutionally obliged to provide such funding in Ontario' (United Nations, 1999: Ss. 2.8, 2.9 and 2.11). The Supreme Court of Canada also ruled that the funding of Catholic schools did not obligate the government to fund other religious schools (Adler *v.* Ontario, 1996).

Parents representing a wide spectrum of small independent religious schools in Ontario appealed, in 1997, directly to the United Nations. These parental groups claimed discrimination because Roman Catholics were no longer a minority in Ontario. The parents requested that all funding be withdrawn from Catholic schools because 'publicly funded separate schools for Roman Catholic citizens in Ontario represent in real terms a privilege to the largest religious organization in Ontario' (United Nations, 1999: S. 5.5). The United Nations Human Rights Committee ruled their case inadmissible since the totally secular system they requested was already in place. Counsel for the United Nations Committee *commented* that it was not bound by the Constitution of Canada and that the multicultural fabric of current Canadian Society strongly suggests that a rationale no longer exists for the flagrant discrimination in the educational laws of the Province of Ontario vis à vis one religious denomination over all other denominations (United Nations, 1999: 5. 1).

The present position of the Ontario government is that 'the existence of the separate schools system is [...] a historical artefact of the political and social realities of Canada's past [since] denominational schools are never funded *as denominational schools*, but as independent schools' (emphasis added, Johnston & Swift, 2000).

The Charter's right of freedom of religion in today's context

Since the implementation of Canada's *Charter of Rights and Freedoms* in 1982, freedom of religion and freedom from religious discrimination are the right, whether or not you are a citizen, of all who reside in Canada. This may be seen as consonant with the 1774 decision of the British Parliament, before the 1829 *Emancipation Act* in England, to permit Roman Catholicism in Upper Canada. Today, in Alberta, Ontario and Saskatchewan, the Roman Catholic separate schools guaranteed under Section 93 of the 1867 Constitution are supported by their provincial governments. Additionally, Alberta, British Colombia, Manitoba and Saskatchewan provide partial funding for religious independent schools that follow their respective provincial curricula. For historical reasons, Nova Scotia provides $400 per Twelfth Grade student in four private high schools only; in Prince Edward Island, Canada's smallest province with a population of 141,000, all private schools receive free textbooks in the same manner as in the public system. Ontario, New Brunswick and Newfoundland alone provide no funding of any kind to private or independent schools (Johnston & Swift, 2000).

The perceived and real inequity across Canada has been noted by the Roman Catholic hierarchy, particularly since the 1985 completion of funding for Catholic schools in Ontario. In an address to the Liberal Forum of the Senate in 1986, G. Emmett, Cardinal Carter stated (emphasis added; Carter, 1986):

> I maintain that the school situation is exceptional and unique because of our [Canadian] history but as I would expect my opinion to be respected in this regard and at least considered as honest, *I am prepared to accept the honesty of the opposite position of total voluntaryism. I feel that the weakness is that historically it was the state that decided to enter the field of education. There was a time when the church was the educator.* In assuming that role the state made the total voluntary system impossible.

In other words, the situation in 1986 before the changes in Newfoundland and Québec, with regard to religious schools in Canada was a result of Section 93 of the *British North America Act, 1867*. This included the initial provisions for Catholic schools in Ontario and Protestant schools in Québec.

In 2007, Conservative leader John Tory campaigned for the premiership of Ontario on the promise of equal funding for all faith-based schools. (As noted above, currently parents must provide the full costs of educating their children in these faith-based schools.) At the time there were '53,000 Ontario students in privately funded faith-based education [in Ontario] who would have [had] the right to re-enter the province's public system at any time' (Macleans, 2007). An Environics poll in the fall of 2007 found that 48 per cent of Ontarians supported the Tory plan and 44 per cent were opposed (Wilson, 2007). The provincial Conservatives lost the election, but the Editors of Macleans, Canada's national news magazine were quick to express the opinion of many (Macleans, 2007):

> Full funding … is consistent with our heritage. When the framers of the 1867 Constitution explicitly protected Catholic education in Ontario, their intent was not to privilege one religion above others. No one in 1867 could have anticipated the

dizzying array of faiths that now fill our country. Rather, the protection of Catholic rights spoke to their belief in defending minorities in their nascent country. We should honour their impulse towards tolerance and pluralism by supporting diversity in religious education.

Canada's national news magazine said it well. Moreover, many of the worldviews which make up the Canadian mosaic have as an integral part of them an integration of specific cultures, ethnicities and religions. In 2011, it would seem that the privileged position of Catholic education, not only in Ontario but also in Alberta and Saskatchewan, that is rooted in the Canadian Constitution, should be shared with other faith communities who are also committed to the religious education of their children. Only when this takes place will the true spirit of the *British North America Act, 1867*, incorporated into the *Constitution Act, 1982* and the *Charter of Rights and Freedoms, 1982* be responsive to the fabric of Canada's contemporary religio-ethnic and cultural mosaic.

References

Adler *v.* Ontario. (1996). 3 s.c.r. 609. Retrieved March 13, 2012, from http://scc.lexum. org/en/1996/1996scr3-609/1996scr3-609.html

Bowman, L. (2007). G. Emmett Carter. *Talbot School of Theology*. Retrieved March 8, 2012, from http://www2.talbot.edu/ce20/educators/view.cfm?n= emmet_carter.

Canadian Jewish Congress. (1945). *For children in a democracy*. Toronto: Morris Printing Company.

Canadian Jewish Congress. (1967). *Brief of the Canadian Jewish Congress central region to the committee on religious education in public schools*. Privately printed.

Carter, G. (1986). Church and state: Freedom and responsibility. In *Pastoral letters, communications, postsynodal legislation* (pp. 1430–1444). Toronto: Archdiocese of Toronto.

Catholic Hierarchy. (2005). Canada, statistics by province, by Catholic Population. Retrieved March 8, 2012, from http://www.catholic-hierarchy.org/country/ spcca1.html

Constitution Act. (1982). Retrieved March 8, 2012, from http://www.solon.org/ Constitutions/Canada/English/ca_1982.html

Constitution Act. (1867/1996). Retrieved March 8, 2012, from http://www.solon. org/Constitutions/Canada/English/ca_1867.html

Constitution Amendment, 1997 (Québec). (1997). Retrieved March 8, 2012, from http://www.sfu.ca/~aheard/queamend.html

Fagan, B. (2004). *Trail: The loss of constitutional rights in education in Newfoundland and Labrador*. St John's, NL: ADDA Press.

Houston, S., & Prentice, A. (1988). *Schooling and scholars in nineteenth-century Ontario*. Toronto: Ontario Historical Studies for the Government of Ontario.

Johnston, L., & Swift, S. (2000). *Public funding of private denominational schools in Canada*. Toronto: Ontario Legislative Library. Retrieved March 12, 2010 (source later withdrawn), from http://www.ontla.on.ca/library/b39tx.htm.

Kim, S. (1996). Seeking a home in North America: Colonialism in Asia. In D. Ng (Ed.), *People on the way*. Valley Forge: Judson Press.

Kutnik, J. (1989). Jewish education in Canada. *Jewish Population Studies, 21*, 135–169. Retrieved March 8, 2012, from http://www.policyarchive.org/handle/10207/ bitstreams/15006.pdf

Mackay, J. et al. (1969). *Religious information and moral development: The report of the committee on religious education in the public schools of the Province of Ontario*. Toronto: Department of Education.

Macleans. (2007, September 27). Equality in education: Funding faith-based schools. *Macleans. CA.* Retrieved March 8, 2012, from http://www.macleans.ca/educa-tion/postsecondary/article.jsp?content=20071001_110024_110024

Newfoundland Act. (1949). Retrieved March 13, 2012, from http://www.solon.org/ Constitutions/Canada/English/nfa.html

Piper, L. (2000). The Salvation Army. *Newfoundland and Labrador Heritage*. Retrieved March 8, 2012, from http://www.heritage.nf.ca/society/salvation_army.html

Québec Ministry of Education. (2007). Ethics and Religious Culture Program. Retrieved March 8, 2012, from https://www7.mels.gouv.qc.ca/DC/ECR/ index_en.php

Sanneh, L. (1983). *West African Christianity: The religious impact*. New York: Orbis Press.

Statistics Canada. (2001). Population by religion, by province and territory (2001 Census) (Newfoundland and Labrador, Prince Edward Island, Nova Scotia, New Brunswick). Retrieved March 8, 2012, from http://www40.statcan.gc.ca/ l01/cst01/demo30a-eng.htm

Statistics Canada. (2006). Table 1. Population of Canada, provinces and territories in the last 50 years. Retrieved March 8, 2012, from http://www12.statcan.gc.ca/census-recensement/2006/as-sa/97-553/table/t1-eng.cfm

Tholfsen, T. (Ed.). (1974). *Sir James Kay-Shuttleworth on popular education*. New York: Teachers College Press.

United Nations. (1999). CCPR/C/67/D/816/1998. Retrieved March 13, 2012, from http://www.worldlii.org/int/cases/UNHRC/1999/49.html

Walker, F. (1955). *Catholic education and politics in Upper Canada: Vol. I*. Toronto: The Catholic Education Foundation of Ontario.

Walker, F. (1964). *Catholic politics in Ontario: Vol. II*. Toronto: The Catholic Education Foundation of Ontario.

Wilson, J. (2007). Faith-based schools. *cbc.ca*. Retrieved March 8, 2012, from http://www.cbc.ca/ontariovotes2007/features/features-faith.html

DZINTRA ILIŠKO

3 Religious Freedom in a Democratic Latvia

Abstract

In the past two decades, Latvian society has changed from a monolithic soviet worldview to a state of religious diversity. This transition has been accompanied by social disorder and a reorientation to Western ideologies and various global trends. The rapid disintegration of society and the particularization of identities has led to a growing entropy in the social system. This chapter highlights the major tendencies in post-soviet Latvian society, including an initial renewal of interest in religion, morality, norms and values, and then, decline in religious practices and an emergence of secularism. The chapter shows the new role of religion operating within a framework of diversity in which various narratives co-exist on a relatively equal footing. It also notes how the transition from an atheist ideology to relative religious freedom has changed public perceptions of religion in quantitative and qualitative ways. Finally, it describes the impact of the above trends upon Religious Education in Latvian schools since 1991.

Introduction

Latvia is a multi-religious country, located in Eastern Europe close to the borders of Russia and Lithuania, with a population of 2.3 million. In 2002, the Latvian Justice Ministry registered more than 1,000 religious congregations. Among them were Lutheran, Roman Catholic, Russian Orthodox,

Baptist, Old Believer, Seventh-day Adventist, Jehovah's Witnesses, and other denominations. A large portion of the Latvian population is atheist. Latvia is effectively a secular state. Yet the official laws of Latvia, like the *Constitution of Latvia* and *The Law of Religious Freedom*, defend the free practice of religion. The law protects the rights of religious groups against any abuse, either by governmental or private actors. However, bureaucratic problems persist for some minority religious groups. The government distinguishes between 'traditional' – Lutheran, Catholic, Orthodox Christian, Old Believers, Baptist, Methodist, Adventist, and Jewish believers – and 'new' religious groups. In practice this has resulted in increased bureaucratic regulation and requirements for new religious groups to register with the government. Latvia, in common with other Baltic countries, has a difficult task of implementing laws that will guarantee fundamental rights and freedoms whilst preserving national culture.

All three Baltic countries guarantee freedom of religion in their constitutions. The law of all three states reflects the European Convention on Human Rights, which clearly states that: 'everyone has the right to freedom of thought, conscience and religion; this right includes the freedom to change one's religion or belief, either alone or in community with others and in public or in private, to manifest one's religion or belief, in worship, teaching, practice and observance' (Article Nine). Post-communist laws on religion are more favourable toward individual expressions of religion than institutional religious freedom, perhaps because of a fear of institutional opposition. Organized religion is perceived to be more dangerous than the personal search for transcendence.

The peoples of all three Baltic countries are struggling to comprehend, and to live within, the new situation of freedom. More often, the idea of freedom remains merely declarative and in practice does not receive sufficient attention. The rapid disintegration of society since 1991 has led to a degree of entropy in the societal system. Bells (2000: 23) describes changes that have occurred in Baltic societies in the following way:

[...] at the end of the scale is democracy, but at the other – totalitarianism. In the middle one finds a complete chaos in which people try out revolutionary, monarchic, anarchic and utopian ways of thinking. Totalitarianism relies on the cage model, but democracy permits people to wander in labyrinths full of complexity by walking alone, stumbling, and making false turns.

People have found themselves at the crossroads of two ideological systems: on the one hand, the recently ended communist experiment – characterized by a totalitarian control and denial of individual freedom – on the other hand, the intrusion of western culture, characterized by individualism, and a pursuit of technological progress. Latvia has been bombarded with western images and commodities that were unavailable during the soviet decades, which now abound for those who can afford them. While such physical changes of the landscape are immediately visible, the psychological transformations and emotional response of these transformations are harder to discern; these changes are profoundly reshaping people's identities and mentalities.

As a result of having their nationality suppressed for fifty years, the Baltic people were quite eager to assert their particular nationality and spirituality in the post-communist setting of the 1990s. National symbols, memorials and holidays played an important role in people's everyday lives during what came to be known as the *'singing revolution'*. As the new millennium approached, however, such patriotic displays become increasingly less prevalent, gradually mutating into more – by western standards – acceptable or conventional expressions of national identity. The process of national reconstruction in Latvia lacks a precedent, and scholars acknowledge difficulties when it comes to predicting where Latvia may be heading.

As Geertz (1963) observed, the people of new states have both the desire to act as free citizens whose opinions matter, and the desire to build a contemporary country. They aim to develop a new identity, to raise living standards and to establish a greater sense of social justice.

The scenario and the challenges of post-soviet Latvia

The people of post-communist Latvia and other Baltic states appear to be searching for new symbols and narratives that can help them find meaning in new circumstances. The following questions need to be raised (Merdjaeva, 2001: 272):

1. How can pluralism in Latvia be effectively combined with intra-societal integration? and
2. How can the western concepts of democracy, liberty and human rights be applied in the different socio-cultural contexts of Baltic countries?

Implementing the ideals of religious freedom and democracy in the post-communist Baltic states requires a creative approach which is dependent upon the specific historical and cultural contexts of each country. Transformation processes and problems posed by multiculturality, migration, globalization, the end of ideologies, and changing identities, bring with them a sense of uncertainty and 'dislocation, rapture, discontinuity, protest and dissatisfaction' to the majority of the population (Martin & Pison, 2005). Some people view the time of transition as an opportunity, whilst others view it as a crisis in which newly found freedoms turn out to be fraught with difficulties.

The transition to a new social order has proven to be a complicated and an ongoing process. Individuals who grew up during the stable and well-defined order provided by communism now have different qualities demanded of them, namely a willingness for cooperation, to be in dialogue, to be open, and to share a sense of collective responsibility. The democratization, liberalization and individualization of society has provoked feelings of nostalgia for the previously well-defined social order for the majority of people in the Baltic region. As nations, Latvia, Lithuania and Estonia have set their priority as the maintenance of their national identity and sovereignty against super-national organizations like the European Union and North Atlantic Treaty Organization. The particularization of society created by the end of communism has led to entropy in systems of meaning. A natural outcome of this has been the growth of new ethnic, linguistic and religious identities. However, these new identities still relate to the past as opposed to the needs of people living within modern civic societies.

The mainstream churches have similarly found themselves in a difficult situation. They have had to recover from spiritual deprivation and to face new realities and challenges. The role of the churches in Baltic states in 1990s has been limited, however, because they were generally normalized during the communist period and thus have been unable to fill the moral vacuum. One of the reasons for this has been that in promoting the ideal of freedom, freedom has been romanticized, so that the reality does not necessarily match the ideal. The churches critique freedom on the basis that it presents new social challenges, but they still idealize it. This attitude toward freedom can be explained by noting that the churches are standing at the crossroads of two ideological systems. On the one hand, there is a recently ended communist experiment, and on the other hand, there is the intrusion of western culture. The former system aspired to a totalitarian control and the denial of individual liberties, the other exaggerated individualism. In these conditions, when the churches failed to provide constructive help to those adjusting to developments in society, and failed to help individuals with their problems, they risked a further loss of their authority. The 'fortress mentality' (Merdjanova, 2001), typical of communist times, widely persists as the churches have not been able to meet the needs of the emergent societies.

From the soviet past to religious pluralism

The process of transformation at the beginning of the 1990s cannot be explained as a miraculous awakening of a mysterious national spirit. Scientific atheism brought in during the fifty years of soviet annexation became an alternative for religion. This had a huge impact on Latvian society. Scientific atheism, as a Marxist-inspired faith, was taught in schools and was promoted in all spheres of public life with the aim to free citizens from outdated religious beliefs.

Marxism can be seen as a complex, multidimensional cultural code. Like all theoretical codes, its practical applications can become tolerant, democratic and liberal or authoritarian, bureaucratic, centralist and despotic, depending on the particular context. However, Marxism became vulgar and simple. The 'new person' that it created was superficial, with no roots in tradition and history, and lacking in conscience. The proponents of Marxist-Leninist regimes deny that their ideology involves god, religion or cult. Still, one can trace some similarities. The followers of Marxism have constructed their own unique rituals, demonology, eschatology and morality in a search for moral meanings in political activity. This included cults, like the 'Lenin cult', and specific socialist rituals. These ritualizations of Marxist civil religion developed as social rites conducted by party-designated specialists. In order to combat traditional religions and to promote the growth of the 'new socialist person', the government institutionalized the practice of public rituals in special buildings. The soviet government replaced religious practices with atheist holidays and ceremonies, thus providing citizens with a new symbolism, meaning and morality.

The awakening of religious pluralism

In a way, by attacking and weakening institutional religious communities, the soviet policy allowed more space for religious pluralism and alternative spiritualities. Thus, indirectly, religious life was revived and found a wider cultural context. People became enthusiastic to regain their lost Christian values, to seek religious experiences, or in other ways to find spiritual nourishment. New religious identities provided a new frame of reference, as well as serving as a means of socialization. This became a source of consolidation in collective identity.

As the result of soviet policy, smaller religious groups became more desirable and evident in the religious landscape in Latvia. Kule (2002) describes the situation with the emergence of numerous forms of religious expression. Some people were carried away by young Lutheran priests' essays on morality; others admired the exotic nature of Hare Krishna or became fascinated by New Age teachings. After fifty years of persecution, the traditional Churches had declined intellectually and limited themselves to the core activities of distributing the sacraments and preaching. Religious pluralism in Latvia grew not only as a result of the efforts of small religious groups, but also due to the migration of people within the borders of the Soviet Union. When the atheist ideology lost its power in 1991, numerous charismatic religious groups began to flourish. These unique circumstances fostered religious growth in Latvia in the absence of religious pluralism.

Numerous western religious sects gained ground in Latvia, though many did not succeed because they were not familiar with the specific historical circumstances of their future converts. The largest religious movements in Latvia included Jehovah's Witnesses and the New Apostolic Church of North Rhine – Westphalia (Krumina-Konkova, 2001). The media created concern around the appearance of eastern religious movements. In reality, the ideology of these movements did not cause any danger to the society of Latvia. The only exception was neo-pagan movements that attracted people through folk tradition (Tēraudkalns, 2003).

Religion played the role of providing moral legitimacy for the democratic transition. One of the major reasons why people turned to new religions was a search for identity. By failing to find their place in the current social order, many people were looking for meaning by joining non-traditional religions. Sects attracted people by offering a feeling of togetherness and by emotionally highly-charged atmosphere in contrast to the one offered by the traditional denominations (Tēraudkalns, 2003). The rituals offered by religious sects seemed to be attractive as a result of their strong emotional component, speaking in tongues, non-verbal forms of communication and distinctive prayer postures. They had a 'therapeutic' effect on the people who participated in the ceremonies. Still, by remaining pessimistic in their evaluation of contemporary society, these charismatic movements preached apocalyptic pessimism. Thereby, in a manner which is similar to that of other Baltic countries, post-soviet Latvia has undergone several waves of religious appraisal: renewed pride for the pre-soviet heritage; the desire for a new set of values; and a search for a new worldview. Berger (2001: 425) describes the current transformations in terms of a decrease in 'the unifying force of the nation-state, and the revival of local forms of identity and sociality (ethnic, religious, cultural)'.

Religion in the Latvian society

The religious revival in Latvia, as in other Baltic countries, was related to the search for symbols. The challenge for Latvia now is how religious liberty can be practiced in these new circumstances. After the first wave of religious revival in Latvia, one can notice the following tendencies (Herbert, 1999):

1. a decreasing number of religious believers;
2. a decreasing number of participants in religious rituals; and
3. an increasingly personal, individual vision of God.

People in Latvia also began displaying tendencies in religiosity similar to those in the majority of western countries. All three Baltic countries, namely, Latvia, Estonia and Lithuania, have undergone similar processes in their search for identity and existence in the new conditions of freedom. A comparative overview of the situation in Baltic countries after the collapse of the Soviet Union enables us to trace some differences. Mattusch (1997: 81–82) has made the following observations. First, Lithuanians remained very religious despite soviet atheism and took guidance from traditional values in family life. They are more traditional-ist and have internalized capitalist culture to the least extent. By contrast, Estonians are the most anti-traditionalist and most strongly attracted to capitalist culture. Meanwhile, Latvian culture is characterized by a mixture of different traditions. As Dreifelds (1996) argues, Latvia is one of the few former soviet countries in which the ethnic composition of its population has changed dramatically during the post-soviet era. Indeed, intensive migration transformed Latvia into a bi-cultural country. Capitalism in Latvia is described as of the 'wild' Russian variety, with comparative indexes demonstrating that corruption in Latvia is even worse than in Lithuania (Norkus, 2007: 34; see Table 1).

Table 1: *Value orientation*

	Latvi %	Lithu %	Eston %
Religion is important in my life	30	44	22
I gained my religious upbringing in my family	37	68	18
I believe in a personal God	21	52	15
Death is inevitable, it is pointless to worry about it	79	28	90
If an unjust law were passed by the government I could do nothing about it	71	75	60

Note. Source: Mattusch (1997). Latvi = Latvians, Lithu = Lithuanians, Eston = Estonians.

The changes reflect the impact of cultural / traditional mentali-ties. Today, all three Baltic countries face similar challenges in defining their national identity. According to a European Values Study (Halman, 1999/2000), a huge number of people in Latvia and Lithuania consider themselves to be religious (see Table 2).

Table 2: *Religious self-identification*

	Latvi %	Lithu %	Eston %
Would you say you are			
a religious person	77	85	42
not a religious person	20	14	52
a convinced atheist	3	2	7

Note. Source: European Values Study 1999/2000. Latvi = Latvians, Lithu = Lithuanians, Eston = Estonians.

There is a need to stress that religious self-identification cannot be made on the basis of affiliation to a particular religion, but rather on the basis of whether one assigns oneself to a particular culture or national way of life. Actual levels of religiosity are determined by a combination of subjective and objective indicators of religiosity. Particular attention needs to be paid to the secular and religious components that form the unique culture of Latvia as well as to the individual's value orientation. Representatives of the younger generation identify themselves as believers by allowing some elements of the Christian religious culture to come into their consciousness, but the secular culture still shapes their consciousness. The religiosity of young people in Latvia is more often reduced to a private matter affording freedom to the individual to understand faith in his or her own way. Religion intertwines with the socio-cultural nature of the Latvian context which shapes people's way of thinking and gives them a sense of security (see Table 3).

Table 3: *Belief in God*

	Latvi %	Lithu %	Eston %
Do you believe in God?			
yes	80	87	51
no	21	14	49

Note. Latvi = Latvians, Lithu = Lithuanians, Eston = Estonians.

The religiosity of the population in Latvia and Lithuania is quite high, but as a rule it is not associated with institutional affiliation. Survey data points to a relatively high level of non-traditional/alternative beliefs in Latvia. The number of people who affiliate themselves with specific religious denominations is also not so high. There are people who fall between denominational categories who do not seek to nourish their spiritual life within a structured religion. There is also a group of people who are happy to belong to certain confessions and who choose a particular church because it is a safe place to be (see Table 4).

Table 4: *Religious denomination*

	Latvi %	Lithu %	Eston %
Do you belong to a religious denomination?			
yes	59	81	25
no	41	19	75

Note. Latvi = Latvians, Lithu = Lithuanians, Eston = Estonians.

This number allows one to see the heterogeneous religious situation in the Baltic region. There is a clear distinction between belonging and believing. The situation in Latvia can be well described by the phenomena of 'believing without belonging' and 'belonging without believing'.

Latvians used to live within an ideology dictated by the soviet government that functioned as a guiding set of values. Now citizens of Latvia are not equipped to live in the conditions of freedom. After the fall of the Soviet Union, the older generation perceives the new order of ideological diversity and freedom as representing moral disorder and as being potentially destructive. They view western ideas of pluralism as artificially imposed and display some resistance. Many of them resist invasive forms that challenge and undermine everything that was 'theirs' or national. By contrast, the younger generation perceives the new situation as part of modern Latvia. Liberated from previous dependencies, some Latvians have fallen into increased dependency on religious groups and sects, with many perceiving religion to be no more than a set of moral and behavioural guidelines. Furthermore, religion in the Baltic countries has undergone a process of secularization which has brought about, first, the withdrawal of religious institutions and norms from the public sphere and relegated them to the private sphere, and second, a decline in institutional religion leading to more individualistic and syncretistic forms of religiosity.

As a rule, secularization processes led to a decline in religious activities (Bruce, 1992; Gautier, 1997). Secularization is 'a process when religious thinking and practice become marginal' (Merdjanova, 2001: 279), when 'religion is reduced to a subsystem of society alongside other subsystems' (Dobelaere, 1984: 200) or when the 'dissolution of sacred cosmos' makes religion 'invisible' (Luckmann, 1967: 101). A number of studies highlight clear trends of secularization in Latvia. Secularization does not mean that only fewer people are genuinely or even nominally religious. In Latvia, religion stops functioning, as Berger (2001) argues, as a 'sacred canopy'. The culture of Latvia presents a mixture of different types of cultures: the secular culture and the denominational culture, which, as Lebedev (2008) argues, is being artificially imbedded into the consciousness of children. For Lebedev, contemporary religious culture is not internalized any more in childhood or through natural assimilation of some particular religious tradition, but is formed as a result of one's conscious and personal choice at a mature age (Lebedev, 2008: 73). When a person turns to religion, it produces a dramatic clash between the acquired religious meanings and secular patterns of life. Religiosity requires not only the replacement of secular structures with religious ones within an individual's consciousness, but also for the religious structures to be placed 'above' the secular ones because the religious sphere is linked to certain overarching values. Without this dominance, as Lebedev (2008) argues, religious structures lose their meaning and become assimilated into secular values and meanings.

Conclusion

The soviet regime in which Latvia lived for forty years was ideologically opposed to religion and religious activity. Religion re-entered as one of the narratives that occupied the discursive space in society after the fall of communism. Presently, Latvia can be described as a discursive space characterized by ideological diversity. Latvia has become open to global systems as a new sphere of influence for various religious charismatic religious groups.

Post-soviet Latvia is undergoing a transition that has been liberating as well as deeply destructive. The rapid disintegration of society has led to entropy of the societal system of meaning and symbols. People have entered a new democracy in which they are expected to express their opinion and exercise their freedom. The diversity of worldviews around them is shocking. The identity crisis shows that old collective values and symbols are no longer working and that new social categories (e.g. ethnicity) are emerging.

The religious landscape of Latvia can be described with reference to such notions as syncretism, eclecticism and pluralism. Baltic countries are experiencing the emergence of religious freedom as a new cultural phenomenon. Religion and religious freedom in post-soviet countries can be seen as one of the major fields in which political, ideological and cultural transitions are occurring and being resolved. In the transition toward the new democracy, the mainstream churches need to recover from spiritual and institutional stagnation and overcome their 'fortress mentality' (Merdjanova, 2001).

References

Bells, A. (2000). *Būris* [Cage]. Rīga: Zvaigzne ABC.
Berger, P. (2001). *The sacred canopy*. New York: Doubleday.
Bruce, S. (1992). *Religion and modernization*. Oxford: Clarendon.

Dobbelaere, K. (1984). Secularization theories and sociological paradigms: Convergences and divergences. *Social Compass, 31*(2), 199–219.

Dreifelds, J. (1996). *Latvia in transition.* Cambridge: Cambridge University Press.

Gautier, M. (1997). Church attendance and religious belief in post-communist societies. *Journal for the Scientific Study of Religion, 36*(2), 289–296.

Halman, L. (1999/2000). *European values study: A third wave.* Tilburg: Tilburg University.

Herbert, D. (1999). Christianity, democratization and secularization in Central and Eastern Europe. *Religion, State and Society, 27*(314), 277–293.

Krumina-Konkova, S. (2001). New religious minorities in the Baltic states. *Nova Religion, 4*(2), 289–297.

Kule, M. (2002). *Phenomenology and culture.* Riga: Institute of Philosophy and Sociology.

Lebedev, S. (2008). Students' attitudes toward religion. *Russian Education and Society, 50*(8), 71–90.

Luckmann, T. (1967). *The invisible religion: The problem of religion in modern society.* New York: Macmillan Publishing Company.

Martin, M. K., & Pison, R. M. (2005). From knowledge to wisdom: A new challenge to the educational milieu with implications for religious education. *Religious Education, 99*(1), 157–168.

Mattusch, K. (1997). Weltbilder als weichensteller für die richtung des wandels. Zur aktualität der 'protestantischen ethik' am beispiel des Baltikums. In A. Sterbling & H. Zipprian (Eds), *Max Weber und Osteuropa* (pp. 73–93). Hamburg: Heinz Zipprian.

Merdjanova, I. (2001). Religious liberty, new religious movements and traditional Christian churches in Eastern Europe. *Religion, State and Society, 29*(4), 266–302.

Norkus, Z. (2007). Why did Estonia perform best? The north-socialist economic transition of the Baltic states. *Journal of Baltic Studies, 38*(1), 21–42.

Tēraudkalns, V. (2003). Echoes of modernity in the theologies and praxis of churches in contemporay Latvia. *International Review of Mission, 92*(364), 55–65.

PETA GOLDBURG

4 Religious Education: A Foundation for Freedom of Religion and Belief

Abstract

The teaching of religion in Australian schools was originally influenced by a series of Education Acts passed by various Australian States in the late 1800s which eventually initiated free, compulsory and secular education for all children. While Australia openly promotes freedom of religion and belief, there is no formal Religious Education programme for students aged between five and fifteen in government schools other than an optional thirty-minute, faith-based class taught by volunteers from local religious groups. In the late 1980s, *Studies of Religion* programmes, which were educational and multi-faith in nature, became available, but not mandatory, for senior secondary students in all Australian states. While they are popular in religiously affiliated schools, few government schools have taken this option. The educational challenges of a rapidly growing multicultural society are beginning to be felt in Australia. At the same time, the development of a national curriculum has just begun. Therefore, it is important to use this opportunity to re-open discussion regarding the teaching of religion with the aim of developing a multi-religious curricula which is child-oriented and acknowledges plurality. This chapter promotes the teaching of religion to all children and, building on current research in Europe and the United Kingdom, presents a case for how this might be achieved in Australia.

Introduction

In December 1872, ninety years after British settlement in Australia, the state parliament of Victoria, one of the six states in Australia, passed a law which provided free, compulsory and secular schooling for all children. Six years later, the 1880 State Public Instruction Act of New South Wales followed suit, stating that all teaching should be secular instruction but also indicating that general religious teaching could take place as long as it was free from dogmatic or polemic theology. The Act decreed that during each school day:

> [...] children will spend four hours devoted to secular instruction and not more than one hour shall be set apart when children may be instructed by a clergyman or other religious teacher ... and in all cases the pupils who receive religious instruction shall be separated from the other pupils of the school. (ACT Parliamentary Counsel, 2005/1880)

The Act provided opportunity for students to study religion but the Catholic Church considered that a system founded on the principle of secularist education and controlled by secular authorities would be inadequate for the complete education of Catholic children. It continued, therefore, to establish separate schools where the teaching of religion was carried out using a confessional approach according to the teachings of the Catholic Church. The separation of church (private or independent) schools from government (public) schools virtually ended the general teaching of religion in public schools.

The current situation

Today, the teaching of religion is not part of the formal school curriculum for students between the ages of five and fifteen. Nevertheless, every State and Territory in Australia has the provision for voluntary confessional religious instruction on a weekly basis if a religious tradition or denomination is able to provide people to teach it. In most instances, ministers of religion or their accredited representatives are the only people approved to enter the school to provide these classes. The confessional instructors are volunteers and, on the whole, have no formal qualifications in religion or education. In some schools, a cooperative programme, which is ecumenically Christian in nature, and designed in such a way that Catholic, Anglican, Lutheran and Uniting Church students are able to participate together, is provided, rather than denominational religious education.

Religiously based schools, which constitute the majority of the non-government (private or independent) school sector, have always offered some form of religious education to their students. The time allocated to Religious Education varies across systems with Catholic schools allocating approximately three hours per week while denominational schools may only offer thirty minutes per week of Religious Education. Originally, the classroom teaching of religion had a mono-religious approach (Hermans, 2003) focusing exclusively on one religion with the aim of transmitting a particular tradition, for example, Catholic or Anglican tradition. Gradually these 'enfaithing' approaches have moved toward informative approaches which endeavour to teach about religion rather than teaching people to be religious in a particular way (Moran, 1991).

During the early 1980s Australian religious educators such as Basil Moore, Norman Habel and Terence Lovat promoted religion programmes that enable students to learn about religion without necessarily requiring them to profess a belief in a particular religion. They were concerned that a religion programme should increase students' religious literacy and ultimately increase tolerance and understanding of a variety of religions including Christianity. Their writings ultimately influenced the development of *Study of Religion* programmes which emerged during the mid-1980s and explored world religions and were offered as elective subjects in Australian senior secondary schools.

Each Australian State now offers some form of *Study of Religion* as an elective subject to students in senior secondary (sixteen to eighteen years of age) and enrolments for the subject are at an all-time high. Although the subject is offered in independent schools, only a few public schools offer it.

Study of Religion programmes have advanced the overall study of religion in senior secondary schools in Australia and have established religion as a subject worth studying and as a valid matriculation subject.

Of all the Australian *Study of Religion* syllabi, the 2008 Queensland syllabus (Queensland Studies Authority, 2008) is distinctive for its acknowledgement of religious plurality and its student-centred approach to learning and teaching. Using an inquiry-based approach, it focuses on the development of critical religious literacy which requires participants to move through three phases: recognition, reproduction and reflection (Unsworth, 2002). Recognition literacy involves learning to recognize and produce the codes that are used to construct and communicate meaning as well as cultural practices present and central to common experience of everyday life. Reproduction literacy involves understanding and producing the conventional visual and verbal text forms that construct and communicate the established systematic knowledge of cultural institutions. Reflection literacy involves learning how to read inclusion and exclusion, analysing and interrogating verbal and visual codes to expose how choice of language and image privilege certain viewpoints and how other choices of visual and verbal resources could construct alternative views. Students and teachers are challenged to examine how they read the world, to examine what they take for granted and to critique the particular culture in which texts are constructed. Such an approach enables people to look at written, visual, spoken and multimodal texts and to question and challenge attitudes, values and beliefs that lie beneath the surface. The approach emerges from critical pedagogy, which Freire says we need to evaluate and critique received ideas, particularly those presented in student texts.

A unique opportunity for the teaching of religion in all Australian schools is presented with the introduction of a national curriculum. The Australian Curriculum Assessment and Reporting Authority (ACARA) has been charged with development of a national curriculum guided by the 2008 *Melbourne Declaration on Educational Goals for Young Australians* which commits 'to supporting all young Australians to become successful learners, confident and creative individuals, and active and informed citizens' (Ministerial Council on Education, Employment, Training and Youth Affairs, 2008). After twelve months of consultation, the national curriculum will be introduced into schools in three phases. English, Mathematics, Science and History (Phase 1) curricula was released in March 2010, and are currently being 'road tested' in 150 schools across Australia. Phase two is being developed for Languages, Geography and the Arts, but Phase three, Design and Technology, Health and Physical Education, ICT, Economics, Business, and Civics and Citizenship, is on hold. The teaching of religion is not, to date, part of the national curriculum but religion and religious diversity are specifically mentioned in the *Melbourne Declaration* (2008) which states '... this heightens the need to nurture an appreciation of and respect for social, cultural and religious diversity, and a sense of global citizenship ... Australians need to become "Asia literate" ... ensure that schooling contributes to a socially cohesive society and respects and appreciates cultural, social and religious diversity' (Ministerial Council on Education, Employment, Training and Youth Affairs, 2008).

The inclusion of religion as part of citizenship education would not only provide the opportunity to teach about religion, but also address Goal 2 of the *Melbourne Declaration* which focuses on 'active and informed citizens' who 'act with moral and ethical integrity, appreciate Australia's social, cultural, linguistic and religious diversity ... understand and acknowledge the value of Indigenous cultures ... communicate across cultures' and '... are responsible global and local citizens' (Ministerial Council on Education, Employment, Training and Youth Affairs, 2008).

Given the Australian government's and ACARA's allusion to religion and religious diversity, it is timely to draw some insight from research related to international citizenship education programmes and education about religion within citizenship education. The forming of citizens for a global world is important, and internationally the place of citizenship education within the overall curriculum has taken on new significance given the climate of increased globalization, migration and pluralism. Making citizenship education explicit is one way of responding to rapid changes we have experienced in the world in recent times. Kerr identifies the following as impacting on citizenship education: the rapid movement of people within and across national boundaries; the growing recognition of the rights of Indigenous peoples and minorities; the collapse of existing political structures and the growth of new ones; the changing role and

status of women in society; the impact of the global economy and changing patterns of work and trade on social, economic and political ties; the
effects of the revolution in information and communications technologies;
the increasing global population and the consequences for the environment; and the emergence of new forms of community and protest (Kerr,
2003: 9). We could also add to this list growing religious diversity within
communities that once considered themselves to be homogeneous and
mono-religious.

Dimitrov and Boyadjieva describe citizenship as 'the system of values,
efforts and institutionalized practices required for creating and main-
taining conditions for living together in a complex society' (2009: 156).
Citizenship education in most countries promotes social order and control
by cultivating civic values. Two questions which have yet to be addressed
regarding citizenship education in Australia are the following: How will
citizenship education address religious diversity? and What conceptions
of citizenship will promote religious diversity?

A variety of understandings of citizenship and citizenship education
exist and they are particularly complex because they differ according to
place and historico-political culture. Kiwan identifies five constructions of
citizenship which she labels as moral, legal, identity-based, participatory and
cosmopolitan. *Moral citizenship* can be traced back to Plato's *The Republic*
where the notion of justice was central to society and individuals, and while
it is not a legalistic conception it does, nevertheless, relate to the social
nature of the individual (Kiwan, 2005). Contemporary expressions of
moral citizenship appear in the discourse related to citizenship and values,
but the contemporary expression does not address the political nature of
humankind. *Legal citizenship*, first developed by the Romans, entailed six
privileges (four community-based privileges and two private privileges),
namely serving in the military, voting, eligibility to public office, the legal
right to action and appeal, rights of intermarriage, and trade with other
Roman citizens. Modern conceptions of free and equal citizens can also be
traced back to Hobbes and Locke, whose theories became a central tenet
of modern European liberalism. According to Kiwan and Kiwan (2005),
legal conceptions of citizenship are evidenced in France where citizenship
is expressed in abstract universal terms with no reference to personal or

group attributes, such as ethnicity or religion. *Identity-based* conceptions of citizenship emerge from communitarian theories and can be seen in Germany where citizenship is 'particularist and Volk-Centred' (Kiwan, 2005: 42), in other words, citizenship is conceptualized in terms of descent. *Participatory* conceptions of citizenship advocate an active citizenry whose humanity is actualized through participation in civil society. This idea of citizenship reflects the ideas and ideals of the eighteenth-century philosopher Rousseau who focused on the importance of community and shared values. Rousseau was an 'advocate of "participatory" democracy and an active citizenry, an idea that subsequently had an influence on ideas during the French revolution' (Kiwan, 2005: 42). *Cosmopolitan* conceptions of citizenship are universalist in approach rather than state-oriented. The idea emerges from the Stoics who argued that all human beings are equal and that the cultivation of wisdom was the only requirement for citizenship. More recently, other theories have emerged which include transnational, digital, global and multiple citizenships. Modern citizenship is concerned with being an active member of the modern world from an individual and collective dimension. Citizens are required to be 'morally and existentially self-reliant on the one hand, and contributing to the "common good" and to social cohesion on the other hand' (Roebben, 2008: 207).

Hudson argues for broadening understandings of citizenship to include differential citizenship, which acknowledges that people have access to a vast diversity of citizenships rather than a single citizenship. Differential citizenship, Hudson says, is 'different on different sites and in different contexts and domains; involves multiple capacities; and cannot be totalized by the citizenships people possess as members of a nation-state' (Hudson, 2000: 15–16). The pluralization of citizenship has major implications depending on race, religion, age and gender. One such citizenship, Religious Citizenship, enables people to exercise religious freedoms on the condition that they extend this right to others, at the same time recognizing religious difference in the ways in which they enact their social life (Hudson, 2000).

Religious Citizenship would be an interesting concept for Australians to engage with as it goes beyond anything envisaged by existing legal frameworks in Australia. Because of our colonial origins, Australians were British subjects and we were not granted Australian citizenship until 1949. Australia has only recently grappled with notions of citizenship and does not have a developed understanding of Religious Citizenship, but the Australian Constitution (1900: Section 116) does refer to religion, albeit negatively:

> The Commonwealth shall not make any law for establishing any religion, or for imposing any religious observance, or for prohibiting the free exercise of any religion, and no religious test shall be required as a qualification for any office or public trust under the Commonwealth.

As society becomes more overtly multicultural and therefore multi-religious, we need to develop an understanding of Religious Citizenship which is indigenous to Australia. It would, according to Hudson (2000), involve developing inter-religious understanding nationally and internationally, as well as involving the development of a concern for the good management of faith relations worldwide. It would also require Australia to identify herself as multi-faith rather than secular, and to acknowledge the diversity of religious, anti-religious and secular commitments in society.

Citizenship education in Europe

European citizenship education programmes are very broad and include topics such as human rights education, civic education, peace education, global education, religious education and intercultural education. Central and Eastern European regions have developed citizenship programmes which focus on their status as newly established democracies, while Western European societies are facing different challenges related to changes in demography, increased migration and voter apathy, so their programmes tend to focus more on the need to address the diverse mix of demographies and religions. Regardless of the approaches taken, citizenship education is nevertheless 'central to the idea of a modern, integrated, yet diverse Europe' (Jackson & Steele, 2005: 55).

At least two international projects have focused on religious diversity in relation to social and personal values in the light of the events of 11 September 2001, Bali 2002, Jakarta 2003, Madrid 2004, and the London bombings in 2005. *Teaching for Tolerance and Freedom of Religion or Belief* (Oslo coalition, 2001) concentrated on developing strategies for combating religious intolerance and discrimination and promoting freedom of religion or belief through education. The Council of Europe's project on *Intercultural Education and the Challenge of Religious Diversity and Dialogue* produced materials for practitioners and policy makers across the forty-six member states. The aim of both projects was to focus on 'school education that increases understanding and respect between people of different religions or world-views and foster knowledge about and respect for freedom of religion or belief as a human right' (Larsen & Plesner, 2002). The Council of Europe and the European Commission identify their project, *Education for Democratic Citizenship*, as creating responsible and informed citizens in the context of European integration. Thus, in today's world, Citizenship Education and Religious Education programmes need not only to address issues of intercultural education and religious diversity, but also to promote social cohesion through understanding and respect between peoples.

In England, citizenship education was considered in 1998 through a consultation process led by Professor Bernard Crick. The need to include religion in citizenship education programmes in the UK was reinforced when, in 2001, race riots, expressed in religious terms, occurred in a number of northern English towns. In 2002, English schools introduced Citizenship as a statutory national curriculum foundation subject for eleven- to sixteen-year-olds and as a non-statutory subject for five- to eleven-year-olds. The model of citizenship education on which the Crick report was based, draws on the work of Marshall (1997) and consists of three elements: civic, political and social. While the Crick report modified the first element, civics, to emphasize reciprocity between rights and duties, the report nevertheless focused on national identity and common citizenship, ignoring contexts such as cultural racism and cultural diversity. By ignoring the distinctive features within a multicultural and multi-religious society, the report failed to respect the politics of difference so evident in modern societies.

Pedagogically, the Crick report presented a model of citizenship education which advocated civic participation, social and moral responsibility, and political literacy (McKenna, 2005), all of which require knowledge and understanding of 'the diversity of national, regional, religious and ethnic identities in the United Kingdom and the need for mutual respect and understanding' (DfEE/QCA, 1999).

Citizenship education in Australia

In Australia, citizenship education has tended to focus on understanding Australia's system of government and Australian history, and has not, to date, addressed the growing religious diversity evident within local and national communities. Historically, schools promoted two forms of citizenship: loyalty to Great Britain and the British Empire through the singing of the national anthem, *God Save the King/Queen*, and a developing sense of nationalism through the teaching of poetry, particularly bush ballads (Reid & Gill, 2010). Post 1945, the influx of migrants from Europe, combined with the cultural and social upheaval of the 1960s, and the eventual acknowledgement of Indigenous Australians in the census of 1967, paved the way for a minimal recognition of multiculturalism in the 1970s, but it still did not recognize that multiculturalism also implies religious diversity.

In the early 1980s, with the relaxation of regimented military-style school parades and the shift in formal curricula, civics and citizenship education as expressed within the hidden curricula of school structures shifted, and citizenship education changed to reflect more of a social studies approach focusing on current realities rather than a civic and governmental focus. The Labour governments of the 1980s and early 1990s worked to continue the Whitlam government project of moving Australia from a British colony to an independent nation.

The 1996 election of a Liberal/National Coalition government led by John Howard marked a significant shift in how citizenship was understood:

there was a narrowing of the citizenship education curriculum away from multiculturalism to a distinct focus on Australian values. In 2004, Mr Howard claimed that schools were too value neutral and proposed a focus on values education. The *National Framework for Values* identified nine values for Australian schools: freedom, honesty, respect, care and compassion, fair go, doing your best, integrity, understanding and tolerance, and inclusion. The government spent $29 million on school-based projects to foster these nine values. Many educationists criticized the government for trying to re-create, through school education, individual citizens who were 'loyal, competitive and compliant' (Reid & Gill, 2010: 27) rather than global citizens. In 2006, John Howard stated: 'We've drawn back from being too obsessed with diversity ... Australians are now better able to appreciate the enduring values of the national character that we proudly celebrate and preserve' (cited in Reid & Gill, 2010: 23). During the Howard government, understandings of citizenship were narrowed. The 'other' emerged as a threat. Within the context of '9/11' and the 'war on terror', border protection was emphasized, ideas of multiculturalism diminished and consequently greater emphasis was placed on 'sameness' rather than 'difference'. Australian citizenship was expressed in the language of 'us' and 'them' and schools were left to deal with changing ideas regarding citizenship.

At no stage, however, in the history of Australian citizenship education has there been any serious discussion regarding the place of religion in Australian culture and society. The neglect of religion can be identified on a number of levels: first, religion has been ignored as an aspect of cultural diversity and is left out even at the level of multicultural education. When racism is addressed, little or no attention is paid to religion and religious diversity. Second, education about religion does not occur in state schools even though events such as 11 September and the Bali bombings may be addressed. Religious diversity as a part of cultural diversity cannot be ignored and, unless the religious factor is addressed, values held by many people will not be fully understood. Australian education has had a brief encounter with values education in the recent past, but there has been no serious attempt to address values within a pluralistic context using a sophisticated and rich vocabulary which included values influenced from both religious and non-religious perspectives. While *The Melbourne Declaration* acknowledges cultural and religious diversity, it appears to separate religious diversity from citizenship, and by doing so presents citizenship purely from a legal perspective rather than presenting a broader form of citizenship which embraces cultural, social and religious aspects.

Approaches to teaching citizenship education and religious education

The tension between knowledge-centred education and learner-centred education is important when examining citizenship education. In today's world, the teaching and learning approaches required for the promotion of active citizenship need to be oriented toward developing social cohesion. McLaughlin's (1992) distinction between 'maximal' and 'minimal' interpretations of citizenship education provides a useful distinction. Maximal approaches emphasize active learning which is process-led, allowing students to develop and articulate their own opinions and to engage in debate. Minimal approaches, on the other hand, present civics-related subject knowledge in a formal and didactic manner. An examination of current Australian citizenship programmes indicates that a minimal rather than maximal approach is taken.

Kerr (1999) makes the distinction between citizenship programmes which teach *about, through* and *for* citizenship. Education *about* citizenship is focused on developing knowledge and understanding of national history and the structures and process of government. This style of citizenship education is the easiest to present but is at the 'minimal' end of the continuum because it does not require students to critique their current situation, nor does it question the status quo. Education *through* citizenship is active and participative because it links practical experience with knowledge development and is moving toward the 'maximal' end of the continuum. Education *for* citizenship is a combination of the two approaches 'about and through' and also works to develop skills, attitudes and values which enable students to take an active role in society.

Kerr's analysis and categorization of citizenship education programmes has some parallels with Grimmitt's (2000) three models for teaching religion. The first, education *into* religion, is confessional in approach; focused on one religion only; and taught by insiders of that tradition. Educating *about* religion is an approach which involves learning about the beliefs and practices of a variety of religions through descriptive and/or other lenses and which attempts to examine how religion shapes communities. Learning about religion is valuable in itself and makes it possible to communicate and operate effectively in a multicultural world. Education *from* religion involves encouraging students to ask 'autobiographical questions and to engage in both personal and impersonal evaluations of religious beliefs, values and practices' (Grimmitt, 2000: 35). The strength of the third approach, according to Hull (2002: 109), is that by studying religion in this way students are exposed to 'wider issues with which government and the community at large are rightly concerned'.

Conservative confessional approaches to the teaching of religion, which focus on the unchanging nature of religion and which do not engage in reflection and critique, are close to the 'minimal' end of McLaughlin's continuum. A more liberal approach to teaching religion which focuses on diversified cultural and religious identity and also raises ethical and political issues would, according to Jackson and Steel (2005), contribute to a 'maximal' form of education, but even more effective forms of religious education are those which are contextual and dialogical and pay attention to diversity, plurality and the globalized nature of communities. In Europe, over the past five years there has been increased focus on issues of religious and cultural diversity and plurality and the contribution religious education can make to people's understanding of citizenship. The *Citizenship Education at School in Europe* report recommends that citizenship education embrace 'all members in a given society, regardless of their nationality, sex, racial, social or education background' (cited in Jackson, 2007: 31). There is also widespread support for developing political literacy through citizenship education and in 'linking citizenship education with religious education to reflect the range of conceptions of both fields found across Europe' (p. 31). The report recommended that students should have 'education in religious and secular diversity as part of their intercultural education' and that this should include 'encouraging tolerance for different religious and secular points of view, education in human rights, citizenship and conflict management, and strategies to counter racism and discrimination in a religiously diverse world' (Jackson, 2007: 38). In addition, the report also recommended that schools develop policies with respect to religious diversity; develop curricula that reflects cultural, religious and linguistic diversity; develop a critical attitude toward textbooks and develop criteria for the selection and use of resources (Jackson, 2007). The project established procedures for including learning about religion and religious diversity as an essential part of intercultural education in Europe. Such procedures as these could readily be applied and adapted for use in Australian schools.

Papastephanou (2008) says that religious education can contribute to the development of political identity and the enrichment of citizenship. She sees citizenship as more than learning about fairness, social justice, respect for democracy and diversity at the local and global levels. She believes that in most instances, the political dimension of religious education is ignored. By political, she is not referring to the politics of government but rather 'politics' in its fullest sense of *polis* which requires active involvement in public affairs and action for justice. Papastephanou (2008: 126) argues that robust religious education which is political can 'assist cosmopolitan identity and citizenship ... by emphasizing international and restorative justice and by cultivating a spirit of forgiveness, forgetting and mutual understanding'. By acknowledging, teaching about, and engaging the political in religious education, we avoid presenting religions as being shallow and reified.

Citizenship education could learn a great deal from contemporary pedagogies of religious education, particularly inter-religious education which focuses on developing hermeneutic awareness and critical communication about religion and religious perspectives. Learning happens when differences in interpretation surface and when students recognize difference within particularity. In particular, a model such as the inquiry-based approach developed for *Study of Religion* (Queensland Studies Authority,

2008) in Queensland, which actively involves students in the learning process and encourages them to move beyond the acquisition of facts to metacognition and to take responsibility for their own learning, could be employed (Goldburg, 2010).

Conclusion

Given the developments in expanding understandings of citizenships, a 'Copernican revolution' regarding citizenship education needs to take place in Australia. The revolution would necessitate incorporating the serious study of religion in all schools, both public and independent, from Preparatory year through to year twelve. By including religion as central to education, we would not only be broadening understandings of citizenship, but we would also be acknowledging the place of religion in society and culture 'because the matter of religion – whatever orientation we each adopt – goes to the heart of our emotion and identities ...' (Battaini-Dragoni, 2004: 13 in Jackson et al., 2007: 21).

An understanding of citizenship which encompasses differential citizenships and recognizes social, cultural and religious diversity broadens perceptions by acknowledging that religious identities operate beyond the private sphere and indeed have a place in the public sphere, including public education. Religious education and citizenship programmes which only concentrate on shared, common or national values as a means of initiating dialogue are insufficient because they do not acknowledge difference, nor do they address power imbalances between groups. Programmes which are solely based on principles of empathy and tolerance have also been criticized because they lack critical engagement when issues of human rights or issues of religious beliefs and morals are concerned.

Public education in a pluralist society must deal with difference and religious diversity from a variety of inter-disciplinary perspectives. Developments in the teaching of religion in recent times have focused on pedagogies which enable students not only to learn about religions but also to learn from religions, thereby operationalizing pedagogies of process (Kalantzis & Cope, 1999) which are critical and participative rather than didactic, static and accepting. What Australia needs through the national curriculum is a maximal form of citizenship education which is grounded in critical pedagogy and embraces a political form of religious education resulting in a citizenship-rich programme.

Pragmatically, given Australia's history and its emphasis on secular education which excludes religion from the formal curriculum, we have not addressed the 'impact that religious belief has had on our understanding of humans and their place in the world' (Trigg, 2008: 91), nor have we had a rational debate about the place of religion in the curriculum. Trigg (2008: 92) argues that, 'Whilst a free society cannot, and should not, enforce any religious belief, it should not go to the other extreme, and pretend that religion is of no account from a public perspective, but is a private matter. If education colludes in that approach, some of the strongest roots of democracy may thereby in the end be destroyed.' The recent development of a national curriculum has presented educators with a window of opportunity to reconceptualize citizenship education and to include a study of religion for all students in public schools. It is time to initiate that conversation, take action and revolutionize the teaching of religious education and citizenship education in Australia.

References

ACT Parliamentary Counsel. (2005). NSW Public Instruction Act 1880 (repealed). Retrieved March 8, 2012, from http://www.legislation.act.gov.au/a/1880-23/20050101-17485/pdf/1880-23.pdf

Australian constitution. (1900). *Australianpolitics.com*. Retrieved March 8, 2012, from http://australianpolitics.com/constitution-aus/text/chapter-5-the-states

Battaini-Dragoni, G. (2004). Opening. In Council of Europe (Ed.), *The religious dimension of intercultural education* (pp. 11–14). Strasbourg: Council of Europe Publishing.

DfEE/QCA. (1999). *The national curriculum for England.* London: Department for Education and Employment and Qualification and Curriculum Authority.

Dimitrov, G., & Boyadjieva, P. (2009). Citizenship education as an instrument for strengthening the state's supremacy: An apparent paradox? *Citizenship Studies, 13*(2), 153–169.

Goldburg, P. M. (2010). Developing pedagogies for inter-religious teaching and learning. In K. Engebretson, M. de Souza, G. Durka & L. Gearon (Eds), *International handbook of inter-religious education* (pp. 341–360). Dordrecht: Springer.

Grimmitt, M. (Ed.). (2000). *Pedagogies of religious education: Case studies in the research and development of good pedagogic practice in RE.* Great Wakering: McCrimmon Publishing.

Hermans, C. A. M. (2003). Interreligious learning. In C. A. M. Hermans (Ed.), *Participatory learning: Religious education in a globalizing society* (pp. 334–379). Leiden: Brill.

Hudson, W. (2000). Differential citizenship. In W. Hudson & J. Kane (Eds), *Rethinking Australian citizenship* (pp. 15–25). Cambridge: Cambridge University Press.

Hull, J. M. (2002). The contribution of religious education to religious freedom: A global perspective. In H. Spinder, J. Taylor & W. Westerman (Eds), *Committed to Europe's future: Contributions from education and religious education: A reader* (pp. 107–110). Munster: Coordinating Group for Religious Education in Europe and the Comenius Institute.

Jackson, R. (2007). European institutions and the contribution of studies of religious diversity to education for democratic citizenship. In R. Jackson, S. Miedema, W. Weisse & J. Willaime (Eds), *Religion and education in Europe* (pp. 27–46). Munster: Waxmann.

Jackson, R., & Steele, K. (2005). Citizenship education and religious education: A European perspective. In R. Jackson and U. McKenna (Eds), *Intercultural education and religious plurality* (pp. 53–64). Oslo: Oslo Coalition on Freedom of Religion or Belief.

Kalantzis, M., & Cope, B. (1999). Multicultural education: Transforming the mainstream. In S. May (Ed.), *Critical multiculturalism: Rethinking multicultural and anti-racist education* (pp. 245–276). London: Falmer Press.

Kerr, D. (1999). *Re-examining citizenship education: The case of England.* Slough: NFER.

Kerr, D. (2003). Citizenship education in international perspective. In L. Gearon (Ed.), *Learning to teach citizenship in the secondary school* (pp. 5–27). London: Routledge.

Kiwan, D. (2005). Human rights and citizenship: An unjustifable conflation. *Journal of Philosophy of Education, 39*(1), 37–50.

Kiwan, D., & Kiwan, D. (2005). Citizenship education: The French and English experiences. In C. Pole, J. Pilcher & J. Williams (Eds), *Young people in transition: Becoming citizens* (pp. 136–158). Basingstoke: Palgrave Macmillan.

Larsen, L., & Plesner, I. T. (2002). *Teaching for tolerance and freedom of religion or belief.* Oslo: Oslo Coalition on Freedom of Religion and Belief.

McKenna, U. (2005). A discussion of the relationship between intercultural education, religious diversity and religious education. In R. Jackson & U. McKenna (Eds), *Intercultural education and religious plurality* (pp. 63–76). Oslo: Oslo Coalition on Freedom of Religion or Belief.

McLaughlin, T. (1992). Citizenship, diversity and education: A philosophical perspective. *Journal of Moral Education, 21*(3), 235–250.

Marshall, T. H. (1997). Citizenship and social class. In R. E. Goodin & P. Pettit (Eds), *Contemporary political philosophy* (pp. 291–319). Oxford: Blackwell.

Ministerial Council on Education, Employment, Training and Youth Affairs. (2008). *Melbourne declaration on educational goals for young Australians.* Retrieved March 9, 2012, from http://www.mceecdya.edu.au/verve/_resources/National_Declaration_on_the_Educational_Goals_for_Young_Australians.pdf

Moran, G. (1991). Understanding religion and being religious. *PACE, 21,* 249–252.

Oslo Coalition. (2001). *Teaching for tolerance and freedom of religion or belief.* Retrieved March 8, 2012, from http://www.oslocoalition.org/html/project_school_education/index.html

Papastephanou, M. (2008). Religious education for political thinking and citizenship. *Journal of Beliefs and Values, 29*(2), 125–137.

Queensland Studies Authority. (2008). Study of religion. Retrieved March 8, 2012, from http://www.qsa.qld.edu.au/downloads/senior/snr_study_religion_syll_08.pdf

Reid, A., & Gill, J. (2010). In whose interest? Australian schooling and the changing contexts of citizenship. In A. Reid, J. Gill & A. Sears (Eds), *Globalization, the nation-state and the citizen: Dilemmas and directions for civics and citizenship education* (pp. 19–34). London: Routledge.

Roebben, B. (2008). Fellowship of fate and fellowship of faith: Religious education and citizenship education in Europe. *Journal of Beliefs and Values, 29*(2), 207–211.

Trigg, R. (2008). Private faith and public education. *Journal of Beliefs and Values, 29*(1), 87–92.

Unsworth, L. (2002). *Teaching multiliteracies across the curriculum: Changing contexts of text and image in classroom practice.* Buckingham: Open University Press.

PART II

Theoretical Perspectives

JEFF ASTLEY

5 Can We Choose our Beliefs?
A Philosophical Question for Religious Education

Abstract

In this chapter Astley first distinguishes a freedom *for* religious belief from a deeper freedom *of* belief, in the sense of an 'inner freedom' of human beings to control their religious states of mind, heart and spirit.

There is a considerable literature in philosophy and the philosophy of religion devoted to the issue of the role of the will in belief; and the topic has also been of historical concern to Christian theologians. In exploring these ideas, Astley argues against certain assumptions that are widespread in the debates concerning religious education, especially those that utilize the concepts of intellectual autonomy, decision and choice in ways that imply or directly assert a radical freedom of belief. By contrast, he develops the claim that we possess no more than an indirect freedom in our believing, and that the employment of the language of choice is often misleading as we can only exercise choice at the level of choosing to examine the grounds for our beliefs. We may choose our path to belief; but we cannot directly choose our beliefs.

The implications of these claims for both non-confessional and confessional religious education are discussed.

Freedom 'for' and freedom 'of' belief

In considering the relationship between freedom, on the one hand, and religious beliefs, on the other, discussion normally centres on what I would call *freedom for belief.* This is the concern of most writers in this area, although they frequently describe it as freedom *of* religious belief (or of worship). It is the freedom to express one's religious beliefs by engaging in certain actions, including linguistic actions (confession, evangelism, etc.) and other overt behaviour such as public prayer.

Freedom for belief is frequently characterized as one of the values of the Enlightenment, although it surely has a more ancient lineage and its provenance does not only lie in the West. It is often said to include an unrestrained freedom of enquiry, expression, and public debate; freedom of worship; and freedom 'to pursue one's own vision of the good life in one's own way' (Cupitt, 2008: 50). The 'right to freedom of thought, conscience and religion' of Article 18 of the 1948 *Universal Declaration of Human Rights*, like the 'right to ... religious belief' of Article 18 of the UN's 1981 *Declaration on the Elimination of All Forms of Intolerance and of Discrimination Based on Religion or Belief*, advocates freedom to *exercise* one's religion. Such documents therefore routinely make reference to the freedom to maintain and manifest the religion or beliefs that a person has and holds. This is an 'outer freedom': a freedom *to act out* one's desires, beliefs, and convictions. It is rightly a matter of considerable moral, political, religious and educational concern.

In this chapter, however, I am more interested in a rather different and deeper form of freedom. This is our *freedom of belief* in the sense of the 'inner freedom' of human beings to control these (religious) states of mind, heart and spirit. The value we place on religious liberty in terms of freedom from external restrictions with respect to activities such as worship and evangelism leads many to assume that people also have (and strongly value) an inner freedom to control what they believe and worship. But do we possess that sort of freedom?

Arguments against freedom of belief

In the literature on the nature of belief, some have written of a 'will to believe', or at least they have assumed a strong, direct volitional element in belief, particularly in religious belief, together with a concomitant duty to believe certain things and not to believe others. I shall argue, against this view, that we possess no more than an *indirect* freedom in our believing; and that employing the language of choice in this context – as many religionists and religious educators quite commonly do – can be misleading. My thesis, in brief, is that although we may choose our paths to belief, we cannot directly choose any of our beliefs.

Now, the view that we can give or withhold assent to some beliefs by a direct act of will has received reputable endorsement from several philosophers. Thomas Aquinas distinguished religious faith (*fides*) from scientific knowledge (*scientia*) on the grounds that the assent of the intellect in the case of faith is not wholly coerced by the object of reason or by rational evidence, but requires an additional voluntary act of the will (moved by God's grace). 'Mere hearing is not a sufficient cause. The assent is caused by the will, not by any necessity of reason' (*de Veritate*, 3 *ad* 12, quoted in Gilby, 1955: 198). René Descartes held an even stronger position. The Cartesian view is that *all* believing involves our free action. We are free to decide to perform this activity or not. In affirming or denying propositions – other than those that are clear, distinct, and indubitable (propositions about the existence of the thinking self and of God) – we are acting wholly freely (*Meditations on the First Philosophy*, IV).

On accounts such as these, we are directly responsible for any false cognitions that we may hold.

There are, however, two arguments against this position that seem to me to be decisive. The first argument is essentially phenomenological, in that it appeals to the actual phenomenon of belief – that is, to its psychology. Believing something appears to be a passive state, something that happens to us rather than something that we do. Coming to a belief, it has been said, 'seems more like falling than jumping, catching a cold than catching a ball' (Pojman, 1986: 160). Indeed, it is 'psychologically impossible' to believe at will (Alston, 1989: 122).

If you doubt this, just try it. Try straining yourself to believe something that you presently do not believe, simply by an act of will rather than by ruminating on arguments or evidence. We cannot manufacture belief in that sense. We cannot even manufacture the reasons for our beliefs – or even for our actions. As Galen Strawson has put the matter:

> [H]owever much one deliberates, and whatever one does finally do when one actually acts, one does what one does for reasons ... that one just finds one has (or finds occurring to one or seeming right or relevant to one) in the situation in which one then is. And whatever the precise nature of the processes by which one has come to have these reasons ... there is a simple and fundamental sense in which one is demonstrably not truly or ultimately responsible for the fact that one has them. (Strawson, 1986: 313)

Many philosophers tend to place even more weight on a second argument. This is the argument that there is something incoherent, or at least logically odd, in the claim that one can obtain or sustain a belief in full consciousness by any act of one's own will. The meaning of a belief appears to preclude its being the direct product of any volition. If that is the case, it would seem to be essential that our control over our own believing should be limited if it is to remain a form of 'believing' at all. According to Bernard Williams:

> If I could acquire a belief at will, I could acquire it whether it was true or not; moreover I would know that I could acquire it whether it was true or not ... I could not then, in full consciousness, regard this as a belief of mine, i.e. something I take to be true, and also know that I acquired it at will. (Williams, 1973: 148)

On this view, it follows from the very logic of belief that 'one does not want to be self-determining either with respect to (simple, factual) belief or with respect to one's canons of reasoning, but [one] simply wants truth in beliefs and validity in reasoning' (Strawson, 1986: 47–48). As beliefs aim at truth, I cannot wholly control my beliefs – or they would no longer count as beliefs.

The position that we cannot directly will what we believe is one that has been adopted by many philosophers of religion. In addition to those cited elsewhere in the paper, see Griffiths (2001: xiv, 28), Plantinga (1987), Price (1969: 221–240; 1975), Swinburne (2005: 24–28, 264–268) and Ward (1994: 323–324). Most of these authors, however, are unwilling to go along with the radical position that was held by David Hume that the will *never* plays a role in the formation of belief. Hume's blanket claim that belief 'depends not on the will, but must arise from certain determinate causes and principles, of which we are not masters' (*A Treatise of Human Nature,* Appendix) may be true of our *perceptual beliefs*; but surely the will plays some role in many of those beliefs that we characterize as religious? After all, religious beliefs are mostly not beliefs about the direct objects or data of sense experience. They are more abstract beliefs that bear only a complex and distanced relationship, if any, to such experiences (although some may ultimately be grounded in cognate mystical or numinous experiences). On account of their abstraction and their complex structures, many religious beliefs are best classified as metaphysical or ideological. In such cases, as well as in many more ordinary forms of non-perceptual believing, it would appear to be the case that we can – at least on occasions – obtain or sustain a belief by the *indirect* operation of various acts of will. In cases like this, we are able to perform certain actions that can lead to changes in our beliefs. I am thinking here of such operations as selectively directing our attention onto certain evidence and arguments, or even imagining what things would be like if the proposition under consideration were true. We can and do perform these acts, and as a consequence our beliefs often change. In this respect, therefore, we may *indirectly* affect what we believe.

> It is primarily because we judge that our beliefs are to some significant degree the indirect results of our actions that we speak of being responsible for them. Although we cannot be said to be directly responsible for them, as though they were actions, we can be said to be indirectly responsible for many of them. If we had chosen differently, if we had been better moral agents, paid attention to the evidence, and so forth, we would have different beliefs than we in fact do have. (Pojman, 1986: 180)

In other words, we are not directly free to believe or to disbelieve something; but we *are* free to engage in trying to understand certain arguments, or to seek out certain sorts of evidence, or to engage in other forms of behaviour that may themselves change what we believe.

As Kevin Kinghorn has argued (2005: 47), this 'notion of *in*direct belief acquisition is less problematic – but only inasmuch as we assume a person's efforts to carry no guarantee of success' in this area. This feature is key. It means that there may still be 'no decision open to [the believer] by which he can ultimately control whether or not he holds the belief'. *Indirect volitionalism*, as this position has been called, does allow for some element of choice in believing. But our choice remains at some distance from – and certainly cannot be guaranteed to deliver – the moment of assent. *That* remains beyond our power to control. Our beliefs are (ultimately) forced into us – or, if you prefer, they are forced out of us – by something else. At their rational best, our beliefs are determined by good arguments and convincing evidence. They are not *our* direct creations; nor should they be.

> [T]he freedom that the learner can exercise is not a freedom to adopt one belief and reject another, but a freedom to engage in actions that have much more indirect, and sometimes unpredictable, consequences on her beliefs. (Astley, 1994: 200)

And the same may be said, with the appropriate qualifications, of the learner's affective states: for example, her religious values and dispositions to act, and her attitudes and feelings of trust and commitment. As these attributes, alongside her beliefs about religious realities, together make up her *religious faith* (her religious 'belief-in'), then that faith can only be affected by the learner's will indirectly and in an uncertain fashion. So we cannot directly control our faith either. Whom or what we believe in depends on (a) whom or what we believe to be real; (b) our evaluation of and commitment in trust to these objects of belief; and (c) our decisions to act on these beliefs, attitudes, and commitments. In a theistic context, while category (c) may be said to represent our free active trust or belief in God, categories (a) and (b) – on which (c) depends – are determined by passive states over which we have no direct control.

Implications for religious learning

What follows from these claims? Theologically, what follows is that religious faith and religious belief are states of human beings that are not culpable or meritorious, or at least not in any straightforward way. We do not, because we cannot, directly choose or control our religious believing. It may be, as many religions claim, that God will judge our actions, including those actions that may indirectly lead toward (or away from) religious conviction. But who can judge us for either possessing or not possessing the consequent *passive* states of assent to 'God's truths', or affective trust in 'God's promises'? This question is, of course, a matter of contentious *theological* debate, and therefore belongs in a different collection of essays. In such a book we should surely be instructed that some theologians and religious traditions that embrace theological determinism hold that we are responsible for our beliefs and actions even though God ultimately determines everything we believe and do. (As if *that* helps ...)

Our concern here, however, is with what follows for the practice of religious education from these claims concerning the place of freedom of belief.

Religious education may be viewed as a broad category that includes both confessional and non-confessional modes. Confessional religious education involves educating students *into* religious belief ('forming' or 'nurturing' their beliefs); whereas non-confessional religious education teaches students *about* these beliefs, without seeking from its students any commitment to them. As it happens, both modes of religious education speak warmly of the learners' responsibility for their own learning, as a crucial aspect of their autonomy. But these claims are often seriously overstated.

Central to the idea of autonomy is the notion of individual learners forming beliefs and making judgements for themselves on criteria that these learners have themselves accepted, while doing this in a self-critical way by keeping these criteria under review and acting on their decisions. Both in its moral and intellectual designation, autonomy comes down to the idea of 'personal choice'. In employing that phrase I have always stressed the word 'personal' rather than the word 'choice'. In the case of intellectual autonomy, the learning outcome is very largely forced on us. The belief under consideration has certainly become 'my' belief, but this belief does not result (or, rather, it does not *directly* result) from any choices that I have made. Belief is not a matter of my 'deciding to believe'. 'Autonomy here can mean no more than that it is the *real I*, not-less-than-I, who comes to have a belief; and who perhaps exercises choice only at the level of choosing to examine the evidence' at an earlier stage in the process (Astley, 1994: 206). We choose the pathways that lead to our beliefs; we do not (because we cannot) directly choose those beliefs themselves. We should therefore not construe intellectual autonomy as incorporating an untrammelled cognitive freedom, for that is simply not plausible as an account of what it is to come to believe anything.

Elmer Thiessen (1993, ch. 5) has argued for a *properly qualified* notion of autonomy, while opposing the seductive educational rhetoric of other writers about the possibility and desirability of any full rational autonomy – that is, of an absolute independence of mind and unrestricted critical competence within the learner. Thiessen dismisses the latter notion as a romanticized, unrealistic ideal, preferring Lawrence Haworth's (1986) account of our *normal* rational autonomy or critical competence. Haworth recognizes a tradition-bound autonomy that sets realistic limits to demands for critical reflection, and which takes for granted the other values and beliefs that we acquire by means of our (inevitable) nurture within a determinate culture. In a later work, Thiessen adds:

> A more defensible approach to choice in regard to religious belief would make reference to dispositions to believe, and this will lead to a more moderate assessment of the place of the will in religious commitment. ...
> Human beings have only limited free will. ... While in nearly all cases involving voluntary behavior, the agent has a degree of independence and choice, freedom is limited to some degree by such constraints as heredity, psychology, environment, and social context. (Thiessen, 2011: 96, 167–168)

The term 'normal autonomy' is also used by the psychologist of religion, Heije Faber (1975), to signal his belief that self-confidence and creativity can only properly develop on the foundation of a more passive and dependent basic trust. Outside these limits, he claims, it would become 'perverted self-justification' and 'desperate self-assertion'.

Taking up these insights, I have argued that the issue of autonomy in confessional religious education is best situated in the context of a balance between a *formative education* that forms the learners' beliefs (and their attitudes, values, feelings, and dispositions to act and experience), on the one hand; and a *critical education* that enables them critically to evaluate such learning outcomes from their own standpoint, on the other hand (Astley, 1994, ch. 5; 2000: 2, 37–53).

At the risk of repetition, I wish to underscore one particular point. Although we do not choose our beliefs, this does not mean that we cannot *change* our beliefs, and especially that we cannot change them on the basis of our decision to subject them to critical appraisal. Vincent Brümmer (1981: 154–157) agrees that 'it is not possible to choose whether or not to become convinced by the evidence'; but he insists that it is possible for us to choose whether or not we will allow ourselves to consider that evidence. Being rational, he adds (p. 194), is a matter of adopting 'an open and critical attitude towards those beliefs which we have' (which is one of the learning outcomes of a critical education). Thus 'critical rationality' is as much dependent on an affective stance as is any other way of life. It requires a positive attitude toward rational believing, in addition to a certain sort of cognitive behaviour.

But we must be cautious here, too, because – as I have claimed above – our attitudes are not under the direct control of our will either. The affective dimensions of a critical attitude (as 'open', 'tentative', and 'cautious') are not aspects of ourselves that we can *directly* choose. Nevertheless, as Aristotle insisted, we can develop certain attitudes by an indirect route, by freely engaging in certain sorts of behaviour; and once it has been formed an attitude is, or includes, a disposition to act in a certain manner. And we may certainly be said to be free in our decision whether or not to adopt such policies of behaviour. So 'it is by doing just acts that the just man is produced, and by doing temperate acts the temperate man' (*Nicomachean Ethics*, II: 4). Or, to quote Friedrich von Hügel, 'I kiss my child not only because I love it; I kiss it also in order to love it' (von Hügel, 1921: 251).

To translate this into action relevant to our present example, we may decide to search for and steadfastly examine any evidence and arguments that appear to conflict with the beliefs that we presently hold. If that is all that is meant by being 'open-minded' or 'rational', then it is true that we *can* 'decide to be' open-minded or rational by deciding to engage in the sort of behaviour that forms us in open-minded or rational attitudes and dispositions. We are also, of course, free to *refuse* to seek out material that conflicts with our current beliefs; and in that sense we can decide not only *not* to treat certain beliefs in a rational way, but also to form ourselves in an uncritical cognitive orientation or stance. By exercising our choices in these different ways we may thus develop attitudes that are either more critical and open, or more uncritical and closed.

Such attitudes may be formed in us, therefore, as other virtues are, by habitual behaviour. But that is not their main source. Mostly they arise as learning outcomes of some form of critical or 'liberal' education. Critical education not only needs to give its learners the opportunity of adopting critical enquiry by equipping them with the appropriate critical skills of rational evaluation. It must also make them *feel* tentative and open about their beliefs. Critical learners must be formed in a critical stance toward their beliefs. It should also evoke in them some degree of love for critical reflection – in particular, a desire for and disposition toward critical exploration and reflective evaluation. Paradoxically, therefore, critical education must include a formative dimension.

All this is as true of religious education as it is of other areas of learning. Confessional religious education naturally involves a considerable amount of formation in religious beliefs, as well as in religious attitudes, values, feelings, and dispositions to act and experience. But non-confessional religious education must also include an element of formation, if its students are to learn critically to evaluate the religions that they study. They must be formed in the dispositions and virtues, as well as in the intellectual skills, of the critical learner.

Many argue that other formative components are integral to non-confessional religious education. The development of tolerance is one candidate that is much beloved of religious educators. In a survey of secondary Religious Education teachers in England, 'becoming tolerant of other religions and world views' featured at the top of the priority list of the proper aims of Religious Education for teachers in both secular ('community') and Catholic schools (Astley, Francis, Burton, & Wilcox, 1997: 172, 183 n. 2; cf. Astley, Francis, Wilcox, & Burton, 2000). Additionally, as I have argued elsewhere, a proper emphatic *understanding* of religious attitudes, experiences, and emotions – and of the beliefs with which they are so intimately associated – also requires a religious education that helps develop elements of these affective states in its learners, or at least something closely akin to them (Astley, 2007, 2012).

In both forms of religious education, the confessional and the non-confessional, the weaker the view of freedom of belief that we adopt, the more the learner's responsibility for her own beliefs diminishes and the educator's liability for that learner's beliefs increases. My thesis thus increases the burden of accountability that lies on the shoulders of those who structure, facilitate, and enable religious learning (even though neither the learner nor her teacher has any direct and certain effect on the learner's learning). It must be stressed, however, that to acknowledge the power and responsibility that all teachers have with regard to other people's beliefs does not imply that they are exercising any improper control over those learners, nor that they are putting at risk the learners' *real* autonomy. It is simply a matter of being realistic about what happens in the real world, including the real world of teaching and learning. To insist on name-calling by describing all such facilitated-learning 'manipulation' or 'indoctrination', rather than 'education', would leave us without any contenders for the titles of proper educators and the properly educated.

The educator's indirect responsibility for the beliefs of those in his or her charge is a responsibility that is shared with the learner. It is also shared with Nature and society (and, according to theists, with God). We should not, therefore, blame their teachers for *everything* that learners of religion learn or religious believers believe.

But nor can teachers transfer all of their own responsibility onto the shoulders even of their adult students, however loudly they bully them with the refrain, 'Take responsibility for your own learning!' The responsibility for learning is more widely shared than many seem to allow. As no one can come to believe anything by any direct act of will, we should certainly stop implying or assuming in our educational (and our religious) rhetoric that whether a learner learns (or believes) or not is somehow entirely his or her own fault.

References

Alston, W. P. (1989). *Epistemic justification*. Ithaca, NY: Cornell University Press.

Astley, J. (1994). *The philosophy of Christian religious education*. Birmingham, Alabama: Religious Education Press.

Astley, J. (Ed.). (2000). *Learning in the way: Research and reflection on adult Christian education*. Leominster: Gracewing.

Astley, J. (2007). Crossing the divide? In M. Felderhof, P. Thompson, & D. Torevell (Eds), *Inspiring faith in schools: Studies in religious education* (pp. 175–186). Aldershot: Ashgate.

Astley, J. (2012). A theological reflection on the nature of religious truth. In J. Astley, L. J. Francis, M. Robbins, & M. Selçuk (Eds), *Teaching religion, teaching truth: Theoretical and empirical perspectives* (pp. 241–262). Bern: Peter Lang.

Astley, J., Francis, L. J., Burton, L., & Wilcox, C. (1997). Distinguishing between aims and methods in RE: A study among secondary RE teachers. *British Journal of Religious Education, 19*(3), 171–185.

Astley, J., Francis, L. J., Wilcox, C., & Burton, L. (2000). How different is religious education in Catholic schools? A study of teacher aims in England. *International Journal of Education and Religion, 1*(2), 267–281.

Brümmer, V. (1981). *Theology and philosophical inquiry*. London and Basingstoke: Macmillan.

Cupitt, D. (2008). *The Meaning of the West: An apologia for secular Christianity*. London: SCM.

Faber, H. (1975). *Psychology of religion*. ET London: SCM.

Gilby, T. (Ed.). (1955). *St. Thomas Aquinas: Theological texts*. ET London: Oxford University Press.

Griffiths, P. J. (2001). *Problems of religious diversity*. Oxford: Blackwell.

Haworth, L. (1986). *Autonomy: An essay in philosophical psychology and ethics*. New Haven, CT: Yale University Press.

Kinghorn, K. (2005). *The decision of faith: Can Christian beliefs be freely chosen?* London: T. & T. Clark International.

Plantinga, A. (1987). Justification and theism. *Faith and Philosophy, 4*, 403–426.

Pojman, L. P. (1986). *Religious belief and the will*. London: Routledge & Kegan Paul.

Price, H. H. (1969). *Belief*. London: Allen & Unwin.

Price, H. H. (1975). Belief and will. In R. F. Dearden, P. H. Hirst, & R. S. Peters (Eds), *Reason* (pp. 198–217). London: Routledge & Kegan Paul.

Strawson, G. (1986). *Freedom and belief*. Oxford: Clarendon Press.

Swinburne, R. (2005). *Faith and reason*. Oxford: Clarendon Press.

Thiessen, E. J. (1993). *Teaching for commitment: Liberal education, indoctrination, and Christian nurture*. Montreal: McGill-Queen's University Press.

Thiessen, E. (2011). *The ethics of evangelism: A philosophical defence of ethical proselytizing and persuasion*. Milton Keynes: Paternoster.

von Hügel, F. (1921). *Essays and addresses in the philosophy of religion*, First Series. London: Dent.

Ward, K. (1994). *Religion and revelation: A theology of revelation in the world's religions*. Oxford: Oxford University Press.

Williams, B. (1973). Deciding to believe. In B. Williams, *Problems of the Self*. Cambridge: Cambridge University Press.

PETRO DU PREEZ

6 Toward a Curriculum for Morality, Human Rights and Freedom of Religion(s) and Belief(s)

Abstract

Curriculum structure and practice in pre-modern and modern contexts have demonized religions, silenced the vulnerable and created a culture where human wrongs are ideologically justifiable. In this chapter, I will explore this statement and aim to justify a postmodern conception of curriculum that is profoundly moral and human rights-orientated and creates enabling spaces for human beings to express their freedom of religion(s) and belief(s). Such a conception of curriculum necessitates that human rights and freedom of religion(s) and belief(s) should not exclusively be addressed in Religious Education, but that they should be infused into the whole curriculum. Furthermore, the aim will not be to investigate the nature of, and the relationship between, morality, human rights and freedom of religion(s) and belief(s). Rather, the aim is to generate a profound moral curriculum theory that enables human begins to bring their private lives into the public domain through expressing freedom of religion(s) and belief(s), so as to better understand the life-worlds of fellow human beings in a human rights culture.

Past wisdoms – Present conditions

> The trouble with the wisdom of the past is that it dies, so to speak, on
> our hands as soon as we try to apply it honestly to the central political
> experiences of our time.
>
> — ARENDT, 1994: 309

It has been argued that education is by its very nature a moral endeavour.
For philosophers such as Socrates and Plato 'reflection on the purposes
and methods of education was inseparable from reflection on morality,
knowledge, or the nature of a just society' (Burbules & Warnick, n.d.: 1).
However, one might argue that modern education has annihilated the moral
potential of education and has, in many instances, perpetuated a conception of education devoid of morals. This is largely due to neo-liberalist
ideologies, global politics and market-driven rhetoric that frames modern
education (Apple, 2010; Sörlin and Vessuri, 2007; Slattery, 2006) and that
has, to my mind, led to the loss of these philosophers' *sophia* (or wisdom).
With this loss came an ontology of education devoid of a profound moral
nature. Slattery (2006: 73) argues that in such conditions '[t]he curriculum is often used as a cultural bomb to eradicate beliefs'. Given this, one
might question whether discourses *vis-à-vis* morality, human rights and
freedom of religion(s) and belief(s) receive ample attention in curriculum
theorizing. Or are they only superficially included in official curricula to
silence those who advocate the inclusion of morality and justice in the
curriculum? These questions require a critical exploration into the nature
of leading curriculum theories, how they relate to theories about moral
education, and the extent to which these theories could accommodate
such discourses.

   Given that the nature of, and relationship between, morality, human
rights and religion (freedom of religion(s) and belief(s)) has been widely
researched from a variety of perspectives (Morrison, 2000; Gearon, 2002;
Du Preez, 2005), this chapter will explore curriculum theories in relation to
moral education theories that might serve as a context to unite and infuse

discourses regarding morality, human rights and freedom of religion(s) and belief(s) in the curriculum. From a curriculum point of view, I support Bernstein's (2009: 290) notion of the integrated curriculum, which seeks to develop curricula through integrating contents and discourses, instead of isolating them. Therefore, I will not exclusively focus on morality, human rights and freedom of religion(s) and belief(s) in the context of the Religious Education curriculum, but in terms of how these discourses could infuse the curriculum as a whole. I will not refer to the curriculum as merely a syllabus, but as a comprehensive phenomenon embracing an integrated set of activities that includes learning-teaching practices, assessment and the general school climate (Graham-Jolly, 2009).

The explorations in this study will attempt to shed light on the following question: what is the nature of a postmodern theory of curriculum for morality, human rights and freedom of religion(s) and belief(s)? I will argue that freedom of religion(s) and belief(s) cannot be realized in the context of pre-modern and modern conceptions of curriculum, especially when it comes to pre-modern and modern views of religion in education, and mainly due to the moral theories that underpin these conceptions of curriculum. It will be argued that a postmodern conception of curriculum (Slattery, 2006) might better account for freedom of religion(s) and belief(s) due to the moral nature of such a conception and its receptiveness toward human rights discourses.

Curriculum as moral habituation:
Freedom of religion and belief to the uncritical masses

> Is it not generally true that one is not in a good position to judge the conception of the good one has been raised in, since one will tend to see what one has grown accustomed to as good?
>
> — CURREN, 2008: 510

Due to the influx of political refugees, immigrants and migrant workers from different African countries into South Africa, the country has become a volatile xenophobic battleground. Various violent incidents have occurred in poverty-stricken township areas. These include the burning of immigrants' and migrant workers' houses, small businesses and human beings themselves. In many instances, it is argued that these immigrants and migrant workers *steal* the work of South Africans and that their presence leads to a loss of culture and religion in the local communities. This situation is disconcerting, given the fact that many of these human perpetrators were once, during apartheid, victims of discrimination and inhuman treatment, due to their cultural and religious orientations. Hence, one would anticipate affection and empathy: instead, one sees fear, brutal action and hatred. Also, the value of *ubuntu* (a caring, communitarian value meaning: I am because you are) seems to have lost credence. This phenomenon confirms Moore's claim that 'for very many human beings, especially the mass of human beings at the bottom of the pyramid in stratified societies, social order is a good thing in its own right, one for which they will often sacrifice other values' (1978; cited in Dlamini, 2010: 11).

Some might argue that the phenomenon described above is *normal*: the values of the oppressor leave their traces behind long after the roles have changed, and that the oppressed often becomes the oppressor. I would argue that this is not enough, it is a mere polarization of the victim and the victor, and that a possible explanation for this lies in our politico-historical background. Under apartheid the nationalist education system socially regulated, intimidated and indoctrinated the majority black culture into the hegemonic discourses of the minority white cultures' cultural, religious and political views. Slattery (2006: 73) confirms this, arguing that schools have for many years been the gate-keepers of social regulation, intimidation and indoctrination; places where dominant, hegemonic cultures are bred and nurtured, and counter-hegemonic cultures are trivialized through processes of systematic assimilation and oppression. The latter is described by Valenzuela as *subtractive schooling*. This refers to how schooling and the nature of the curriculum often 'adds a second culture' (a dominant, hegemonic culture) and 'subtracts an original culture' (the counter-hegemonic cultures) (Valenzuela, 2009: 339). This phenomenon has led to the rise of an uncritical mass: a mass that are granted freedom of religion and belief based on their (un)conscious conformity to the more powerful culture's beliefs and views. This systematic process has also left *a knowledge in the blood* (Jansen, 2009) – *a* knowledge of *one* unquestionable narrative.

I would argue that the situation described above is mostly attributed to systematic, prolonged moral habituation (Curren, 2008: 510). That is the approach to moral education in which a set of values are inculcated in learners to change their behaviour (Joseph & Efron, 2005: 525). Virtue-ethicists, the proponents of this approach, contend that moral decisions are based on the communal or shared values and virtues in a community. This approach is character-building orientated and realized when learn-ers are provided with clear directions, good role models and incentives for good behavioural change (Joseph & Efron, 2005: 525–526). This neo-Aristotelian approach focuses on the notion that moral education ought to encourage good habits since this will nurture good character (Curren, 2008: 508). Noddings and Slote (2005) argue that character education dominated the history of moral education both in western and eastern philosophies for many years. Empirical studies (especially in the USA) and criticisms related to the assumption that it is possible to establish a set of values that everyone adheres to and understands led to the decline of this approach (Noddings & Slote, 2005: 350). However, it should be noted that the traces of moral habituation are still prominent in the hidden curriculum of a country like South Africa that has for so long been totally focused on this approach.

Curren (2008: 510–511), who refers to the weakness of the assump-tion made by character education as the problem of local variation, raises five more criticisms of this approach to moral education. First, he warns of possible indoctrination in that the values or virtues that are prioritized could manipulate and mould learners' perceptions and foster a disposition of uncritical acceptance. Second, he argues that moral habituation might foreclose the life options of children and usurp their right to an open future. Third, he cautions that moral habituation is driven by force and not established through rational persuasion. Fourth, he raises the prob-lem of scepticism which is concerned with the logicality and rationality of moral issues. Finally, Curren argues that character education does not allow human beings to evaluate or revise the set of values or virtues that are imposed on them: '[t]he problem ... is how morality can both command our fidelity and be open to effective public scrutiny and appropriate revision. It would seem that [character education] can only have one of these properties at the expense of the other' (Curren, 2008: 513). The weaknesses of moral habituation, as described above, become a reality when stories of xenophobic attacks and behaviours occur. What is most prominent is this approach's inability to awaken the affective, empathetic potential in human beings, which is needed when human beings are faced with the inherent otherness of co-humans.

I would further like to propose that this theory of moral education correlates to Slattery's idea of *theology as curriculum text* (2006: 101). Theology as curriculum text refers to a curriculum that is based on a value system, one that is based on a particular hegemonic religious or ideological narrative. He describes such an approach to the development of a curriculum as autocratic, dogmatic and fundamentalist in orientation (Slattery, 2006). Such a traditionalist interpretation of curriculum development is not only bureaucratic and based on a technological rationality (Pinar, 2009: 169), but is also one that welcomes the less complex nature of a universal metanarrative. The biggest problem with this approach is that it renders a chosen group, usually those adhering to the hegemonic viewpoints, with a responsibility to construct a curriculum for human beings of diverse contexts – human beings who might differ in their viewpoints. The questions arising then are: how morally honest is a curriculum developed by the uncritical mass? How can such an approach to curriculum development create a space for expressing freedom of religion(s) and belief(s) if it is centred upon one meta-narrative? How can we teach human rights as a just, moral construct in a diverse society epitomized by moral monism? I agree with Slattery who argues that '... the pre-modern paradigm of the theological text as curriculum ... will lead only to further ideological conflagration' (2006: 104–105).

Curriculum as rationality:
Freedom of religion and belief to the secular individual

> 'My life was better during apartheid', said Mr Ntswayi. 'Freedom turned out to be just a word. Real freedom, real power, that comes from money – and I haven't got any money.'
>   — NARRATIVE EXCERPT FROM DLAMINI, 2010: 5

Xenophobic behaviour is not only attributed to moral habituation, but also to classism, racism, colonization and empire-building (Slattery, 2006: 79). Neo-liberal forces in the curriculum perpetuate these actions by reinforcing neo-liberal virtues such as the importance of individual rights, competitiveness, universalism and impersonalism (Bridges & Jonathan, 2005; Smith, 2009). A conception of morality built on such virtues might be problematic in that it rationalizes complex moral issues to simplistic matters – matters devoid of humanity and based on the survival of the privileged. Such a conception of morality is visible in the liberalist paradigm, which draws on Lawrence Kohlberg's cognitive development theory. This paradigm maintains that humans make moral decisions based on their individual rationality. Kohlberg, whose theory is derived from a liberal-democratic ideal of justice, strongly opposed character education. He argues that human beings seldom agree on values, even if they belong to the same culture, and that not enough attention is given to the essential worth and meaning of the set of values in this approach (Noddings & Slote, 2005: 351). In Kohlberg's view, moral education should lead learners through six progressive stages (Fullinwider, 2008: 502). These phases could be described as follows: human beings take morally right action to (1) avoid punishment, (2) satisfy their desires, (3) obtain approval of others, (4) obey laws or conventions, (5) judge right and wrong in terms of a social contract, and (6) respond to their self-constructed ethical principles based on logical comprehensiveness, universality and consistency (Fullinwider, 2008: 501–502). After a lengthy critique of Kohlberg's theory, Fullinwider (2008: 505) arrives at the conclusion that these stages are in fact not stages of moral development, but stages of intellectual or theoretical sophistication. For Gareth Matthews, however, the chief problem of such models is the constraints they impose: 'we must guard against letting those models caricature our children and limit the possibilities we are willing to recognize in our dealings with them' (1995: 29). It seems, however, that character educators in general are critical of the liberal paradigm's fixation with the moral process and methodology (or stages) and its neglect of moral content (or a predefined set of values) (Noddings & Slote, 2005: 351).

The curriculum tradition that corresponds to this conception of morality is described by Slattery (2006: 101) as *curriculum as technological text*. This curriculum promotes learners as independent, secular individuals who should place their trust in individual rationality to successfully participate in a global economic environment. However, it might be argued that a liberalist approach to curriculum development might be inherently oppressive in that it assumes that 'human reason is the same everywhere' and 'all reasonable people will abide by the version of reality that reason draws and maps for them' (Smith, 2009: 372). This rationalized attempt to level the playing field does not take diversity into consideration, as can be demonstrated in violent xenophobic attacks, for instance. Another example is how some, privileged under apartheid, constructed an apartheid reality by reinforcing the othering process with their neo-liberal virtues. For example, in describing 'the problem of blacks in modern contexts', Marais and Van der Kooy (1978; cited in Dlamini, 2010: 131) writes the following:

> The seriousness of this problem is due: first, to the urban blacks who themselves are in a most difficult stage of their adjustment; the difficulty of adjusting from being tribesmen to becoming city-dwellers. It is the difficulty of adjusting to differences between tribal discipline and individualism, between a subsistence economy and a highly competitive market economy, between African religions and Christianity, between rural security and urban insecurity and between tribal realisation and self-realisation.

This also represents thinking that aims to subtract an original culture and add a second hegemonic culture (Valenzuela, 2009: 339).

One might also argue that the liberalist approach artificially reduces religion(s) and belief(s) to the private sphere, not acknowledging how human beings inevitably bring their religions and beliefs into the public sphere. In this regard, Arendt says: 'Nothing proved easier to destroy than the privacy and private morality of people who thought of nothing but safeguarding their private lives' (1978: 338). This time one might ask: how morally honest is a curriculum dictated by individual rationality that is driven by the self-constructed reality of the privileged and the powerful who have the means to participate in a global economy? How can a curriculum grant a space for morality if it demonizes religion(s) and belief(s) (that often act as human beings' moral construct) by reducing it to the private sphere? Does this mean that freedom of religion and belief are only limited to the private life-world? Slattery postulates that '... the modern theological approach to curriculum development will continue to avoid the questions of morality, spirituality, and theology as essential elements of schooling because these issues are considered outside the modern scientific parameters of the school' (2006: 105).

Curriculum as care:
Freedom of religion(s) and belief(s) to the affective human being

> To treat people, including strangers, with kindness is to treat people as ends in themselves, rather than as means to my ends; to treat them with respect and politeness.
> — DLAMINI, 2010: 98

Research conducted by Valenzuela indicated that 'youth prefer to be *cared for* before they *care about* school, especially [in contexts] when the curriculum is impersonal, irrelevant, and test driven' (2009: 342). This finding does not only bring a liberalist approach to moral education and a neo-liberalist curriculum ideology into question, but suggests a different way of thinking about morality when it comes to curriculum work. It suggests a curriculum for care, based on caring relations between *the caring* and *the cared for* (Noddings, 1984; cited in Valenzuela, 2009: 342). Expanding on this, one might argue that human beings will care for or respect the religion(s) and belief(s) of others if they feel that their own religions and beliefs are cared about and respected. This reasoning requires a space where caring relations can be established and where human beings are free to express and dialogue their freedom of religion(s) and belief(s). Such an approach to curriculum is described by Slattery (2006: 101) as *curriculum as theological text*. This process-orientated, communitarian curriculum is strongly based on the design element integration (Slattery, 2006). It also seems to place religion(s) and belief(s) in the public space – the space where they can be critically dialogued to create profound wisdom of significant Others. In this conception of curriculum 'the educational enterprise will include the metaphysical dialogue. In this proposal, self-reflection, intuition, nonrational discourse, nonlinear teaching methodologies, meditation, and wisdom are all encouraged and nurtured in the curriculum' (Slattery, 2006: 105).

Such conceptions of curriculum are morally illuminated by the work of the ethicists of care who argue that the moral decisions human beings make are based on their affective and intellectual understanding of a situation that requires them to respond to their caring self and to prioritize the significant Other when making such decisions. According to Noddings and Slote (2005: 345), care theorists, whose arguments are often deeply embedded in feminist theory, contend that moral education should sensitize human beings to consult their constructed caring self (or identity) in the absence of a spontaneous inclination to care. In line with this, Tronto states the following: 'The moral question an ethic of care takes as central is not – What, if anything, do I (we) owe to others? but rather – How can I (we) best meet my (our) caring responsibilities?' (2007: 256). Noddings and Slote (2005: 346) further argue that moral education should allow learners to experience moral interdependence and avoid self-righteousness when moral decisions are made. Care theorists are generally critical of character education's failure to accommodate diversity. But they are also critical of the liberalist's trust in individual rationality. Ruiz (2004: 283), for instance, underlines that:

> the origin of this morality is not reason, as in idealist morality, but feeling, 'pathos', solidarity with other human beings who deserve happiness and recognition. It is not the faculty of reason which moves us to act without duty, but neither is it a mere irrational feeling. Rather, it is an *affection* [...]

Taking a similar view to Korczak (2001), Wilson (1998), Weldon (2009) and Ruiz (2004: 272) argue that ethicists of care are not concerned with the 'utilitarian and communal morality of Rawls and Rorty', but with the process of prioritizing and empathizing with a significant Other. It seems that in this concept, freedom of religion(s) and belief(s) might be expressed more prominently, since it demands human beings to dialogue about their private life-worlds in public spaces.

However good this proposal might seem for a curriculum for morality, human rights and freedom of religion(s) and belief(s), it might appear equally naive and unrealistic. This is mostly attributable to the observable modernist traces left in society and in schools, which are often fortified by our uncritical engagements. Greeley (1992; cited in Slattery, 2006: 105–106) argues that postmodern attempts to conceptualize a curriculum are arduous for two reasons: first, because of a loss of identity due to minority groups being systematically immersed in modernist ideologies, and second, because of modernist attempts to invalidate theological self-reflection by refuting the power of autobiography, ethnography, narrative research, and so forth. One might wonder to what extent black South Africans experience a loss of identity due to the apartheid ideology, and how this experience influences their reasoning when brutal xenophobic attacks occur. Therefore, I would argue that our curriculum work should aim to uncover these opaque traces in the curriculum through deconstruction and critique since it has an impact well beyond the official curriculum. In the last section, I will propose a normative conception of a curriculum for morality and human rights that renders a space for human beings to express their freedom of religion(s) and belief(s).

Toward a curriculum for morality, human rights and freedom of religion(s) and belief(s): A hybridic justification

> [We should] … explore curriculum in a way that gives possibility to the living word [narratives], in all its mystery, ambiguity, and complexity.
> — SLATTERY, 2006: 112

In this concluding section, I would like to propose and discuss two essential, but inseparable, features for conceptualizing a curriculum for morality, human rights and freedom of religion(s) and belief(s). These include the notions *curriculum as a caring, web-like bond* and *curriculum as an enmeshed, disciplinary fusion.* Conceptually these notions are based on Slattery's (2006) postmodern idea of curriculum and Jansen's (2009) idea of a critical, post-conflict pedagogy, which I shall broadly describe as a deconstructive perspective to curriculum. Both of these authors argue against the essentialization of concepts and realities, such as described earlier in the quote by Marais and Van der Kooy (1978; cited in Dlamini, 2010: 131). In fact, Jansen (2009: 256) criticizes critical theorists for their inclination to create simplistic dualities to assist them in making sense of the world, and then to select a dualist position from which to argue. He argues that this is not helpful in a post-conflict pedagogy which aims to build a bridge between such superficial dualities and to create spaces for dealing with complex moral issues. He states: 'in any oppressive situation the moral world is a lot more complex than critical theory suggests' (Jansen, 2009: 259). With this in mind, I will now turn to discussing the above notions of curriculum and its respective potential to contribute toward a profound moral curriculum based on human rights, open to freedom of religion(s) and belief(s).

Curriculum as a caring, web-like bond

The nature of a curriculum as a caring, web-like bond is cooperative (Slattery, 2006) and responsive to caring relations (Noddings, 1984; cited in Valenzuela, 2009). This caring, cooperative nature is epitomized by the acknowledgement of brokenness and the significance of hope (Jansen, 2009). Jansen describes brokenness as the realization of imperfection and 'the profound outward acknowledgement of inward struggle done in such a way as to invite communion with other people' (2009: 269). Hope, he argues, 'begins with the quest for individual and collective understanding within the classroom' (Jansen, 2009: 271). An ontological understanding of the curriculum as caring and cooperative, epitomized by hope and brokenness, cannot rely on the methodology of corporate competition.

Rather, it should be based on 'sustainable learning environments ... and just community models of schooling' (Slattery, 2006: 108). Jansen (2009: 274) refers to these as risk-accommodating environments which create enabling spaces for human beings to engage in the difficult task to unburden themselves. This requires a learning-teaching methodology committed to, for example, Socratic dialogue, critical thinking, discovery learning and autobiographical forms of learning (Slattery, 2006: 109). This learning-teaching methodology should be characterized by demonstrative leadership, focus on listening to a significant Other, and aims to reframe dualist notions such as victors and victims (Jansen, 2009).

Curriculum as an enmeshed, disciplinary fusion

Slattery quotes T. S. Eliot who asks 'where is the wisdom we have lost in knowledge' (Eliot, 1971; Slattery, 2006: 111)? He argues that modern ideas about science have created a condition where epistemology is devoid of the wisdom that allows us to create alternative ways of knowing (Slattery, 2006: 109). I shall refer to this wisdom as intuitive knowledge. Intuitive knowledge arises when human beings intuitively argue in an attempt to seek alternative ways of knowing and in the process 'draw on their life-worlds and related experiences to confront (dis)similar situations. The value of intuitive argumentation ... lies in its nature that necessitates the use of familiar situations to respond to dissimilar situations' (Du Preez, 2008: 77). Jansen refers to this as 'the power of indirect knowledge' (2009: 260). He argues that human beings possess 'powerful ideas and constructs about the past, present, and future' that are deeply embedded in their ethnic, cultural and religious traditions and beliefs; and are therefore both cognitive and emotional in nature (2009: 260–261). The emotional nature of this knowledge necessitates a curriculum methodology that could surpass the traditional, rationalized ways of teaching; it requires an affective-reflective space where autobiographical learning is equally acceptable with other forms of learning–teaching. On the part of the teacher, this requires delving into her imagination as a means to produce this space (Dlamini,

2010: 107). Jansen goes as far as to argue that '[a]ny teacher who fails to recognize the existence and the influence of indirect knowledge ... might as well be in a minefield' (2009: 262), playing with the metaphorical 'cultural bomb' that has the potential to annihilate religions and beliefs in the curriculum (Slattery, 2006: 73). Furthermore, intuitive knowledge requires that received knowledge be disrupted within a pedagogy of dissonance (Jansen, 2009: 264–267). This requires learning-teaching methodologies and epistemologies that obstruct and challenge our accustomed knowledge constructs in order to open pathways to alternative ways of knowing. However, Jansen warns that '[a] single incident of pedagogic dissonance does not ... lead to personal change, but it can *begin* to erode sure knowledge' (2009: 266). To accommodate such an approach to curriculum, one has to view the curriculum holistically and not reduce it to neatly packaged knowledge constructs. In similar vein, Slattery argues for a multi-layered, interdisciplinary curriculum that integrates and infuses elements of morality, spirituality and humaneness throughout the curriculum (2006: 109–110). By its nature, such a curriculum might lead to situations where freedom of religion(s) and belief(s) could be expressed, dialogued and challenged in a risk-accommodative environment.

In summary, the curriculum lens that we use determines the extent to which morality and human rights, as well as freedom of religion(s) and belief(s), could be seen. I have argued that traditional lenses to curriculum make morality, human rights and freedom of religion and belief appear opaque and even barely visible. The hybridic curriculum lens proposed above evinces the potential to make morality, human rights and freedom of religion(s) and belief(s) more conspicuous. To disclose this potential, it is not enough to merely adopt a care-theorist approach to morality in the curriculum. We need to challenge and deconstruct the devastating pre-modern and modern debris, such as the loss of identity and the delegitimization of theological self-reflection, in curriculum theorizing. This will require that we too rely on our intuitive knowledge to unleash the potential of such a hybridic curriculum theory. For the moment, I would describe the above justification of a moral curriculum as an intricately webbed cocoon awaiting the liberation of an enigmatic butterfly: the realization of freedom of religion(s) and belief(s) in a human-rights orientated society.

Future intuitions

Curriculum structure and practice based on pre-modern and modern conceptions have demonized religions, silenced the vulnerable and created a culture where human wrongs are ideologically justifiable. In this chapter, I have proposed a postmodern, hybridic justification of curriculum that is inherently moral and that renders a space for human beings to express freedom of religion(s) and belief(s) based on a human rights culture. This was done in an attempt to reposition religions and beliefs in the curriculum, to create spaces for dialogue between significant Others, and to create a human rights culture. This hybridic conception of curriculum necessitates a different ontological, methodological and epistemological take on schooling – one that returns to ancient wisdoms and intuitive knowledges to challenge accustomed ways of knowing, one that allows for classrooms to become spaces where diverse narratives could meet and embrace mystery, ambiguity and complexity in a risk-accommodating environment.

References

Apple, M. (Ed.). (2010). *Global crises, social justice, and education.* New York and London: Routledge.

Arendt, H. (1978). *The origins of totalitarianism.* New York: Meridian Books.

Arendt, H. (1994). *Essays in understanding, 1930–1954* (trans. and ed. Jerome Kohn). New York: Harcourt Brace.

Bernstein, B. (2009). On the curriculum. In U. Hoadley & J. Jansen (Eds), *Curriculum: Organizing knowledge for the classroom* (pp. 287–291). Cape Town, South Africa: Oxford University Press.

Bridges, D., & Jonathan, R. (2005). Education and the Market. In N. Blake, P. Smeyers, R. Smith & P. Standish (Eds), *The Blackwell guide to the philosophy of education* (pp. 126–145). USA, UK and Australia: Blackwell Publishing.

Burbules, N., & Warnick, B. (n.d.). Ten Methods of Philosophy of Education. Unpublished paper prepared as the introductory chapter for The International

Handbook on Methods in Philosophy of Education, Kluwer Publication, forthcoming.

Curren, R. (2008). Cultivating the moral and intellectual virtues. In R. Curren (Ed.), *Philosophy of education: An anthology* (pp. 507–516). Malden, MA: Blackwell Publishing.

Dlamini, J. (2010). *Native nostalgia*. South Africa: Jacana Media.

Du Preez, P. (2005). Facilitating human rights values across the OBE and Waldorf Education Curricula. Unpublished master's thesis, University of Stellenbosch, South Africa.

Du Preez, P. (2008). Dialogue as facilitation strategy: Infusing the classroom with a culture of human rights. Unpublished PhD dissertation, University of Stellenbosch, South Africa.

Eliot, T. S. (1971). *The collected poems and plays of T. S. Eliot: 1909–1950*. New York: Harcourt, Brace & World.

Fullinwider, R. K. (2008). Moral Conventions and Moral Lessons. In R. Curren (Ed.), *Philosophy of education: An anthology* (pp. 498–506). Malden, MA: Blackwell Publishing.

Gearon, L. (Ed.). (2002). *Human rights and religion: A reader*. Brighton and Portland: Sussex Academic Press.

Graham-Jolly, M. (2009). The nature of curriculum. In U. Hoadley & J. Jansen (Eds), *Curriculum: Organizing knowledge for the classroom* (pp. 247–252). Cape Town, South Africa: Oxford University Press.

Greeley, A. M. (1992). A modest proposal for the reform of Catholic schools. *America*, *166*(10), 234–238.

Jansen, J. (2009). *Knowledge in the blood. Confronting race and the apartheid past*. Palo Alto, CA: Stanford University Press.

Joseph, P. B., & Efron, S. E. (2005, March). Seven worlds of moral education. *Phi Delta Kappan*, 525–533.

Korczak, J. (2001). Selected writings of Janusz Korczak – the educator of educators. *Dialogue and Universalism*, *9/10*, 47–73.

Marais, G., & Van der Kooy, R. (1978). *South Africa's urban blacks: Problems and challenges*. Pretoria: University of South Africa.

Matthews, G. B. (1995). *The philosophy of childhood*. Cambridge, MA: Harvard University Press.

Moore, B. (1978). *Injustice: The social bases of obedience and revolt*. London: Macmillan.

Morrison, D. (2000). Cultural values, human rights and religion in the curriculum. In J. Cairns, R. Gardner & D. Lawton (Eds), *Values and the curriculum* (pp. 123–133). London: Woburn Press.

Noddings, N. (1984). *Caring: A feminine approach to ethics and moral education.* London: University of California Press.

Noddings, N., & Slote, M. (2005). Changing notions of the moral and of moral education. In N. Blake, P. Smeyers, R. Smith & P. Standish (Eds), *The Blackwell guide to the philosophy of education* (pp. 341–355). Malden, MA: Blackwell Publishing.

Pinar, W. (2009). The reconceptualization of curriculum studies. In D. Flinders & S. Thornton (Eds), *The curriculum studies reader* (pp. 168–175). New York: Routledge.

Ruiz, P. (2004). Moral education as pedagogy of alterity. *Journal of Moral Education, 33*(3), 271–289.

Slattery, P. (2006). *Curriculum development in the postmodern era.* New York and London: Routledge.

Smith, D. (2009). Curriculum and teaching face globalization. In D. Flinders & S. Thornton (Eds), *The curriculum studies reader* (pp. 368–384). New York: Routledge.

Sörlin, S., & Vessuri, H. (2007). *Knowledge society vs. knowledge economy: Knowledge, power, and politics.* Basingstoke: Palgrave Macmillan.

Tronto, J. (2007). An ethic of care. In A. Cudd & R. Andreasen (Eds), *Feminist theory: A philosophical anthology* (pp. 251–263). Malden, MA: Blackwell Publishing.

Valenzuela, A. (2009). Subtractive schooling, caring relations, and social capital in the schooling of U. S.–Mexican youth. In D. Flinders & S. Thornton (Eds), *The curriculum studies reader* (pp. 336–347). New York: Routledge.

Weldon, G. (2009). Memory, identity and the politics of curriculum construction in transition societies: Rwanda and South Africa. *Perspectives in Education, 27*(2), 177–189.

Wilson, J. (1998). Moral education for beginners. *The Curriculum Journal, 9*(1), 41–50.

MARIO O. D'SOUZA

7 Pluralist Societies, First Principles, and the Freedom of Religion and Belief

Abstract

This chapter inquires into the possibility, place and implications of first principles in the context of religious and cultural pluralism. Western democratic societies do not claim to possess intellectual principles or a political elasticity to accommodate religious differences. Diversity for diversity's sake seems to be a rallying cry, but it appears to be a hollow one for it does not further the discussion about the nature and purpose of democratic society. Credal and doctrinal claims are by their nature distinct, but their distinctiveness can also tear at the fabric of democratic society. A proposal of first principles must be secured upon some general agreement on the unity of human nature. Such first principles also draw attention to the end of political society, an end that neither requires the exclusive dominance of religion nor is held captive by religious differences. Though the freedom of religion and belief rise above the terrestrial limits of political society, they are neither independent of such a society, nor are the dispositions and convictions of one's religion and belief unrelated to the terrestrial pursuit of the common good.

Introduction

As the clever line has it, 'When all is said and done, there is more said than done'. Over the last decade, and perhaps particularly since the attack of the twin-towers in New York, now commonly known as *9/11*, western governments, think-tanks, political theorists, religious leaders, educators and citizens in general have all been paying sustained and close attention to the health of democracy within increasingly pluralist societies, particularly with regard to the relationship between religious pluralism and democracy. While much has been written, thought and spoken about this relationship, the bringing together of religiously pluralist societies into some form of democratic harmony has been much more difficult. The difficulty is marked by cultural, ethnic and social differences certainly, but particularly marked, on the one hand, by the primacy of differing religious worldviews (and often by substantial theological and doctrinal differences) and, on the other hand, in reaching some agreement as to the nature of political community and how it influences democratic fellowship in working and striving for the common good. These difficulties are exacerbated by a common, and mistaken, understanding of the common good as a collection of individual goods simply piled together, and/or the collective material and the social services' patrimony of the state (see Maritain, 1966: 52–53). Rather, the common good consists of the collective good of human society, comprising citizens who are, first and foremost, human persons in possession of a human nature (see Maritain, 1966: 49). But even this seemingly minimal reference to human personhood is rife with philosophical, theological and cultural differences which prevent it from being a foundational collective reference in political discourse.

Pluralist societies also experience these tensions in the nature and purpose of education and schooling, presupposing, of course, the non-negotiable minimum of the primacy of literacy and the intellectual and technical competency of citizens within this educational nature and purpose. Today, the intellectual, social, cultural and religious differences and questions all stand against a backdrop in what has been succinctly described as an incredulity toward meta-narratives, which is Jean-Francois Lyotard's pocket-sized description of postmodernism. Apart from their legal, constitutional, civic and political identities, western democratic societies are marked by the absence of strong theoretical principles that characterize their nature and purpose. In short, such societies do not possess some ultimate *telos*, some principle or principles that situate(s) society in more final terms, and their governments do not see themselves as being either responsible or qualified in providing such principles. Alasdair Macintyre confirms the relationship between first principles and ends: 'Genuinely first principles ... can have a place only within a universe characterized in terms of certain determinate, fixed and unalterable ends, ends which provide a standard by reference to which our individual purposes, desires, interests and decisions can be evaluated as well or badly directed' (Macintyre, 1990: 7). Consequently, the identification of first principles may seem to be pointless, particularly as there is no agreed theoretical foundation and worldview upon which they may be secured. Furthermore, a variety of pluralisms makes it difficult to determine a course of action even for the individual. Stacy Smith sums this up well:

> In the midst of a host of pluralisms, and absent grand narratives to provide us with absolute explanations, it is often difficult to determine the right course of action. Often it is even more difficult to fathom convincing someone else that a course of action that *I* have determined to be right is also right for *you*. Contemporary celebrations of individuality and differences make such assertions not only unpopular but downright dangerous. (Smith, 2000: 408)

The possibility of first principles

In light of recent cultural and intellectual forces that have shaped society, a shaping that has gone on with particular intensity over the last three or four decades, any attempt to speak about first principles might seem like the proverbial ostrich burying its head in the comforting sand; an intentional, and perhaps even fearful, ignoring of things as they are. In the world of education, Alan Bloom's *The Closing of the American Mind* (1987) is a watershed analysis as to the collapse of an intellectual and cultural edifice that has led to the disappearance of educational first principles able to unite and integrate a diverse society, even, as in Bloom's case, when that cultural diversity is contained geographically and politically within a particular country. For his part, and with a different focus and purpose, the Canadian Catholic theologian and philosopher Bernard Lonergan is critical of the term first principles and all its accompanying historical baggage, though he certainly does not refute the central place of cognitional, epistemological and metaphysical structures that play a more active and dynamic role in confirming and attaining truth compared with the seemingly staid picture that tends to be associated with first principles (see Ryan & Tyrrell, 1974: 39, 48, 50).

Communal living, however, does require some basic forms of agreement, and in that context one might say that a first-principle is a fundamental truth, which, in turn, should guide individual and collective actions. First principles are fundamental in constructing a worldview, and again, any form of communal living entails some basic worldview, without which harmonious civic interaction would be impossible. Jacques Maritain's approach is to situate this unity in 'the equality of human nature', saying that there are three philosophical approaches to such an understanding of equality: nominalist (or empiricist), idealist or realist. He chooses the third realist position because it is the 'true philosophy of equality which does not suppress inequalities, but bases them indeed on equality, as something more fundamental, and turns them, by virtue of justice, into an equality concerned with the use and the fruition of the common good' (Maritain, 1972: 2–3). In the context of pluralism, Maritain is interested in exploring equality secured upon justice and friendship, but also upon the conviction that human persons need the community of other persons for their 'material, intellectual, and moral life' (Maritain, 1947: 5). Maritain recognizes the various inequalities in society, be they biological, ethical or social, but he sees these inequalities as accidental to the nature of society *per se*. He is concerned, rather, with social equality secured upon the fundamental rights of the human person, rights that prescind from religious differences or any other *accidental* inequalities. As a believing Catholic, Maritain understands accidental not as questioning his own conviction that the Christian religion is *the* true religion (a conviction, incidentally, that all religious believers would hold of their particular traditions, without which there would be an epistemological collapse of religious belief) but, rather, as accidental to the nature of civic cooperation and unity, which should not be dependent upon someone governing religion, nor subject to the intolerance of the religious majority.

In basing his idea of society upon human equality, Maritain, among other matters, wishes to stress two points in particular. First, in the face of religious differences, human equality is not dependent upon a common fellowship of belief, but upon a common fellowship of human persons who believe. Second, that difference in religious beliefs does not render the pursuit of the common good to be an impossible, endless Sisyphean task, or one simply subordinate and inferior to religious convictions. The striving for the common good is an end in itself, certainly a temporal and time-bound end when compared with the finality and eternity of religious or theological ends, but an end nonetheless, and worthy to be independently pursued. He says that the 'ontological mystery of personality and freedom' is the genuine foundation for tolerance and fellowship within a pluralist political society, and a foundation for that temporal end (Maritain, 1961: 34–36).

The nature of social life, in the face of religious pluralism, should be grounded upon reason and virtue. Thus social equality is not ready-made; it requires the constant attention of human persons seeking fellowship and truth. Maritain reminds us that it is a great pity that men and women who believe in the supernatural continue to be 'enchained ... by so many sociological prejudices' (Maritain, 1972: 127). Accordingly, he separates the ultimate religious and theological destiny of human persons from the temporal community of human life with its natural activities, virtues and the common good, and says that the unity of such a society is neither dependent nor secured upon a common religious creed (Maritain, 1947: 24), but upon a fellowship of truth, justice and human dignity, all secured upon substantial unity of human equality and not upon the accidental differences of religious beliefs. The political, civic and social cooperation of men and women of different religious beliefs stems from a concern for the good of political society and the perennial striving for the common good.

First principles

In elaborating on his understanding of human equality, Maritain makes a crucial philosophical claim. He says that human unity and equality cannot be 'visibly perceived because it is something perceivable only by the intellect' (Maritain, 1972: 3). Accordingly, for the empiricist, the unity and equality of human nature is less basic than the observable inequalities. However, in opting for the realist position, and in saying that human unity and equality cannot be visibly perceived as it can only be perceived by the intellect, Maritain is basing his conviction on the place of truth, fellowship, justice and dignity, none of which are perceivable to the intellect *per se*, but the manifestation of these virtues poured into actions and choices and decisions are. So the conviction of the equality and unity of human nature is manifested through human intentions, choices and willing, all of which are dependent upon the intellect.

Finally, when it comes to communal, civic and political living, first principles are of an order that cannot fall prey to a mindset requiring proof leading to a position of infinite regress. There must come a point when some principles no longer require further proof, for the continual requirement of proof would question the foundations of political society itself. Macintyre puts it as follows: 'argument *to* first principles cannot be demonstrative, for demonstration is from first principles' (Macintyre, 1990: 35). John Henry Newman also provides some valuable insights as to the centrality of first principles. He describes them as 'starting points of reason'; as 'the propositions with which we start in reasoning on any given subject matter'; as 'initial truths'; as 'primary principles, the general fundamental cardinal truths'; and 'principles taken for granted' (Williams, 1992: 58). Like Maritain, Newman understands first principles as a 'foundationalism' of a quite different order compared with the clear and distinct ideas of Cartesianism. Williams states:

> Newman is concerned to show that there *are* certainties, that we give fundamental assent to a variety of fundamental truths, and that these, although themselves lacking justification, provide unquestioned starting-points for inferring other propositions: the fundamental starting-points of reasoning are also the stopping-points

of justification. In justifying an inference we are 'thrown back' to prior inferences in which assumptions are proved, and beyond those to inferences to proving yet prior assumptions, and so on. And Newman, like so many philosophers before and since, asks the obvious questions: 'Where is this process to stop?' Justification must come to an end, but not as some quite arbitrary point; if first principles are both expressions of our human nature and conditions of inquiry and knowledge, then the infinite regress that would undermine justification can be avoided and the sceptic silenced. What Newman saw very clearly ... was that the natural can act as a 'sanction' for particular kinds of human judgment and practice precisely because what is natural is not arbitrary, contingent perhaps, but not arbitrary, or, for that matter, conventional. (Williams, 1992: 58–59)

Newman and Maritain may not necessarily be advocating some form of phenomenology. However, while even a partial examination of the phenomenological method is not possible here, a phenomenological approach does offer a context for the identification of first principles. Phenomenology studies the structures of the individual's experience or consciousness with regard to phenomena, that is, the appearance of things as they are, or as they appear in experience, the way we experience things, and the meaning of experience. Communal political and civic life does provide a common experience and is observable in the various manifestations of that experience. So rather than approach the question of experience from the subjective or first-person point of view, could one propose a communal phenomenological method for life in political society? Second, is it possible to apply the phenomenological reduction or bracketing in a communal way? This reduction would call for the suspension of all preconceptions in a pluralist context, that is, communities would try to free themselves from theories and presuppositions and attempt to engage the political and civic context with fresh eyes. Thus, one would approach the questions about the very presuppositions of citizenship through the precise use of language. Bernard Crick says that, whether in school or in wider terms, all education:

[...] consists of increasing an initial understanding of language and increasing ability to use it to adjust to more complex external relationships and events, to extend one's range of choice within them, and finally in the case of citizenship to influence them. At all times we have some general image of the world in which we live, some understanding however tentative, primitive or even false, and the slightest degree of education consists in forming explanations of these images or offering generalizations, however simple, about alternate images or modifications of earlier ones, with some argument or some appeal to external evidence. (Crick, 1999: 340–341)

However, what is needed is a context or field in which religious and cultural communities would practise this phenomenological method and phenomenological reduction from where they would examine their experience for agreements of certain first principles. That context or field would have to be a democratic community itself, as it is the very site and possibility of the citizen's freedom, indeed it is the very foundation and possibility of citizenship as understood in western pluralist democracies. Such a society is the very basis, the foundation upon which first principles may be secured, so any criticism that such a conception of society brings with it prior meaning or preconceptions to this examination is ultimately groundless, as political society is both the condition for citizenship and makes for the possibility of cultural and religious pluralism.

Having attended to the possibility of first principles, one can list some suggested first principles without too much further qualification. The first is reason. Reason unites us as human beings, and apart from any prior religious or cultural or ideological preconceptions, and recognizing the philosophical critique of reason (for example, Jurgen Habermas' interest in the retrieval of reason in the face of its overwhelming historical, social and cultural impurity is worth noting; see Habermas, 1992 and 1993), it does unite human beings in a practical fellowship. Citizenship and political fellowship would be inconceivable without the primacy of reason. We are reasoning beings. Reason enables us to recognize the other – persons or contexts – even though we may disagree. The second principle is peace. Though it has many expressions, peace is realized in the communal pursuit of the common good, a pursuit by human persons. Peace is made possible through dialogue, through generosity of spirit, and through a common striving for justice, all of which could also be counted as the fruits of peace. Apart from the obvious manifestations of a freedom from bodily harm, from political intimidation, from armed conflict, peace is essential to the inherent structural dignity of human persons. Without it, many other manifestations and actualization of human personhood, particularly the virtues and all that one associates with human flourishing, would be very difficult to realize. The third principle is religious freedom. As this freedom is part of the nature of western democracies, the communal practice of different religious traditions is an obvious means by which citizens manifest themselves in pluralist societies, as well as manifesting themselves as human persons. However, this freedom also includes choosing not to believe in the religious tradition that one inherits, choosing to move to another religion, or choosing to reject religious belief altogether. The fourth principle is freedom of speech. It is because freedom of speech is housed in the principle of reason that one can, objectively, question anything, so long as one does not slip into irrationality or into instigating violence and leading to harm, thus contradicting the principle of peace. The fifth principle is freedom of education. While the state offers education through schools and universities, cultural and religious communities can operate their own educational institutions so long as they respect the agreed context of democracy and the public accountability of education. Finally, we have the first principle of human dignity. Placing this principle here may seem like a circular argument: first principles of political society are in response to human dignity and then human dignity becomes a first principle. The place of human dignity here, however, is linked to the more observable manifestations as to how that dignity is recognized, enhanced and served. So while religious and cultural communities can ground this freedom in their various theories, the state secures this dignity through social, economic, medical and other kinds of benefits that it offers citizens, such as healthcare, pensions and social welfare. While there may not be an agreed-upon philosophical or theological narrative that grounds human dignity, the state's initiatives presuppose and guarantee that dignity. There are other principles, of course, but there is a certain primacy to these six principles. While there are varieties of freedoms (to be a pacifist, to ignore moral standards, not to vote, to choose not to be informed, etc.) these six principles can be a means by which a pluralist society can ground its self-revelation, and it is a revelation, as we saw with Newman, that need not be accompanied by a call for a prior theoretical framework or additional proof.

The educational context

Some brief comment should be made about the educational context, but particularly the context of religious education and democratic pluralism. Could we go on to say, then, that the six first principles stated above are also values and that they are non-negotiable? If so, then the following question becomes foundational: 'if educational aims are about values and values are non-negotiable, then how could it be possible to *negotiate* about educational aims?' For if values are indeed negotiable, then the sincerity of abiding by values becomes questionable (see Winch, 1996: 35). Religious education, whether in multi-faith or single denominational schools, should be accountable to the wider democratic community as religious education has undoubted implications for citizenship; hence the importance of educational aims. Democracy depends upon commitments, and this dependence cannot be separated from the advancement of one's own religious beliefs and commitments. Walter Feinberg lays out the breadth of one's democratic commitment in the context of religious education, and it is worth quoting him at some length:

> Religious education is a matter of faith in more than the familiar sense of the term. To fail to broaden the debate about the appropriate aims of religious education in liberal democratic societies, beyond the confines of a single faith community, is to assume that the attitudes, skills, and dispositions required to reproduce liberalism can be placed on automatic and grow themselves. This assumption is false. The skills required for the creation of liberal democracy are multifaceted, the dispositions deep, and the attitudes complex. Having taken centuries of political struggle, philosophical debate, and popular upheaval to shape, they are still subject to revision. They are satisfied not just when people vote. They are expressed in the way citizens treat one another at home, at work, on the street ... in a willingness to share power ... believers and nonbelievers alike ... they are also represented in attitudes towards people of different races, religions, genders, and sexual orientations. There may be a one hundred percent turn out for elections, but if these other requirements are not present, neither is democracy. Democracy cannot survive many free riders. It depends on a general citizenry who is committed to advancing its principles as robustly as any one citizen is to advancing any one particular set of beliefs and commitments. (Feinberg, 2006: xii–xiv)

Of course, this process is never smooth; abortion, for example, deeply divides political societies; however, this disagreement, from a strictly phenomenological perspective, is usually made in the context of religious belief, though suspension of one's beliefs regarding abortion is not easy and often divides a society. Nonetheless, from the perspective of religious education, can it not be maintained that the six principles of reason, peace and the freedoms of religion, speech, education and human dignity are the context within which such an education must be carried out? It has been maintained that some pre-conditions for democracy require a commitment to first principles and to actions flowing from those principles: '... a democracy of pluralism can best be understood when we remember, that to function, democracy must obtain in a group committed to sharing not simply ideals, but the social goods that will perpetuate a willingness to share the ideals' (Worsfold, 1977: 403). This commitment to democratic pluralism, on the one hand, and commitment to one's own religious tradition, on the other, has received a great deal of attention. Apart from Feinberg, cited above, Robert Jackson's analysis is also worth noting. For Jackson, plurality, individual identity and social identity are all linked. He says that in the context of religious plurality, 'religious education's fundamental concern' should be 'in relation to existential and social questions'. Consequently, 'religious education preserves its identity as a field of study, but relates to and can make distinctive contributions to a range of fields' (Jackson, 2004: 18).

This leads to two questions. First, could an agreement upon certain fundamental first principles widen the arena where religious education along distinct denominational lines can be freely and integrally pursued? Second, could the agreement on such principles enable a healthy freedom *of* religion and belief but also a healthy freedom *for* religion and belief?

In response to the first question, it would appear that in pluralist societies the absence of religious and cultural unity results in the emergence of diversity in a variety of areas. For their part, the six basic first principles do oxygenate the atmosphere of doctrinally diverse bodies of religious education. While they are not intended to bring about a philosophical agreement, let alone a theological one, they are intended to provide insight that can lead to 'the rationality of collective decision-making in diverse societies grappling with the problems of the public good' (Enslin, Pendlebury, & Tjiattas, 2001: 116). The difficulty of bringing about some general intellectual agreement appears to be exacerbated by theories of multiculturalism which celebrate diversity of all kinds, and, what's more confusing, the promotion of diversity for diversity's sake. Since it sees no need for any unifying principles, diversity is left to its own devices and gives the impression that it somehow promotes meaning in the context of many differences, which of course it does not. Furthermore, there is the difficulty that if only religious (and cultural) differences are emphasized, they become the *only* lens through which wider societal and communal questions are tackled, and these questions do cry out for wider and larger philosophical, humanistic answers. Amartya Sen's work *Identity and Violence: The Illusion of Destiny* is a passionate appeal as to the dangers that ensue when religious identity becomes the sole or main identity; such an exclusive identity leads to a 'miniaturization' of human persons, a 'reductionism [of] singular affiliation, which takes the form of assuming that any person pre-eminently belongs, for all practical purposes, to one collectivity only – no more and no less' (Sen, 2006: xiv, 20). In this light, Jackson's interest in examining 'the relationship between individuals' accounts of and questions about personal identity and wider issues of social identity and plurality', takes on added and urgent meaning (Jackson, 2004: 17). He goes on to say that this integration of the personal and the social sees religious education not as a 'fixed body of knowledge' but 'as a series of existential and social debates in which pupils are encouraged to participate with a personal stake related to their own developing sense of identity' (Jackson, 2004: 17–18). How religious denominations discern religious education, and whether they understand it as a fixed body of knowledge is another matter. Jackson's position, however, does widen the terrain of religious education and removes it from a hot-house approach where theological and doctrinal teachings are isolated from the living of life and the making of choices in the company of others and in the context of differences. Choosing, deciding and acting are, after all, the blood and pulse of democratic society.

Finally, could the agreement on such principles enable a healthy freedom *of* religion and belief but also a healthy freedom *for* religion and belief? I believe it does, and it does so by the explicit engagement of these six principles. In the context of education, phenomenology is concerned with one of the fundamental questions 'of the relationship between knowledge and experience' (Bottom, 1979: 248). Knowledge and experience are bridges between religious education and communal, civic and societal engagement and responsibilities; anything else runs the risk of being either too abstract or exclusively dependent upon one particular religious tradition or cultural position. In this regard, Bernard Lonergan's four foundational transcendental precepts are very helpful: be attentive; be intelligent; be reasonable; and be responsible. Lonergan is exploring how one deals with one's experience; he is ultimately concerned with consciousness and self-transcendence. Be attentive to your experience, be intelligent in understanding, be reasonable in judgement, and be responsible in judgement (see Lonergan, 1972: 13–16). All of this helps fashion a civic anthropology grounded in personal and communal responsibility. Being present to the other, therefore, is not simply about good intentions and common ground; it is also about responsibility and active choice. In religious education, the knowledge imparted by a particular religious tradition is obviously for the welfare of the student's faith life. But that life does not exist in a vacuum, though there are increasing signs of isolating communal life to the confines of faith and cultural communities. What this confinement does – and it seems to be in response to keeping the young pure and apart from the seeming adulteration of religious and cultural pluralism – is to limit the relational nature of knowledge and experience as imparted in religious education. The challenge is to move from this isolated perspective to seeing religious education in the context of democratic life and religious pluralism, and seeing this diversity as a good. If democratic pluralism is seen as the foundational condition of these six first principles, then these six principles do enable a healthy freedom *of* and *for* religion and belief in drawing attention to other dimensions of the students' lives beyond the singular and solitary identification of religion. Consequently, freedom *of* and *for* religion and belief are better situated in the midst of cultural plurality, particularly religious plurality, as the believer's experience and knowledge are not isolated to the confines of a particular religion and religious practice alone. Students, future citizens and religious believers of particular faith traditions should be educated to be able to engage others by respecting their religious beliefs and by recognizing that they too strive for those same principles that make the freedom of religious expression possible.

Charles Taylor says that liberal democracies defend diversity based not upon a particularistic but upon a universalistic perspective, whose characteristics are freedom and equality (Taylor, 1992: 10). Religious educators need to appreciate that their understanding of freedom shapes students as believers and as future active citizens, and in this they influence and help shape the quality of communal democratic life.

Conclusion

In his work, *The Human Condition*, John Kekes elaborates on his understanding of practical reason and correctly notes that practical reason, which aims at 'human well-being', is complex because 'human well-being takes many forms and depends upon the realization of many different values. But in one form or another, understood in terms of one or another set of values, we all aim at it, unless contingencies prevent it' (Kekes, 2010: 19). Where I must part company with Kekes, however, is in his distinction between practical and theoretical reason:

> Practical reason is not theoretical reason; its requirements are not universal and impersonal; and what is practically reasonable for particular persons to do is likely to be different from what is practically reasonable for other persons to do, especially when what is at stake are conflicts between evaluations on which their well-being depends. It is as unreasonable to expect practical reason to conform to the standards of theoretical reason as it is to expect theoretical reason to conform to the standards of practical reason. (Kekes, 2010: 183)

My disagreement with Kekes arises from his sharp distinctions between these two types of reason, particularly his identification of theoretical reason as impersonal. Bernard Lonergan's distinction comes to mind: 'genuine objectivity is the fruit of authentic subjectivity. It is to be attained only by attaining authentic subjectivity. To seek and employ some alternate prop or crutch invariably leads to some measure of reductionism' (Lonergan, 1972: 292). The view that theoretical reason retains universal truth, whereas practical reason only achieves truth after grappling with various contingencies, seems to ignore the one human subject who searches for truth and knowledge. It is very worthwhile quoting Michael Polanyi here:

> we may distinguish between the personal in us, which actively enters into our commitments, and our subjective states, in which we merely endure our feelings. This distinction establishes the conception of the *personal*, which is neither subjective nor objective. In so far as the personal submits to requirements acknowledged by itself as independent of itself, it is not subjective; but in so far as it is an action guided by individual passions, it is not objective either. It transcends the distinction between subjective and objective. (Polanyi, 1974: 300)

I have admitted earlier that the term human person and personhood are fraught with philosophical and theological difficulties, but surely one would have to agree that political society is made up of human beings, an affirmation that is even prior to any proposed first principles. Maritain's approach to human equality and the equality of human nature allows one to develop a political and civic understanding of human personhood that enables us to move the understanding of human flourishing to a higher level. As it stands, western societies seem to be increasingly trapped between two solitary visions of human flourishing: human flourishing is viewed either through the narrow lens of material welfare, or it is defined in strictly and, increasingly, fundamentalist religious terms. Neither vision can be acceptable in a democratic society or to religious educators anxious to show their students the relationship between religious belief and civic cooperation.

The debate about postmodernism and the ensuing discussion regarding the construction of one's identity has led to the view that human dignity is all about singularity and even fluidity. The metaphysical unrest of contemporary society has been pulled and tugged in many directions by differing cultural positions. Often these differing positions were born in institutions of higher learning, and while their effects are perceptible beyond such institutions, their theoretical and intellectual intricacies are confined to a small group of academic and social elites. However broad and sometimes problematic the categories of modernization and rationalization may be, a communal civic discourse cannot proceed without some general acceptance of the place and role of democratic institutions as a means to secure such a discourse (see Snyder, 2003: 329). It has been maintained that modernism and modernity are at the centre of this discussion of the clash of civilizations. It has been noted, for example, that while Muslims may come to dialogue from a position of 'Modern Islam', they are often confronted by the west's naïve criticism of modernism, naïve in that it is often unaware or does not want to become aware of the implications of such criticism (see Senghaas, 2002: 105).

We have spent enormous attention in the west on religious and cultural differences and possible ways to ease these differences; perhaps more attention needs to be paid to those fundamental characteristics that enable our humanity and our dignity to emerge through our communal choices and actions. A dilution of religious and doctrinal differences is bound to fail. What is of greater importance is how one engages in communal life in spite of those differences. In metaphysical terms, and perhaps in religious terms as well, there is a primacy of being over becoming. But the moral life and life in political society are dependent upon one's own becoming through one's choices and actions. Now, of course, all of this depends upon a vision not only of human becoming but of societal and communal becoming as well, and in this, religious education can play a vital role.

More attention has been paid here on constructing the context of pre- and post-first principles than on the actual attention to first principles themselves. My interest has been to widen the discussion of political community amidst religious and cultural differences, and to do so, and I do not think with naïve optimism, as a means to come to some communal agreement as to the unifying place of human nature. Western academies have been prolific in producing philosophical, cultural and sociological theories meant to deal with the diversity of experiences in the context of so many expressions of pluralism. Political society, at least the minimal conception that we have in the west, cannot flourish without some basic agreement as to the collective pursuit of the common good by human persons; for the citizen is always more than just a citizen. Paulo Freire reminds us that dialogue involves a consciousness of *what* one will dialogue with the other *about* (Freire, 1995: 74). Such awareness and consciousness of the *what* and the *about* have undoubted implications for personal and communal becoming, for they challenge communal political discourse from falling prey either to an exclusively material conception of communal life or to a narrow religious conception.

References

Bloom, A. (1987). *The closing of the American mind*. New York: Simon and Schuster.

Bottom, N. (1979). Phenomenology and education. *British Journal of Educational Studies, XXVII*(3), 245–258.

Crick, B. (1999). The presuppositions of citizenship education. *Journal of Philosophy of Education, 33*(3), 337–352.

Enslin, P., Pendlebury, S., & Tjiattas, M. (2001). Deliberative democracy, diversity, and the challenge of citizenship. *Journal of Philosophy of Education, 35*(1), 115–130.

Feinberg, W. (2006). *For goodness sake: Religious schools and education for democratic citizenry*. New York and London: Routledge.

Freire, P. (1995). *Pedagogy of the oppressed*. (M. B. Ramos, Trans.). New York: Continuum.

Habermas, J. (1992). *Postmetaphysical thinking: Philosophical essays*. (W. M. Hohengarten, Trans.). Cambridge, MA: The MIT Press.

Habermas, J. (1993). *The philosophical discourses of modernity: Twelve lectures*. (F. G. Lawrence, Trans.). Cambridge, MA: The MIT Press.

Jackson, R. (2004). *Rethinking religious education and plurality: Issues in diversity and pedagogy*. London and New York: RoutledgeFalmer.

Kekes, J. (2010). *The human condition*. Oxford: Clarendon Press.

Lonergan, B. (1972). *Method in theology*. New York: The Seabury Press.

Macintyre, A. (1990). *First principles, final ends and contemporary philosophical issues*. Milwaukee, WI: Marquette University Press.

Maritain, J. (1947). *The rights of man and natural law*. (D. C. Anson, Trans.). New York: Charles Scribner's Sons.

Maritain, J. (1961). *On the use of philosophy: Three essays*. Princeton, NJ: Princeton University Press.

Maritain, J. (1966). *The person and the common good.* (J. J. Fitzgerald, Trans.). Notre Dame, IN: University of Notre Dame Press.

Maritain, J. (1972). *Ransoming the time.* (H. L. Binsee, Trans.). New York: Gordian Press.

Polanyi, M. (1974). *Personal knowledge: Towards a post-critical philosopher.* Chicago: University of Chicago Press.

Ryan, W., & Tyrrell, B. (Eds). *Papers by Bernard J. F. Lonergan: Second collection.* London: Darton, Longman and Todd.

Sen, A. (2006). *Identity and violence: The illusion of destiny.* London: Allen Lane.

Senghaas, D. (2002). *The clash with civilization: Coming to terms with cultural conflicts.* London and New York: Routledge.

Smith, S. (2000). Morality, civics, and citizenship: Values and virtues in modern democracies. *Educational Theory, 50*(3), 405–418.

Snyder, R. E. (2003). Hating America: Bin Laden as a civilizational revolutionary. *The Review of Politics, 65*(4), 325–349.

Taylor, C. (1992). *Multiculturalism and the politics of recognition.* Princeton, NJ: Princeton University Press.

Williams, I. (1992). Faith and scepticism: Newman and the naturalist tradition. *Philosophical Investigations, 15*(1), 51–66.

Winch, C. (1996). The *aims of education* revisited. *Journal of Philosophy of Education, 30*(1), 33–44.

Worsfold, V. (1997). Teaching democracy democratically. *Educational Theory, 47*(3), 395–410.

KARIN NORDSTRÖM

8 Can We Educate for Freedom? Ethical Perspectives on the Pedagogic Paradox

Abstract

Within a liberal and democratic setting, education normally consists of a process of promoting increased self-determination or autonomy. By facilitating and encouraging self-determination, we are thereby deemed to be educating for freedom. Yet, paradoxically, to educate means also to restrict freedom. Education may be viewed as a series of planned interventions into someone's free behaviour, norms and habits according to certain ultimate intentions and ideals. The legitimacy of such freedom-restricting educational interventions is deemed morally justified as long as a balance is maintained toward the ends of autonomy and freedom. This chapter examines the relationship between means and ends in educating for freedom. Here, autonomy is viewed, not as opposed to heteronomy, rather as in relationship to dependencies of various kinds. It is argued that education for freedom is more plausible if understood as education *within* autonomy, instead of simply education *toward* autonomy. These theoretical arguments are illustrated by a discussion of the common didactic practice in Swedish schools of contract-signing in connection with individual study plans. The question is asked in what sense contract-signing may be a legitimate didactic means within a context of education for freedom.

Education for freedom and autonomy

From the modern perspective, freedom is a state which humans access through certain capacities associated with autonomy, and education and autonomy are paradigmatically linked. Education is founded on the fundamental aim of facilitating the autonomy of the person to be educated. Autonomy is thought to be the result of education as a process, developing from dependency toward autonomy. Kant's conceptualization of moral autonomy has had a significant influence on pedagogic theories about moral education. The impact of his work has earned him the title, the 'inventor of autonomy' (Schneewind, 1998). Of course, many other philosophers of his time were working with questions about human freedom and autonomy. What characterizes Kant's concept of autonomy is his polarized understanding of the moral capacity of human beings. While he is optimistic about humankind (what humans *essentially* are), he is quite pessimistic about how humans *actually* behave. Kant defines autonomy within this divergence as the – very radical – categorical imperative, that humans should be what they essentially are. Education is, according to Kant, the means by which humans become human, and to be human is to be autonomous (Kant, 1961/1788, 1984/1785). In consequence, ethics and pedagogy are intertwined, and education is unalterably oriented toward autonomy as a fundamental pedagogic ideal.

Kant's pessimism about the ability of humans to act in accordance with their proper nature as reasonable beings is shaped by his view that human beings find it difficult to withstand the pervasive impact of *Neigungen* (inclinations). For Kant autonomy means withstanding inclinations and being guided by reason (Kant, 1961/1788, 1984/1785). His exclusive emphasis on autonomy as reasonable may of course be criticized. But Kant's understanding of autonomy and reasonableness contains an important interactive aspect. Being reasonable is acting in accordance with a fundamental respect for the human in one's own person and in other humans (Kant, 1961/1788, 1984/1785). Kant's definition of the reasonable as respect for the human opposes any interpretation of his ethics as exhausted by the isolated moral agent. Onora O'Neill has, focusing on this aspect of his theory, summarized Kant's understanding of autonomy as 'principled autonomy' (O'Neill, 2002). She interprets Kant's interest in self-determination not as related to the self as a psychological entity, but merely as an expression of internal reflection, and accordingly, as a term for independence from external dependencies. She concludes: 'self-legislation is legislation that does not refer to or derive from anything else; it is *non-derivative legislation*' (O'Neill, 2002: 85). Kantian autonomy is thus self-related moral responsibility, where the moral subject is, in a self-sufficient manner, obliged only to itself and its own moral standards. Due to the identity of humans as reasonable beings, the moral duty of the individual toward itself is first and foremost owed to the 'self' as the human (for example, as in a general and fundamental sense belonging to humankind). What is at stake is therefore not an orientation toward individual preferences: autonomy is not just doing what pleases me. To be autonomous, in Kantian terms, means to dispose of one's individual freedom by engaging in respectful interaction with others. This interactive dimension is a decisive feature of Kant's ethics when considering the relationship between autonomy and education. From a Kantian perspective, we can and must educate for freedom, because of the ethical duty of humans to liberate themselves from their *selbstverschuldeten Unmündigkeit* (the self-caused heteronomy), and because autonomy is the morally mature or competent way of exercising freedom (Kant, 1974/1783). It is this ethical and pedagogical imperative that forms the presuppositions for the paradigmatic link between autonomy and education explored here.

From an ethical perspective, the issue of autonomy as a pedagogic ideal must be looked at in relation to autonomy as a value, as a right, and as a competence. While the understanding and valuation of all three dimensions of autonomy are related to one another, it is autonomy as a competence that is specifically relevant in relation to the pedagogic question about education for freedom. Autonomy as a competence focuses not only on the question of the definition of autonomy (the content of such a competence), but also on questions about how such a competence is achieved. The purpose of this chapter is to examine and critically discuss the structure of the legitimacy that informs the paradigmatic link between education and autonomy. The normativity that forms the link between education and autonomy is identified as being based on a balance between heteronomy and autonomy. The argument is that it is legitimate to restrict freedom temporarily in educational situations, as long as the long-term goal is to promote the autonomy of the person to be educated. This normativity is analysed and critically discussed. The idea explored here is that those claims made for education being ultimately about autonomy need to be balanced with those interventions that require dependence, mutuality and heteronomy in order to achieve this greater goal. The theoretical analysis of this chapter is illustrated by reference to a common practice in Swedish schools, that of contract-signing in relation to individual study plans, asking whether contract-signing is a legitimate pedagogic expression of education for freedom.

Individual study plans and contract-signing in schools

In recent years, contract-signing has become a common didactic tool in connection with individual study plans. The latter have been mandatory in Sweden since 2006. Twice a year, teachers meet pupils individually, together with a parent/caregiver, in order to talk about the pupil's learning, their results and goals. On these occasions, an individual plan is usually written, documenting the current learning process of the pupil and pointing out specific learning objectives or areas to focus upon. Often the individual plan is designed as a contract, which is signed by the teacher, the pupil and the parent/caregiver. The purpose of individual plans is twofold. It is thought to increase the number of pupils reaching national standards, but it is also said to facilitate and improve the motivation of pupils, encouraging them to focus on the content and the learning process (Vallberg Roth & Månsson, 2008). The practice of documenting individual plans by a contract, signed by the pupil, the teacher and a parent/caregiver, involves several pedagogic ideas, such as respecting the pupil as a competent learner, involving the pupil as an active partner, as well as ascribing to the pupil a

degree of autonomy. Ethically, however, the question arises, how this coun-
terfactual empowering of the pupil as an 'equal' partner in a three-party
agreement (documented as a contract) may be interpreted. With regard
to education for freedom, which is in school contexts expressed in terms
of citizenship education, one can also ask whether a signed contract just
constitutes 'quasi-autonomy', whether it is faking something which is not
really the case, or whether it can be seen as a constructive way of anticipat-
ing and realizing the otherwise remote goal of autonomy.

The pedagogic paradox and the legitimacy question

As I have argued above, a Kantian understanding of autonomy comprises
a pedagogic dimension because it makes autonomy a matter of morality. Moral education[1] is consequently the endeavour to promote moral
maturity through the formation of an individual who is characterized by
an understanding of his/her individual freedom informed by moral principles of mutual respect. The Kantian view, which entails both a radical
idea of human self-determination as moral self-sufficiency and a principled
morality of the reasonable and respectful interaction, not only informs
the paradigmatic link between education and autonomy, as two mutually
related normative entities, but also defines this link as characterized by a
paradox. From a pedagogic perspective, the paradox consists of the tension
between the freedom that the individual is entitled to, and striving for, and
the heteronomy or dependency this individual experiences as the object
of educational intentions and pedagogic aims, defined and articulated by
others (von Oettingen, 2006). The individual who is to be educated is thus

---

[1]   The term moral education is used here with regard to education that has goals relating
    to ethical values or norms. As education, in a more general sense, is hard to separate
    from values, this chapter also relates to education in a wider perspective.

caught in a paradoxical situation. Being educated means to be affected by freedom-restricting interventions in order to achieve ultimate freedom. Even if educational aims consist of a resolute ambition to respect and facilitate autonomy in the person to be educated, and even if this is articulated in terms of a democratic pedagogic approach, moral education still and inevitably creates situations of dependency and restricted freedom. To identify children or young people as individuals to be educated, to have ideas of what is good for them and what is bad for them, to encourage certain behaviours and interests and to discourage others, all of this means to intervene upon, or restrict, freedom. To what degree the actual effect of the interaction between the educating person and the person to be educated is restrictive of freedom is of less importance here. The claim is that any pedagogic situation, because the educator has intentions on behalf of the person to be educated, includes aspects of dependency or heteronomy. The inevitability of dependencies is caused by the fact that any educational situation is constituted by normative claims of asymmetry and direction. These are articulated by the educating person to the person to be educated in various ways. Contained within the pedagogic paradox is also the legitimacy question of moral education, which may be divided into two interrelated questions: can the legitimacy of moral education be based on autonomy as a pedagogic aim, and in what sense is autonomy a legitimate pedagogic aim (Nordström, 2009)?

Postmodern concepts of autonomy that deconstruct the ideal of a rational, detached and autonomous individual in favour of inter-subjective or relational concepts of autonomy, challenge the modern perspectives on education for freedom and autonomy. While the legitimacy of moral education in pre-modern societies depended on authorities and an ideal of obedience, a modern understanding of moral education elevated the ideal of autonomy or self-determination to an absolutely central position. Autonomy was ascribed the status of a fundamental value, as well as a basic legitimating function. Within a liberal understanding, the pedagogic paradox was usually associated with two basic assumptions: autonomy is understood as opposed to heteronomy or dependence and, consequently, a tension was presupposed between the pedagogic situation or method (as expressing dependence) and the educational goal of autonomy (von

Oettingen, 2003). In consequence, the legitimacy of restricting freedom in order to facilitate freedom was conceptualized in terms of the heteronomy of the pedagogic situation being counterbalanced with autonomy as educational goal. The idea of a counterbalance between these was therefore important.

In my view, these underlying antagonisms and the assumed counterbalance are questionable, rendering the pedagogic paradox problematic. If modern concepts of autonomy are challenged by concepts that understand autonomy, not as opposed to, but within dependence, the supposed antagonism captured by the pedagogic paradox fades. Furthermore, a more realistic understanding of moral education adds to the suspension of the paradox, because education then is not viewed as a continuous process with clearly distinguishable means and goals. Rather, a realistic understanding focuses on education as loosely connected situations, where means and effects are not always causally related, and where goals are not always clearly articulated (Oelkers, 2001). Thus, if the antagonism between autonomy and heteronomy – and between means and goals of education – is fading, the idea of counterbalance as the basis for legitimacy no longer seems plausible or necessary. Consequently, the question of the legitimacy of incursions upon freedom can now be viewed differently. 'Coherence orientation', I argue, is a better basis for the question of legitimate interventions because it takes into account the post-modern perspective. It implies striving for coherence in the pedagogic situation by relating pedagogic aims or ideals to normative claims made in the situation.

Autonomy vis-à-vis heteronomy?

Against the background of a Kantian perspective, I have pictured autonomy and education as inseparable entities. Theodor Adorno is among those who have pursued a Kantian perspective by emphasizing the legitimacy of education within a pedagogic ideal of autonomy. Trying to define and legitimate 'education after Auschwitz', Adorno points at the necessity, as well as at the potential of, autonomously detached individuals in a society built on an ideal of freedom. He is firmly convinced of the intention to educate autonomous individuals as the only way to prevent the kind of repression and suffering Auschwitz manifested and still symbolizes. Yet he also questions the legitimacy of education for autonomy. He writes: 'one has to ask, where anyone today retrieves the right to decide what others ought to be educated for' (Adorno, 1971: 107, translation: K. N.). Regardless of the particular contexts or specific goals of educational endeavours, legitimate education is assumed to comprise an overall aim of facilitating the autonomy of the person to be educated. If the person to be educated is pedagogically not envisioned, nor encouraged, to develop skills of self-determination, we would probably not define this as education, but as indoctrination (Ofstad, 1990). Yet, as Adorno's question suggests, the idea of education for autonomy seems to comprise a paradox. The latter, so I argue, is caused by a Kantian understanding of autonomy, construing autonomy as opposed to heteronomy, and viewing the two as mutually exclusive. Once this antagonism is questioned, the pedagogic paradox contained in education for freedom or autonomy, as for instance perceived by Adorno, fades. In consequence, the legitimacy question presents itself in a new light. This does not imply any necessity to abandon autonomy as a crucial pedagogic ideal, but it demands new patterns of argument with regard to its legitimacy.

Käte Meyer-Drawe points to the inevitability of autonomy as a pedagogic ideal. At the same time, she argues for a perspective that takes the problems of a modern concept of the autonomous, detached individual seriously. In spite of her outspoken and far-reaching criticism against a modern concept of autonomy and the ideal of a detached individual, she stresses the distinctive function that autonomy has for legitimate education. Moreover, she emphasizes autonomy as an indisputable value, as a condition *sine qua non* for a humane society. She speaks of autonomy as an efficient and valuable illusion, a 'reality of its own kind'. As an illusion, autonomy is an effective and crucial tool for criticism of society, but it functions this way by reducing or trivializing the reality it tries to grasp. Autonomy is therefore, according to Meyer-Drawe, not a realistic moral competence, describing the actual state of human beings, but it is never-theless valuable as an illusion, a pedagogic ideal, without which criticism would not be possible (Meyer-Drawe, 1990). Thus, the indisputable value of autonomy as an illusion is based upon its trivializing, yet critical, func-tion in relation to structures of heteronomy. If autonomy is an illusion, an unrealistic ideal, which we, according to Meyer-Drawe, naively and at the same time legitimately strive for but never really reach, there is no longer a clear antagonism between the means and goals of education for freedom. The educational goal of autonomy can never be entirely reached; humans are always partially caught in interdependence. Consequently, the educational situation in which the person to be educated is experiencing restriction of freedom is not necessarily in opposition to its goals. If autonomy is an illu-sion, an illusion that actually and positively affects us, the contrast between the educational situation and the educational goal fades. In other words, if autonomy is not an accessible state that is accomplished or materialized as a result of education for autonomy, the person who educates and the person to be educated are not categorically distinguishable with regard to their autonomy. Rather, they find themselves engaged in a common endeavour to strive for autonomy. Consequently, it is not simply the autonomous adult educating the heteronomous child. Both are simultaneously characterized by heteronomous circumstances *and* attempts to self-determination. What distinguishes the two with regard to autonomy is a matter of degree. As Feinberg (2007: 10) states: 'there is no sharp line between the two stages of human life; they are really only useful abstractions from a continuous process of development, every phase of which only differs in degree from that preceding it.' In order to stress the circumstance that autonomy is not a clearly distinguishable and realistic goal or result of a process, it seems more appropriate to speak of autonomy as a pedagogic ideal than as an educationally attainable goal.

The pedagogic paradox does not just encompass the pedagogic assumption that freedom restricting action can facilitate autonomy as a morally competent way of relating to freedom. It is also associated with an assumption concerning the legitimacy of moral education. Autonomy as a goal of moral education is understood as having a legitimizing func-tion. Restricting freedom is legitimate, as long as the (long-term) goal of educational interventions is the autonomy of the person to be educated. I have elsewhere called this legitimizing function of autonomy in relation to moral education, the modern legitimacy paradigm of moral education. It presupposes an argument of counterbalance between the restriction of freedom as means of education and the promotion of autonomy as educational goal (Nordström, 2009). Various postmodern concepts of autonomy constitute challenges to the way autonomy and moral education are related to each other within the modern legitimacy paradigm. If autonomy is understood as not being in opposition to heteronomy, but is situated within dependencies of various kinds, the argument of counterbalance is not plausible anymore. Concepts of relational autonomy (Mackenzie & Stoljar, 2000; Oshana, 2006), for instance, focus on the importance of relationships. With regard to her autonomy, a person is dependent on her relationships with others. According to Oshana, a person is only autonomous if she is treated as an autonomous person by others (Oshana, 2006). Within a relational perspective, freedom is an ideal, which does not imply a detached or isolated individual, but rather emphasizes – pedagogically and ethically – involvement within social, cultural or religious contexts. The autonomy of the individual is thus a function of its relationships. Autonomy appears consequently not as opposed to heteronomy, but as a way of being related to dependencies of various kinds, including social identities. As Anthony K. Appiah has argued, social identities have an ambiguous function in relation to autonomy. They may contribute to the empowerment of the individual, but they may also, due to the normative expectations and frameworks which are attached to them, impose restrictions with regard to the individual's freedom. Appiah highlights the normative or prescriptive contents of social identities, which are articulated through certain 'scripts' (Appiah, 2005). Thus, scripts are normative ideals attached to social identities, and individual freedom is freedom in relation to or within social identities. Autonomy might therefore be conceptualized in ways that highlight the importance of social and relational dimension. This challenges the modern legitimacy paradigm.

Asymmetry and direction – Education as normative claims

In this section, I elaborate upon moral education in terms of a tension between its normative claims (characterized by constant ideals) and its reality of educational experience (characterized by changeable situations). Since education as praxis or experience is characterized by a lack of clear causality or control, normative claims should be made with respect to this uncertainty. To educate means to envision change or transformation in accordance with an image of the 'better'. Because education is neither a linear process with a clear starting point and a definite goal, nor a causally controllable way of influencing people in accordance with intended goals, education presents itself as rather uncertain or changeable, and as a number of loosely connected situations, events, reactions and relationships (Oelkers, 2001; Winkler, 2006). Yet, despite prevailing uncertainties, education means to strive beyond a status quo for something 'better'. Education therefore involves a normative aspect that is not just restricted to moral education and that consists of envisioned change based on certain values. With regard to the values expressed in the explicit definition or implicit idea of pedagogic aims, education necessarily contains an element of constant ideals. This is an inevitable presupposition of the person who educates. Unless her commitment to the pedagogic aims for which she strives with her educational actions are experienced by her as a matter of development for the good or the better, or a matter of improvement in relation to the existing skills or competencies of the person to be educated, the motivation of the educating person appears nothing else but cynical. Therefore, the normative claim of education must be made in terms of constant ideals.

This creates a tension which, rather than identifying an antagonism between autonomy as pedagogic aim and heteronomy as characterizing the pedagogic situation, focuses on the connection between moral education as a praxis, and as a normativity. This tension consists of a contrast between the normative claims made by the educating person toward the person to be educated in the pedagogic situation, and the limited possibility to control the outcome of these situations. To educate means to hold on to good intentions, while being aware of the uncertainties of the endeavour to take influence toward something good. I therefore propose a shift of focus with regard to the legitimacy question of education. Instead of addressing the legitimacy of education as a function of the tension described by the pedagogic paradox, it should be treated as an issue emanating from the tension between making claims in terms of constant ideals and experiencing changeable or uncertain situations. By constant ideals, I refer to the normative necessity of having pedagogic ideals, even if they might be illusions. The pedagogic intention of the educating person must, in order to be legitimate, be guided by constant ideals in the sense that it must be a claim to influence in order to promote something 'good'. Constant ideals describe the normative claim of education. This collides with the changeable reality experienced by educators in pedagogic praxis. Often, an intended pedagogic effect is not reached, or at least it is not reached as a result of the pedagogic intention. In other words, there is not a logical causality between the pedagogic intention and its outcome. Thus, from an ethical point of view, education for freedom is not necessarily problematic because of the circumstances in which one person defines and strives for pedagogic aims. Rather, the ethical issue arises when the educating person, in all sincerity, claims that her intentions are for the better, even though she is uncertain with regard to the outcome of her efforts.

Dialectical asymmetry and open direction

The articulation of educational aims implies two basic claims in any pedagogic situation: *asymmetry* and *direction*. Asymmetry is based on an experienced difference with regard to certain knowledge, skills or maturity. It is articulated in the sense: 'I know something, which you do not know (as well as I do) and which you ought to know more about!' Asymmetry as a normative claim is related to the pedagogic ideal, which the educating person has identified for the person to be educated. This is, of course, not always explicit and consciously articulated, but the legitimacy question may nevertheless be seen as a matter of critically relating the pedagogic aim at stake to the particular features or claims of the pedagogic situation. It might then be discussed to what degree the claim of asymmetry articulated in a particular pedagogic situation reflects in an adequate way the pedagogic aim and vice versa.

With regard to a definition of autonomy as relational, education for freedom may be seen as based on a view that understands pedagogic situations as marked by inter-subjective premises. The implication of inter-subjectivity in pedagogic situations is to be understood not just in terms of learning interaction, but also as essential for the mutual construction of identities (Meyer-Drawe, 1990). Generations meet and exchange knowledge, but what is ethically interesting for the question of education for freedom is the mutual and constitutive impact of inter-subjectivity. The person who educates and the person to be educated are connected to each other by the very identification of the other within their respective pedagogic roles. By relating to the other in the pedagogic situation, positions and identities are ascribed to oneself and the other, and they are inter-subjectively constructed, adjusted and nurtured by the interaction in the situation. The inter-subjective character of the pedagogic situation often manifests itself in negotiations about autonomy in terms of duties and rights (Backett-Millburn & Harden, 2004; Punch, 2001). Leena Alanen (2001) designates inter-subjectivity between generations as 'generationing' and stresses not only the vital impact that representatives of different generations have on each other, but also the dependence of generational identity on the encounter with the other generation. By describing this process in this manner, Alanen also points at the fluidity of identity in relation to generation.

Applying her view to the legitimacy question of education and the normative claims made in pedagogic situations, asymmetry is not to be seen as static but as a function of mutual dependencies. Since generational identity depends upon an encounter with another generation, the impact is mutual and not controlled by any one of the generations. Furthermore, within pedagogic situations it is not simply a dependent child being influenced by an autonomous adult to become more autonomous. Both share in inter-subjectively shaped identities and both participate in a circumstance characterized by relational dependency. Asymmetry is therefore understood to be *dialectical* in that it tries to integrate both an actual, experienced difference, associated with envisioned change, and mutual dependencies due to the inter-subjectivity within the pedagogical situation.

The second constitutive claim is associated with a temporal aspect. Moral education is intended to bring about transformation over time. It is a spontaneous, or time-consuming, movement away from something toward something else. From a pedagogic perspective, education is intended to influence somebody's development in a certain direction, which is related to particular pedagogic ideals. The associated normative claim is therefore a claim about direction. Its normativity may, due to the above described uncertainties, be described in terms of expectations (Oelkers, 2001). Intended influence is marked by uncertainty, since the intended effect – due to the inter-subjective character of the pedagogic situation – quite often is altered or fails altogether. Yet, from an ethical perspective, there is a claim of improvement associated with intended influence. This is articulated in the following sense: 'My intention to influence you is an attempt to help you develop in a good direction, in order to improve your competence.'

With regard to the claim of asymmetry, a claim of direction also has to deal with a tension between constant ideals and changeable situations. Intended influence is marked by constant ideals due to the lack of causality and controllability in moral pedagogic situations. The claim of improvement though, as a claim, has to be fixed or constant if moral education is to be legitimate. A legitimate educational intention has to be sustained by a continuous – and thus constant – conviction that education is promoting a good ideal. Moral education from the perspective of the educating person must be – in one way or another – an attempt to point out a 'good' direction and to reach for the 'better'. Therefore, there is a tension between the pedagogic and the ethical perspective with regard to direction as well. While the actual influence of educational action is uncertain, the idea of direction and the associated claim of improvement are constant, in consequence, I suggest, as an adequate claim to an open *direction*. This expresses a claim of intended influence toward the 'better', which takes into account the fact that, even if the outcomes of moral education are imagined in terms of ideals, this does not imply that they are causally controllable.

Is contract signing in relation to individual study plans legitimate within education for freedom?

In order to discuss in what sense contract-signing might be an expression of legitimate education for freedom, it is necessary to describe and evaluate the claims made in the pedagogic situation. Thus, I focus on the tension between constant ideals, the normative necessity to have pedagogic ideals, and changeable pedagogic situations caused by lack of causally controllable effects. Instead of arguing within a modern legitimacy paradigm, attempting to examine whether freedom-restricting means are properly counterbalanced by corresponding educational goals, I chose to focus on the normative claims within the educational situation. This way autonomy is treated not as a causally reachable goal but as a pedagogic ideal in terms of an efficient illusion. In the latter sense, autonomy should be accurately strived for within the educational situation. Since claims are articulated in the educational situation, the particular circumstances of the situation are significant. For example, with regard to a claim of asymmetry, it matters how old the pupil is; a younger child can hardly be seen as an 'equal' partner in a contract and the preceding negotiation about its learning targets. Younger pupils are probably neither in a position to identify applicable learning goals for the coming term, nor able to evaluate critically suggestions from the teacher or the parent. The asymmetry looks different, though, with older pupils, because the opportunity for dialectic asymmetry, encompassing mutual influence and dependence, is much better. If the pupil is given a fair share in the negotiation of the contract, it may be seen as an expression of dialectic asymmetry and an acknowledgment of a degree of autonomy. Concerning the claim about direction, it matters, for instance, how well-informed the pupil is about the procedure and about the possibility of exercising influence, and how open is the attitude of the adults present toward the differing preferences of the pupils. An open direction would imply a willingness of the teacher to allow the pupil's creativity to actually influence the contract and learning targets. Consequently, the teacher must be ready to partially relinquish control of the direction of learning. By focusing on the tension between constant ideals and changeable pedagogic situations with respect to the claims of asymmetry and direction, I have deliberately neglected the question of the pedagogic paradox: that is, how to justify restriction of freedom in order to promote freedom. Instead of treating the legitimacy question as a matter of counterbalancing an antagonism between autonomy and heteronomy, I attempt rather to deal with the legitimacy question in a manner which makes legitimacy a function of how well a pedagogic ideal harmonizes with the normative claims made in pedagogic situations. This coherence-oriented pattern of legitimacy requires a continual effort to match pedagogic aims with claims made in pedagogic situations, in order to strive for a coherent normativity. With regard to autonomy as a pedagogic ideal, dialectic asymmetry and open direction have been pointed to as reflecting a pedagogic aim of autonomy, understood in terms of relational autonomy.

A coherence-oriented pattern of legitimacy requires an attempt to understand normativity of education as informed both by the experience of realistic conditions and pedagogic ideals. The latter may be more or less accurate, but they often refer to utopian ideals 'yet to come'. Marianna Papastephanou has pointed out the vital function of utopian and dystopian ideals in education. Her argument is important, not least with regard to education for freedom. In her view, education should always encompass a critical dimension. This is lost, she argues, when pedagogic aims are restricted to what is capable of being accomplished (Papastephanou, 2008). A coherence-oriented pattern of legitimacy, as proposed here, contains an attempt to approach the legitimacy question in relation to both the utopian ideal and the experience of particular situations, reflected in the tension between constant ideals and changeable situations of education. The tension between the ideal and experienced reality thus constitutes a permanent challenge to the legitimacy question. Dietrich Benner describes learning not as a process of moving from the 'known' to the 'unknown', but rather as a transformation consisting of parallel experiences of 'the known within the unknown' and 'the unknown within the known' (Benner, 2005/1987). As a result, learning processes and education have to take into account and validate the unpredictable or uncontrollable. This may be applied to the tension between utopia and reality, not only as a mode of explaining the coexistence of the ideal and the real, but also as an argument for basing the legitimate normativity of education on the tension between utopia and reality, and making it a matter of coherence orientation. On the one hand, utopia is defined in contrast to experienced reality; on the other hand, experienced reality provides the imagination with what is 'not yet' or 'nowhere' – utopia. According to a coherence-oriented pattern of legitimacy, the two should be harmonized. Utopia may challenge reality, while reality should confine claims made in relation to utopia. With regard to contract-signing, this means that the utopia of freedom and the moral competence of autonomy should be in harmony with the claims made in an educational situation. If the situation, or the claims articulated within it, reflect the pedagogic ideal of freedom, contract-signing may be considered as a legitimate didactic means of empowerment within education for freedom.

The legitimacy of contract-signing presupposes moderate claims in the educational situation, in line with dialectic asymmetry and open direction. It means that the involved adults are prepared to actually respect and encourage the pupil as having a certain degree of autonomy in the contract situation. This implies willingness to accept the possibility that the pupil's preferences alter the intention of the adults. Otherwise, the didactic means of contract-signing may have the opposite effect. Autonomy is, in that case, merely a pretence and pupils are not empowered and respected as equals, but rather easily manipulated into a situation that they probably do not experience as giving them any real influence over the identification of their learning goals. Individual plans and contracts then reinforce a tendency toward more 'regulated childhood' (Vallberg Roth & Månsson, 2008). In that sense, the method can be ethically problematic.

Conclusions

I have argued that the coexistence of the known and the unknown, of the utopian in terms of normative constant ideals, and of reality of uncertain educational praxis in terms of changeable situations, set aside the relevance of the pedagogic paradox for the legitimacy question. This is treated, therefore, as a matter of normativity of education (articulated as claims in pedagogic situations and as pedagogic aims) in relation to the uncertainties (manifested in changeable situations with regard to causality of pedagogic intentions and learning processes). Generally, this should be reflected in terms of modest claims made on the part of the educating person or institution with regard to the possibility to educate for freedom. If education for freedom means to facilitate autonomy as a competent way of relating to freedom, and if the pedagogic aim of autonomy is understood in relational terms, it seems problematic to refer to education as a linear process of moving from heteronomy *toward* autonomy. By contrast, a coherence-orientated pattern of argument focuses on education for freedom in terms of education *within* autonomy. Autonomy is then not a remote goal, because it is present as an ideal within the normativity of the pedagogic situation. The challenge of education for freedom is to develop pedagogic situations that reflect the aim of autonomy in adequate ways. Such an intention should be expressed in an interaction characterized by an acknowledgment of the inevitable mutual dependencies which are constitutive of any educational situation within education for freedom.

References

Adorno, T. W. (1971). *Erziehung zur mündigkeit*. G. Kadelbach (Ed.). Frankfurt: Suhrkamp.

Alanen, L. (2001). Childhood as a generational condition: Children's daily lives in a central Finland town. In L. Alanen & B. Mayall (Eds), *Conceptualizing child-adult relations* (pp. 129–143). London and New York: Routledge Falmer.

Appiah, K. A. (2005). *The ethics of identity*. Princeton, NJ: Princeton University Press.

Backett-Milburn, K., & Harden, J. (2004). How children and their families construct and negotiate risk, safety and danger. *Childhood, 11*, 429–447.

Benner, D. (2005). *Allgemeine pädagogik. Eine systematisch-problemgeschichtliche einführung in die grundstruktur pädagogischen denkens und handelns*. Weinheim and München: Juventa Verlag. (Original work published 1987.)

Feinberg, J. (2007). The child's right to an open future. In R. Curren (Ed.), *Philosophy of education. An anthology* (pp. 112–123). Oxford: Blackwell Publishing.

Kant, I. (1961). *Kritik der praktischen vernunft*. Stuttgart: Reclam. (Original work published 1788.)

Kant, I. (1974). Beantwortung der frage: Was ist Aufklärung? In *Was ist Aufklärung?* Stuttgart: Reclam. (Original work published 1783.)

Kant, I. (1984). *Grundlegung zur metaphysik der sitten*. Stuttgart: Reclam. (Original work published 1785.)

Mackenzie, C., & Stoljar, N. (Eds). (2000). *Relational autonomy. Feminist perspectives on autonomy, agency, and the social self*. Oxford: Oxford University Press.

Meyer-Drawe, K. (1990). *Illusionen von autonomie. Diesseits von ohnmacht und all-macht des ich*. München: P. Kirchheim.

Nordström, K. (2009). *Autonomie und erziehung. Eine ethische studie*. Freiburg and München: Verlag Karl Alber.

Oelkers, J. (2001). *Einführung in die theorie der erziehung*. Weinheim and Basel: Beltz Verlag.

Ofstad, H. (1990). *Vi kan ändra världen. Hur bör vi ställa frågorna?* Stockholm: Prisma.

O'Neill, O. (2002). *Autonomy and trust in bioethics*. Cambridge: Cambridge University Press.

Oshana, M. (2006). *Personal autonomy in society*. Aldershot & Burlington: Ashgate.

Papastephanou, M. (2008). Dystopian reality, utopian thought and educational practice. *Studies of Philosophy and Education, 27*(2), 89–102.

Punch, S. (2001). Negotiating autonomy: Childhoods in rural Bolivia. In L. Alanen & B. Mayall (Eds), *Conceptualizing child-adult relations* (pp. 23–36). London and New York: Routledge Falmer.

Schneewind, J. B. (1998). *The invention of autonomy. A history of modern moral philosophy*. Cambridge: Cambridge University Press.

Vallberg Roth, A-C., & Månsson, A. (2008). Individuella utvecklingsplaner som uttryck för reglerad barndom. *Pedagogisk Forskning i Sverige, 13*(2), 81–102.

Von Oettingen, A. (2003). *Det paedagogiske paradoks – et grundstudie i almen peda-gogik.* Århus: Klim.

Von Oettingen, A. (2006). *Paedagogisk filosofi som reflekteret omgang med paedagogiske antinomier.* Århus: Klim.

Winkler, M. (2006). *Kritik der pädagogik. Der sinn der erziehung.* Stuttgart: W. Kohlhammer Verlag.

BRIAN GATES

9 How Far is the Notion of 'Conscience' Redundant and 'Consciencing' a Better Alternative?

Abstract

This chapter explores the concept of 'conscience' and contrasts common usage of the word with increasing academic and professional scepticism as to its worth. It then promotes continued use of the term within formal educational discourses surrounding religious, character, moral and citizenship education, by clarifying and amplifying its meaning with recourse to the concept of *consciencing*, which refers to the personally centred process of making moral sense and which is found in both religious and secular traditions.

Introduction

Explicit use of the word conscience in formal educational discourse has become increasingly rare, at least in the UK and USA. Whilst there may be a good reason why this is so, it is worth reflecting on any loss that might be involved. For wherever in the world there is concern for character education or moral education, and debates about how schools might best equip children and young people for active citizenship and making moral judgements, conscience and *consciencing* are properly at its heart.

Common usage

The notion of conscience figures in common usage, both in everyday discourse and in the more formal language of state constitutions and human rights. In terms of *everyday discourse*, many examples come to mind of the ways in which conscience figures in ordinary conversation, for example, 'In all conscience, I cannot go down that road'; 'That leaves me with a guilty conscience'; and 'My conscience tells me this is what I should be doing'. This common usage regularly takes two different forms. These are exemplified in the following stories. The first illustrates the 'advance warning' connotation involving a sense of shame: 'Driving along a three lane highway, a lady encountered a queue of traffic in the inner two lanes along with a flashing signal indicating that the third lane was closed. Other vehicles were already moving into two lanes, but she knew that it would be another mile before the lane was blocked. By continuing in the third lane she could avoid at least ten minutes of delay. She hesitated, but decided not to. Deep down, her conscience wouldn't let her do it.' The second story illustrates a subsequent sense of 'guilty regret' or even 'remorse': 'A job interviewer, at the time when an appointment is being made, leaves unquestioned what he realizes is an exaggerated appearance of superiority in a particular candidate. He does so to camouflage his preference for this individual, which is actually based on sexual attraction or family loyalty. For some time afterwards, his conscience came back to haunt him.' Whilst acknowledging that individuals using the word conscience may have different notions as to what is behind it, it is still extensively taken for granted in everyday use.

In terms of more formal usage, the word conscience also features in the language of *state constitutions* and *human rights*, as in Article 18 of the Universal Declaration of Human Rights: 'the right of freedom of thought, conscience and religion' (United Nations, 1948). The same is true in many state constitutions (Constitution Society, 2011), where it is the home base of personal freedom – of speech/expression, as of religion/ultimate concern (Schinkel, 2007). It figures especially in the realm of health and medicine, and in the realm of war and peace. In health and medicine, conscience features in discretions and judgements on the part of both doctors and patients over abortion, euthanasia, and research on the human embryo (Beauchamp & Childress, 2008). In war and peace, conscience features in terms of the 'conscientious objectors' as pioneered in the First World War, or in military draftings for service in Vietnam (Childress, 1982) or again what Amnesty International (http://www.amnesty.org) has campaigned to assist as 'Prisoners of Conscience'.

This formal usage can be illustrated in cartoon form. First, there is an example which leaves a bitter taste. It shows the mocking attitude on the part of the English establishment toward 'conchies' – conscientious objectors during the Second World War. Taken from the editorial of a war-time edition of the Church of England clerical directory (Crockfords, 1941), the picture is of a wastrel sprawling in comfort whilst members of his family and friends are loyally engaged in military duties to protect him in his freedom. Its caption reads: 'This little piggy stayed at home.'

A second example may or may not taste sweeter. The conversation between Zonker and Boopsie in Garry Trudeau's *Doonesbury* cartoon (http://www.doonesbury.com/strip) is as follows.

Z: I guess my conscience is finally kicking in. The truth is I've served over 3 million calories at McFriendly's – only 800,000 of them necessary for weight maintenance. That's a lot of excess! On the other hand I was but a lowly server. I was just filling orders.

B: But wasn't that the Nuremberg defence?

Z: No, that was following orders.

B: Then you're good to go morally, whew.

There is nothing here that challenges a taken-for-granted assumption that conscience is real. In neither everyday discourse nor in the language of state constitutions and human rights does this appear to be doubted, even if it is sometimes scorned. Moreover, that remains true even when it is acknowledged that reference to conscience may sometimes be associated with arriving at misguided conclusions and eventually exposed as being morally wrong – what is referred to as the 'erring conscience'.

A potent but contentious example is that of Tony Blair deciding 'in all conscience' that the invasion of Iraq was right on both moral and religious grounds (Blair, 2010). Far from lying, as his critics have accused, he genuinely believed and believes in the light of the evidence and intelligence available at the time, and weighing the potential consequences of indecision, not least with the perceived threat to Israel in mind, that he had to act as he did. With the benefit of hindsight that now looks even more questionable than it did to those who, in conscience themselves, concluded differently at the time. However uncomfortable, for his part, in arriving at the particular political judgement, 'he could do no other'.

Academic and professional scepticism

In spite of predominant common usage that indicates conscience as firm reality, general academic and professional opinion might well be suggesting otherwise. This is certainly a judgement conveyed across the most relevant academic disciplines.

Anthropologists and sociologists have reported on the great diversities within human civilization (Westermarck, 1932; Becker & Barnes, 1960), and so have travellers over many centuries. Local variations in culture and mores are such that norms for mating and family life are seen to be demonstrably diverse. So they also are in regard to dietary compunctions, economic and political order, and conflict resolution. At a deeper level, expected degrees of openness about motives and intentions vary enormously. Any notion that humanity is universally endowed with the same sort of conscience appears highly dubious. Evidence of cultural and moral relativism deems it so.

Psychologists, most especially in Freudian hue, have claimed to expose conscience as merely the very limited result of family conditioning. It is no more than the expression of introverted parental inhibition (Freud, 1913, 1962). As such it is variable in content and relative strength, and it is greatly susceptible to the influence of other emotional pressures. The size of prison populations suggests that the phenomenon of 'conscience-less' individuals (Graham, 1972) is not confined to the extremes of psychosis in a tiny number of individuals. If, in a Kohlbergian cognitive developmental perspective, a morally principled conscience only comes into serious play at Stages 6 and 7, does not that also imply extensive irrelevance – conceptually exemplified, but in reality attained by only a minority in any society (Kohlberg, 1976)?

Philosophers add to the scepticism about the existence of conscience. Not only the positivists within their ranks ask 'Where is it located?' and 'What's the evidence of moral consistency on the part of individuals, let alone wider society, such as would support the claim that it is a common human attribute?' They go on to remark that wherever 'conscience' is appealed to, it is often associated with inauthentic and morally questionable judgements and behaviour (Norman, 1983). Appeal to conscience is just as likely to be found in instances of rationalizations for weakness of response as it is for overweening ambition. If it is so elusive and unreliable, what is the point of continuing to refer and defer to it?

Even some theologians show ambivalence over affirming what is meant by conscience, especially as associated with reference to 'voice of God'. Their reservations are principally twofold. They acknowledge that the reality of God is not only repudiated by secularists, but also by some religious believers such as Theravada Buddhists. They also realize that too literal an attribution of divine authority to individual thinking can unintentionally encourage arrogance along with an unhealthy degree of self-consideration. Therefore, as Paul Tillich (1963: 48) observed, 'although it is safer to follow one's conscience, the result may be disastrous, revealing the ambiguity of conscience and leading to the quest for a moral certainty which in temporal life is given only fragmentarily and through anticipation'.

Conscience also has a part to play in the discourse of the law court. Procedurally, giving evidence and responding to questions is normally done 'on oath', presuming that truth will be told. Whilst it might be expected that the 'accused' will sometimes lie, or at least be economical with the truth, it is not unheard of for attorneys and lawyers to encourage clients to plead guilty or not guilty and to give evidence, not according to what actually is true, but in the interests of achieving the minimum possible punishment or indeed being found innocent when actually guilty. The result is that conscience is deliberately skewed and mocked.

A case for clarification, retention and amplification

Each of these centres of academic and professional discourse is illustrative of strong scepticism as to the worth of the term 'conscience', cumulatively, this might lead to the conclusion that the word would be better dropped entirely from here on. Although I recognize the force of these reservations, my own conclusion is that abandonment would actually be quite difficult to achieve, except perhaps in an academic environment. There, for instance amongst psychologists and educationalists, the word conscience may have already become extensively avoided (Langston, 2001), even if elsewhere it is still a term which has common currency.

Most evidently, it all depends what you mean by conscience. Far better therefore to clarify what is intended by any continuing use and then to try to ensure that this becomes generally normative. If that happens, maybe even those who have become abstemious in its use will once again find it valuable. Conscience or the conscience process, which in the interests of clarity I am preferring to refer to as *consciencing*, will be recognized as shorthand for the personally-centred process of making moral sense both as a springboard for actions and as a seat of responsiveness expressive of future being.

Clarification

I think it is important to acknowledge that it is misleading to speak as though conscience is a ready-made faculty with which every human being is born. In that sense academics have made their point. Moreover, cross-culturally there is no exact match for the word in that sense. In turn, it should be recognized that to understand conscience only as 'super-ego' is highly reductionist. It shows no awareness of the richness of the notion in Judaeo-Christian/biblical and Graeco-Roman Aristotelian and Stoic usage, or in the ruminations of subsequent western philosophers, theologians and playwrights, including Shakespeare (Lewis, 1960), let alone insights from non-western sources.

The French existentialist philosopher Jean-Paul Sartre is quite revealing on the subject. Reflecting autobiographically in later life on his father's death, when he himself was only a year old, he says: 'If he had lived, my father would have lain down on me and crushed me. Fortunately, he died young ... Was it a good or a bad thing? I do not know, but I am happy to subscribe to the judgement: I have no Super-Ego' (Sartre, 1964: 14–15). Whilst not supposing that Sartre is claiming that he is devoid of any moral sense, I do wonder if his express repudiation of a childhood nurturing of moral intelligence provides significant explanatory comment on his subsequent behaviour. The recently documented account of his exploitation of young girls besmirches his avowal as humanist, perhaps even more than his decade of ignoring the evidence of the Gulag (Seymour-Jones, 2008). Might he have actually behaved differently and more sensitively and morally had he recognized the relevant force of conscience even in its rejected sense (Coles, 1997: 58–59)? The need for clarification of usage is self-evident.

Retention

The way forward should now be clear. Instead of reifying conscience as a simple singular entity which is inherited, and which one day might be available in the form of a pill or implant, conscience is far better understood as having to do with moral sense as a multi-faceted feature of wider self-awareness, which John Macquarrie refers to as 'synoptic self-understanding' (Macquarrie, 1977: 58). The Greek and Latin terms – *suneidesis* and *conscientia* – both display the connotation of an accompanying awareness of all one thinks and does, and that such consciousness is continuous throughout life. They also point to a fundamental 'aspect of oughtness' within our being and doing – in other words an experiential process that I am calling *consciencing*.

This awareness is as much at the centre of our whole personal being as are the terms 'heart' and 'mind'. The agency of such awareness requires metaphors to convey its subtler resonances – 'knowing in our bones'; 'feeling in our water'; 'registering in our hearts'; 'being conscious deep down'; or even 'moved by the bowels of compassion'. As such, conscience may be associated with inhibiting certain actions and inducing regret, but more positively it is integrally related to finding newer meaning and purpose, resolving future direction, and inspiring immediate actions. Thus, conscience may represent awareness of my relational context, along with a sense of accountability and 'oughtness' within it. This may lead me to say 'I've devalued another person and even in my own interests I've acted wrongly' or 'this is what I might have done and will do in the future'. It has to do with my becoming more aware of the bigger picture within which my own life is set in terms of both time (past inheritance, present givens and opportunities ahead) and space (my neighbour in gender, race, religion and species). It is actually all about who I am and how at the end of the day I determine to act in relation to others and to the collective universe in which I am alive.

I realize that to talk in these terms may well be exasperating to some. They will see that it is no longer so tightly specific for it to be readily amenable to quantifiable measurement. Any potential gain from this reduced specificity they will judge to be illusory. The term has now become so diffuse that to employ it is just playing with words and in effect useless as a significant reference point. Moreover, they will observe that, not only in behaviour but also in mind, many individuals act in ways that are careless of others and therefore against the grain of any conscience-process. Whether such carelessness is the result of ignorance or ignoring, it calls into question the worth of claiming that conscience has universal educational significance. To paraphrase Freud: 'whereas the starry heavens are truly wonderful, conscience is a very dodgy notion' (Freud, 1938: 38). Yet, even though it is possible to whittle away at such words or to recast them so that there is nothing left of the original, conscience does remain measurably real. Certainly this is so in the manifestation of ingredient elements as, for instance, registered in the extensive range of research on socio-moral events and personal and social identity formation – what Coles refers to as the 'moral archaeology of childhood' (Coles, 1997: 61–166; Stilwell, Galvin, & Kopta, 1991). Yet some of this research is itself deficient in that it neglects to attend to what I have called the 'aspect of oughtness'. The existence of some people apparently without conscience does not invalidate the usefulness of affirming conscience-process in the behaviour of the majority. Neither does the more common carelessness toward others, such as is in different degrees evident in the behaviour of most of us, at least some of the time. For in the conscience-process, I would argue, lies the core of both moral and religious sense and sensibility, that is, it is fundamental to both religious and humanist worldviews.

Amplification

Elsewhere I have made the case that there should be acknowledgement of the relative autonomies of both ethics and religion (Gates, 2006, 2007). They each stand on their own ground but they are also open to the check of the other. Religion without the moral reference is easily capable of individual and institutional distortions, but ethics too without the religious reference can be eviscerated of its holistic humanity.

For the same reasons, Moral Education and Religious Education, whether in religion-specific or common school contexts, are diminished if they are not attentive to the mutual challenge from the complementary integrities of both that which is religious and that which is moral. Together, personal sense of 'oughtness' and 'big-picture-awareness' form the basis for the responsive moral sense found within and across religious traditions and other humanist worldviews. There is a shared educational priority in the individual refining of intention and purpose. Children, young people and adults are all involved in a process of continual registration and response – at times in expressly formal settings and more often informal and certainly lifelong ones as well. *Consciencing* is the term I am using to refer to the living springs of each person's being and doing, within both religious and moral frames of reference.

The range and richness of these frames of reference deserve elaboration as follows. First, it is common to the human condition, individually and collectively, to develop and hold beliefs and values regarding the meaning and purpose of life and death. These beliefs and values become agglomerated in traditions that range from the familial and tribal to the trans-continental and universal. The extent to which humans individually identify themselves with specific religious worldviews is astonishing in terms of numbers and plurality of that mode of expression (see http:// www.adherents.com). Within the mainstream teachings of these many religious traditions and comparable secular humanisms, the 'oughtness' aspect, though variously constituted from within or without the individual, is recurrent (Despland, 1993; Hoose, 1999; Thomas, 1997). *Consciencing* looks to be universal. Accordingly, exposure to the best of these inheritances, along with exploration of their current workings, provides a fertile resource for both Religious Education and Moral Education, as also for any effective preparation for self-motivated citizenship. Arguably, the enrichment of *consciencing* is a world-wide urgency in which teachers would be helped by judicious selection which draws on a balancing of local, national and global experience.

Second, very few would balk at the suggestion that *consciencing* is recurrent within the Jewish and Christian traditions. It is thoroughly scriptural – in both Tenak/Hebrew Bible and both Old and New Testaments. It is there in the experience of the model King David when, on hearing the story of another's savage appropriation of a pet lamb, he becomes aware of his own direct responsibility for self-interested murder (2 Samuel 11–12). It is there in the prophetic affirmation of moral sense as a distinguishing characteristic of those in particular relationship with God ('this is the new covenant ... I will set my law within them and write it on their hearts', Jeremiah 31: 33–34). Some 600 years later, this special covenant is affirmed as universal by Paul: 'When Gentiles who do not possess the Torah carry out its precepts by light of nature ... they are their own law for they display the effect of the law inscribed on their hearts. Their conscience is called as witness' (Romans 2: 14–15; cf. Stendahl, 1963). In subsequent traditions, Orthodox (Harakas, 1978; Thomas, 1999), Protestant (Lehman, 1963; Ebeling, 1963) and Roman Catholic (Libreria Editrice Vaticana, 1994:

3:1:6; Curran, 2004) theologians have variously elaborated on the workings of this central moral sense. There is disagreement, however, regarding the extent to which *consciencing* is dependent on scripture, mediated by ecclesiastical authority, and open to personal reasoning – maybe in isolation, maybe in combination. Even so, responding in conscience is presented as fundamental to the true humanity of the biblical revelation.

Third, the view that *consciencing* comes directly from God is found in all Abrahamic traditions, but the scriptural source is strongest in Islam. Qur'anic revelation, and subsequently the Shari'a, are for the most part singularly determinative. They reveal that the basic experience of *taqwa* – awe/reverence for God – is our human guardian against doing what is wrong: 'Remember God's blessing upon you, and his compact which He made with you ... Be you securers of justice, witnesses of God ... and fear God; surely God is aware of the things that you do' (*Qur'an* 5: 8–9). Even so, appeal to God-given reason and natural reflection, both interpreting scripture and supplementary to it, though less common is still there in Islam as a whole, not least in Sufi tradition.

Fourth, the emphasis on special revelation for *consciencing* is also characteristic of Sikhs and Baha'is, each with their own scriptural reference point in the *Adi Granth* and the *Kitab-I-Aqdas*, but expressly open to insights from other traditions and sources and affirmative of the importance of responsive social engagement.

Fifth, what of the wider Indic traditions? Hindus have a strong sense of moral duty (*dharma*) which is set within their consciousness of each being individually part of the greater Being of Brahman – 'the breath, the self of awareness, entering the self that is the body right to the hairs and nails' (*Kausitaki Upanishad* 4: 20). The scriptural revelation of the *Vedas* and the contextual determinants of *varnashramadharma* provide a given backdrop, but the individual is still at the centre of *consciencing* and responsible for the subsequent actions which will build *karma* (Coward, Lipner, & Young, 1989). For Buddhists, intentionality is all-important in generating compassion and good karmic consequences. The concentration of consciousness, aided by meditation, is the primary vehicle for *consciencing*.

Sixth, the Chinese Confucian tradition speaks of *shin* – in the heart and mind sense of knowing to protect the child. Inherited ancestral wisdom is a formative part of the *consciencing* (Fengyan, 2004), as it is also in Taoism (Cleary, 1992). Followers of Shinto, principally in Japan, pursue a supreme morality rooted in sincerity of motive and purpose which is self-refining and other-serving (Hiroike, 2002).

My argument is threefold. The first point is that, without exception, each religious tradition operates with a strong moral sense. Though they do not each replicate a common notion of a 'faculty' of conscience, they all engage in *consciencing* with an 'oughtness' or responsibility-owning aspect, and this is transformative for individual and collective expression. In the interests of educational enhancement, it is the *consciencing* process that cries out for closer cross-cultural and inter-religious attention, as well as practical application. The different sources contributing to *consciencing* all deserve attention. Many come from outside the individual, as in the authority of special scriptural revelation, legal prescription, the wisdom and example of inspirational leaders or, nearer to hand, trusted adults and peers. Any one or several of these sources may be in peril of becoming absolutized exclusively, but there is no less risk from their being consciously or unconsciously relativized as all equally part of an undifferentiated mix of inherited determinants. *Consciencing* is incomplete, however, if these externals are not accompanied also by reference to sources derived more from within each person, whether spoken of as contemplation, enlightenment or more prosaically critical reflection.

The second point is that it is healthy to recognize that highly relevant insights for both ethics and Moral Education are not confined to western sources. The current fashion for Virtue Ethics, especially in Character Education (Lickona, Schaps, & Lewis, 2003) can look to Wisdom traditions not only of the Ancient Near East (Heaton, 1974; Curnow, 2010) and Greece (Thomson, 1953) but also of India and more especially China where the harmony of personal and social well-being has been consistently prioritized (Smart, 1999). At the same time, the contention over the existence of 'common core values' is counterbalanced by the heightened priority given elsewhere to the matter of individual motivation and intention.

The third point is that the common school is neglecting an enrichment opportunity, complementary to faith-specific education, if it does not make space and find time to explore these resources with its students.

They are tried and tested elements of global inheritance. As such they are relevant in addressing the educational priority of helping equip children and young people for making moral judgements and enabling them to live what have the potential to become both other-considering and self-rewarding moral lives.

Conclusion

Far from being redundant, conscience deserves to be affirmed as an intrinsic ingredient for public education provided it is recognized as a continuing process rather than a fixed attribute. My proposal that the active form *consciencing* be used instead of the more static conscience is a way of respecting the relevant diversities within and between different worldviews and at the same time conveying the activity-related focus involved. It recognizes that the springs of moral action are variously charged by a range of external influences and internal ruminations.

How this is translated into the classroom will be shaped by national determinants, but it is reasonable to expect that story and example, custom and law from both religious and secular sources will be quarried. Understanding and empathy, so fundamental to both Religious Education and Moral Education in a plural world (Hoffman, 2000) will be promoted, and opportunities to try out practical expression will be built in. As part of this, some reference to Freire's strategies for liberation by *conscientization* is worth exploring as a link with political education (Freire, 1972). *Consciencing* deliberately gives opportunity for comparable and interrelated attention to personal, social and political outcomes. Similarly, reference to Wilson's *consilience* would supply a biological basis for linking to the Indic and especially Jain worldviews, extending to include all life forms in the frame for *consciencing* (Wilson, 1998). In the context of our contemporary global village, that agenda for effective religious and moral education is one which has ramifications for both public and private domains with each challenging and deepening the other. Thus *consciencing* beckons self-transcendence.

In the years before his election, Barack Obama invited American citizens, in all their religious and non-religious diversity, to dedicate themselves to a new kind of politics – *a politics of conscience* (Obama, 2007). As a next step, I would suggest that a shared educational target of *consciencing* would be a realistic contribution toward this throughout the world.

References

Beauchamp, T. L., & Childress, J. F. (2008). *Principles of biomedical ethics* (6th edn). Oxford: Oxford University Press.
Becker, H., & Barnes, H. (1960). *Social thought from lore to science, 4 Volumes* (3rd edn). New York: Dover Publications.
Blair, T. (2010). *A journey*. London: Random House.
Childress, J. F. (1982). *Moral responsibility in conflicts: Essays on nonviolence, war and conscience*. London: Louisiana State University Press.
Cleary, T. F. (1992). *The essential Tao: An initiation into the heart of Taoism through the authentic Tao Te Ching*. San Francisco: Harper.
Coles, R. (1997). *The moral intelligence of children*. New York: Random House.
Constitution Society. (2011). *National Constitutions*.
Coward, H. G., Lipner, J. J., & Young, K. K. (1989). *Hindu ethics*. New York: State University of New York Press.
Crockfords. (1941). *Clerical directory*. Oxford: Oxford University Press.
Curran, C. E. (Ed.). (2004). *Conscience: Readings in moral theology, 14*. New York: Paulist Press.
Curnow, T. (2010). *Wisdom in the ancient world*. London: G. Duckworth & Co.
de Bary, W. T. (Ed.). (1969). *Sources of Chinese tradition: Vol. 1*. New York: Columbia University Press.
Despland, M. (1993). Conscience. In M. Eliade (Ed.), *Encyclopedia of religion: Vol. 3*. New York: Simon Schuster Macmillan.
Ebeling, G. (1963). *Word and faith*. London: SCM Press.

Fengyan, W. (2004). Confucian thinking in traditional moral education: Key ideas and fundamental features. *Journal of Moral Education. Special Issue: Moral Education in changing Chinese societies, 33*(4), 429–447.

Freire, P. (1972). *Pedagogy of the oppressed*. London: Sheed and Ward.

Freud, S. (1913). *Totem and taboo*. London: Faber & Faber.

Freud, S. (1938). *New introductory lectures on psychoanalysis*. London: Hogarth.

Freud, S. (1962). *Civilisation and its discontents*. New York: W. W. Norton & Co.

Gates, B. E. (2006). Religion as cuckoo or crucible: Beliefs and believing as vital for citizenship and citizenship education. *Journal of Moral Education, 35*(4), 371–394.

Gates, B. E. (2007). *Transforming religious education. Beliefs and values under scrutiny*. London: Continuum.

Graham, D. (1972). *Moral learning and development: Theory and research*. London: Batsford.

Harakas, S. S. (1978). Centrality of conscience in eastern Orthodox ethics. *Greek Orthodox Theological Review, 23*(2), 131–144.

Heaton, E. W. (1974). *Solomon's new men: Emergence of Ancient Israel as a national state (Currents in the history of culture and ideas)*. London: Thames & Hudson.

Hiroike, C. (2002). *Towards supreme morality. An attempt to establish the new science of moralogy: Vol. 3*. Kashiwa: Institute of Moralogy.

Hoffman, M. (2000). *Empathy and moral development: Implications for caring and justice*. New York: Cambridge University Press.

Hoose, J. (Ed.). (1999). *Conscience in world religions*. Leominster: Gracewing.

Kohlberg, L. (1976). Moral stages and moralization: The cognitive developmental approach. In T. Lickona (Ed.), *Moral development and behaviour: Theory, research and social issues* (pp. 31–53). New York: Holt, Rinehart & Winston.

Langston, D. C. (2001). *Conscience and other virtues: From Bonaventure to Macintyre*. University Park, PA: Penn State University Press.

Lehmann, P. (1963). *Ethics in a Christian context*. New York: Harper & Row.

Lewis, C. S. (1960). *Studies in words*. Cambridge: Cambridge University Press.

Libreria Editrice Vaticana. (1994). *Catechism of the Catholic Church*. London: Geoffrey Chapman.

Lickona, T., Schaps, E., & Lewis, C. (2003). *Eleven principles of effective character education*. Washington DC: Character Education Partnership.

Macquarrie, J. (1977). *Principles of Christian theology*. London: SCM Press. Norman, R. (1983). *The moral philosophers*. Oxford: Oxford University Press.

Obama, B. (2007, June 23). A politics of conscience. *United Church of Christ*. Retrieved March 8, 2012, from http://www.ucc.org/news/significant-speeches/a-politics-of-conscience.html

Sartre, J. P. (1964). *The words.* London: Hamish Hamilton.

Schinkel, A. (2007). *Conscience and conscientious objections.* Amsterdam: Pallas Publications.

Seymour-Jones, C. (2008). *A dangerous liaison.* London: Century.

Smart, N. (1999). *World philosophies.* London: Routledge.

Stendahl, K. (1963). The Apostle Paul and the introspective conscience of the West. *Harvard Theological Review, 56,* 199–215.

Stilwell, B. M., Galvin, M., & Kopta, S. M. (1991). Conceptualization of conscience in normal children and adolescents, ages 5 to 17. *Journal of American Child Adolescent Psychiatry, 30*(1), 16–21.

Tillich, P. (1963). *Systematic theology: Vol. 3.* Chicago: Chicago University Press.

Thomas, R. M. (1997). *Moral development theories – secular and religious: A comparative study, part III.* Westport CT: Greenwood Press.

Thomas, S. (1999). Conscience in Orthodox thought. In J. Hoose (Ed.), *Conscience in world religions* (pp. 99–128). Leominster: Gracewing.

Thomson, J. A. K. (1953). *The ethics of Aristotle: The Nicomachean ethics translated.* Harmondsworth: Penguin Books.

United Nations. (1948). *The universal declaration of human rights.* Retrieved March 8, 2012, from http://www.un.org/en/documents/udhr/

Westermarck, E. (1932). *Ethical relativity.* London: Kegan Paul.

Wilson, E. O. (1998). *Consilience: The unity of knowledge.* London: Little, Brown & Co.

MANFRED L. PIRNER

10 Freedom of Religion and Belief in Religious Schools? Toward a Multi-perspective Theory

Abstract

In the recent disputes about religious schools in various western countries, doubts have been raised about whether such schools are able to promote the human right of freedom of religion and belief, and contribute to the common good in an ever more pluralistic society. The author advances five theses to mark basic elements of a multi-perspective theory of religious schools that tries to take pluralism and the freedom of religion and belief seriously. These theses deal with philosophical, socio-ethical, educational and legal perspectives, and lead to a theological perspective that mainly relies on the concepts of representation and translation. On this understanding, it is argued that religious schools represent a pedagogy that goes beyond the uniform and monolithic rationality that used to demand strict neutrality in public education. Moreover, transparency with regard to educational norms, and an emphasis on a communitarian perspective complementing universalistic principles, are the strengths of religious schools. In order to develop these strengths, Christian schools need to draw upon a public theology that is able to translate the language of the Christian faith into secular and educational rationalities, while still representing it as a potential that can never be fully realized.

Introduction

In various countries, religious schools have had an ambivalent image over recent years. On the one hand, religious schools seem to be very popular. In Germany, for example, over the past twenty years, a considerable number of Protestant private schools have been founded; at present – in the year 2011 – two new private Protestant high schools are being planned in Munich alone. In Britain in 2008, the first Hindu religious school was opened (Pigott, 2008). On the other hand, religious schools have been increasingly called into question. In these controversial disputes the human right of freedom of religion and belief has played a decisive role. Is it compatible with the right of freedom that religious schools require their teachers, and at least a substantial part of their student-body, to belong to a specific religion? One concrete example of this debate in Britain, one that made it to the Supreme Court in 2009, was the case of a Jewish boy who was rejected by the Orthodox Jewish JFS school in London on the ground of being not Jewish enough (Romain, 2009). The Court ruled that this was discriminatory. In May 2010, a somewhat similar case happened in Germany when a 17-year-old student was about to be expelled from a Catholic high school in Illertissen, Bavaria, because she had left the Catholic Church. After a fervent public discussion the school allowed her to stay on and finish her exam (merkur-online, 2010).

Apart from the legal problems involved, such cases easily trigger questions about whether or not religious schools are still the right schools to educate young people in an ever more pluralistic society. In 2008, for example, Britiain's biggest teacher union, the National Union of Teachers, debated a call to abolish all religious schools. Its major argument was that education which was segregated on the basis of faith, ethnicity, or social class undermined community cohesion (Daily Mail, 2008). Critical questions have also been raised by a qualitative study among graduates of an evangelical Christian school, showing that some of them felt they had not been properly prepared to face the pluralism in society (ap Siôn et al., 2007).

These examples illustrate that the issue of freedom of religion and belief in religious schools has to be seen in the wider frame of asking whether religious schools – and which kinds of religious schools – are still able to promote the development of the individual student and the common good of society in a pluralistic context. In the following, I will suggest, in the form of theses, five basic elements for a theory of religious schools that tries to take the pluralistic context and the human right of freedom of religion and belief seriously.

Thesis 1

The first thesis proposes that from a philosophical perspective, religious schools are based on the insight that rationality is not uniform but diverse.

Typically, in the English-speaking context, the philosopher Paul Hirst in the 1970s rejected the notion of 'Christian education' as a 'contradiction in terms' (Hirst, 1972, 1974: 81). Education, he argued, is a rational, critical process that can never presuppose a specific ideological truth. Obviously, Hirst for his part implicitly presupposed an incontestable universality and uniformity of rationality. He was not able, or willing, to see at that time that his own concept of rationality – and consequently his concept of education – was one that had its own axiomatic presuppositions, being predominantly informed by western enlightenment thought. Interestingly, Hirst later distanced himself from this form of 'hard rationalism' as he adopted more recent developments in philosophical thinking (Hirst, 1993; see also Astley, 1994: 41f.).[1] Perhaps the most striking aspect of this is that in almost all major currents of philosophy during the twentieth century, the idea of a uniform, universal rationality has been increasingly criticized.

---

1   I owe thanks to Jeff Astley for drawing my attention to Hirst's further development.

It is a merit of the assertions by postmodernists in the 1980s and 1990s that a case was made for different rationalities and a broadening of the concept of rationality itself. According to the Austrian-German philosopher Wolfgang Welsch, rationality can be defined as follows.

> 1. We speak of rationality whenever people follow a specific set of principles which determine the realm of their validity, identify their objectives, define the aims to be achieved, the methods to be followed, and the criteria to be applied. 2. These principles must be coherent with one another in order to allow coherent usage. 3. Therefore, to be rational simply means to follow the rules suggested by these principles. In doing this, we are rational in the sense of the respective version of rationality. (Welsch, 1998: 17).

Within such a framework, cultural realms such as aesthetic discourse, mythical discourse, and also religious discourse are no longer perceived as irrational or non-rational but as having their own rationality, or – to put it in the words of analytical philosophy – as having their own language games with their own grammars. This implies that there are different legitimate ways of looking at – and trying to make sense of – the world, and that each of them is a specific way of accessing the world, rooted in a specific rationality, and informed by a certain social and cultural context. As German philosopher Juergen Habermas puts it: 'There is no pure reason [...] Reason is of its nature always an incarnate reason imbedded in complexes of communicative action and in structures of the lifeworld [Lebenswelt]' (Habermas, 1987: 374).

For education, these insights make it seem problematic to try to build public education exclusively on the foundation of a uniform, universal rationality. Instead, they strengthen the view that public education from diverse perspectives, drawing on diverse rationalities, is legitimate and makes good sense. Thus, a religious perspective on education and educational theory today is likely to gain plausibility more easily than in the 1970s. For scholarship, the philosophical development particularly resulted in relativizing the ideal of 'objectivity', increasingly valuing the obligation to be explicit about the researcher's subjectivity, his or her perspectives, presuppositions and research interests. Similarly, schools and teachers should make explicit from which presuppositions their pedagogies are guided, thus supporting students and their parents in critically assessing the education they are offered. Religious schools doing so, it seems, will be transparent as regards their educational norms and objectives, and in this way will contribute to the students' freedom of religion and belief.

Of course, we cannot neglect the question of how a common ground for communication and cohesion in an increasingly pluralistic and global society can be sustained when we give up the idea of a uniform and universal rationality. In the face of plural forms of rationality, or at least a 'variety of its voices' (Habermas, 1992), dynamic concepts of, for instance, a 'communicative rationality' (Habermas, 1984) or a 'transversal reason' (Welsch, 1995, 1998) seem helpful to theoretically address the tension between the obligation to respect different rationalities, on the one hand, and the necessity to enable communication and understanding across them on the other. Such a dynamic concept of reason also seems best to account for the fact that in the lifeworld ('Lebenswelt') manifold transversal linkings have already taken place and are continuously going on.

For religious schools, as long as they are part of public education, these deliberations imply a two-fold challenge. First, religious schools are challenged to clarify and communicate how their specific religious perspective on (public) education (connected with their religious rationality) comes about, and how it relates to more general – as well as other specific – views of education (in the sense of a transversal rationality). Second, the question is raised of how diverse rationalities find their place in religious schools and how the tension between autonomy and transversality is modelled. In concrete, this refers to the school subjects, or learning domains, the question of how these can be respected in their own right, but also be connected, in the sense of a transversal rationality, and a multidimensional notion of education. For both tasks, a theory of religious schools needs to rely on processes of theological self-clarification, which will be the content of thesis five below. But before that it seems advisable to address the issue of religious schools from more general socio-ethical, pedagogical and legal perspectives.

Thesis 2

The second thesis proposes that from a socio-ethical perspective, religious schools can be seen as emphasizing a communitarian perspective as a legitimate and meaningful complement to liberal universalism.

While in the context of postmodern philosophical discourse the idea of a uniform and universal rationality has been challenged by pointing to diverse rationalities, in the context of the practical-philosophical or socio-ethical discourse it has been challenged by a broadened concept of rationality represented prominently by communitarianism. In the dispute between communitarians and universal liberals since John Rawls' classic book *A Theory of Justice* (Rawls, 1971), several arguments have been exchanged which are of importance for educational issues. Communitarians – probably the most prominent of them at present being Canadian philosopher Charles Taylor – criticized the individualism of classical liberal theory for an 'atomistic' view of man and pointed out that 'man is a social animal' (Taylor, 1985: 190) whose identity necessarily depends on his social relations, on personal commitments, and on communities. Whereas liberalism emphasizes the importance of abstract norms which can be reflectively endorsed by virtually all people in the world, communitarianism underlines the importance of personal social experiences for the development of values within the individual. As a conclusion of his widely read book *The Genesis of Values*, Hans Joas has by-and-large supported such a communitarian approach by pointing out that values are generated by experience – either by special, extraordinary experiences or by continuous experiences over a longer time (Joas, 2001).

It is clear that, according to the communitarian view, concrete, particular communities in which shared meanings can be experienced and communicated become substantial for an individual's identity and morality alike. While liberalism accentuates the individual's cognitive act of choice in moral issues, communitarianism argues that acts of choosing are only possible in a social context of shared meaning and shared practice in which the individual already finds himself and which guides his choosing. Of course it suggests itself that religious communities may serve especially well to constitute such contexts of shared meaning. This is why the communitarian concept, and especially Charles Taylor's thoughts, have been widely and gratefully adopted in theological discourse.

In general, the realization seems to have spread that democratic western societies cannot be built and sustained on the basis of the rather abstract and theoretical norms of human rights and constitutional values alone, but that they need 'dense' or 'thick' forms of underpinning, substantiating and motivating these norms and values in multiple contexts of social experiences and social practice (Schoberth, 2002: 261). It can be seen in this light that John Rawls, in his book *Political Liberalism* (Rawls, 1993), has addressed some of the communitarian critique, and reduces the scope of his idea of justice to a political framework that would allow citizens with conflicting – religious or non-religious – worldviews to find an 'overlapping consensus' in major political issues with the help of a common secular language of 'public reason'. It is interesting to see how Rawls in his late essays has increasingly appreciated comprehensive worldviews such as those entertained by religious communities as a 'vital social basis' of reasonable political conceptions, 'giving them enduring strength and vigor' (Rawls, 1999: 592). However, Rawls also emphasizes that this only goes for 'rational' worldviews and religious communities that remain open to public reason and integrate basic democratic norms so as to not become sectarian and secluded.

Building on this insight, that both approaches, liberalism and communitarianism, are important and complement each other, I suggest understanding state schools and religious schools as placing their emphases differently. Because they are more pluralistic inside, state schools have a stronger emphasis on liberal universalistic principles and ideas – but yet will try to create a school ethos that can be experienced as a context of shared meaning in the school community. Because they can refer to a specific religious basis, religious schools can place a stronger emphasis on particularistic communitarian principles and ideas, and on creating a context of shared meaning. However, they will also correlate their religious perspective with the more abstract and universal principles of general democratic values and human rights – including the right of freedom of religion and belief.

With reference to Christian schools, this means that abstract democratic and human rights and values may be underpinned, substantiated and motivated – but of course also specified, modified or even criticized – by Christian narratives, rituals and social interactions. For instance, the value of 'human dignity' will be brought together with the Judeo-Christian narrative of God creating man and woman in his image, with acts of blessing or baptism and with the social interaction of loving your neighbour as yourself because he or she, too, is God's child. In this process of 'value generalization' (Parsons, 1971: 2–3; see also Joas, 2008), and the specification of universal values, are two sides of the same coin, as will become even clearer below.

Thesis 3

The third thesis proposes that from an educational perspective, religious schools are based on the insight that education in general and school in particular are inevitably based on worldview-related premises and therefore can never be neutral.

It has been one major insight of the approaches of 'critical education' in the 1970s that 'there is no such thing as a neutral educational process' (Shaull, 2007 [orig. 1970]: 34; see also Astley, 1994: 91). Neutrality in the strict sense does not work in education, because there is no education without an implicit – or explicit – concept of what it means to be human, and what this world is all about. In other words, pedagogy is necessarily based on 'indissoluble ideological and religious premises' (Nipkow, 1998: 108), and theories of education cannot exist 'apart from an ideological and religious pluralism' (Dressler, 2006: 60). It is in line with this insight that John I'Anson in his recent article in the *British Journal of Religious Education* argued against neutrality in Religious Education and recommended to develop a 'pedagogy – after neutrality' (I'Anson, 2010). Just as he traces the biases concerning religion in British concepts of Religious Education, one might as well uncover the 'hidden curriculum' in our schools in general in order to critically question the notion of a school that claims to be 'neutral' concerning religious or worldview related aspects. On the one hand, recent educational research, especially in the German context, has shown that educational theories and scientific approaches still carry much of an implicit 'suppressed heritage' of the western Christian tradition with it (Oelkers, 2003; Ziebertz & Schmidt, 2006; Hofmann, 2006). On the other hand, emancipation processes, both of the academic discipline of educational science and of public schools in the nineteenth and twentieth centuries, seem to have led to rather secularistic tendencies in public school education. The analyses presented by a number of scholars in a recent German book on the relationship between religious education and other school subjects (Pirner & Schulte, 2010) reveal that, in several of these subjects, religious aspects of the curriculum topics are improperly neglected or misrepresented. For instance, one of the standard school textbook series for teaching English at German high schools comprising about 1,200 pages deals with religion only on three-quarters of a page, which is typical of other school textbooks for English, too, and corresponds with the neglect of religion on the level of teacher training (Hollm & Pirner, 2010: 75). In other subjects, such as political education and history, religions tend to be represented almost exclusively in a negative, distorting way as sources of conflict, tension and war. The problem here is not only that religious issues are misrepresented in various school subjects, it is also that teachers, textbook authors and academics *do not realize or even deny* that they have an a-religious or anti-religious attitude which influences their pedagogical theories, their teaching materials and their classroom teaching. From the US-American context, similar findings have been reported by Warren Nord (1995). In a comprehensive investigation of school textbooks for history, natural sciences and economical education from elementary school to college, he found that religion was consistently marginalized. Nord speculates that the secular views of pedagogues as well as textbook authors may be one explanation for this result, another may be the impression that religion is a highly controversial topic from which authors and publishers tend to shy away.

From these arguments and findings, it seems advisable to demand more attention to normative questions in educational discourse and school research. In this light, religious schooling offers a special opportunity in that the schools can be more explicit in this respect. They do not, and need not, pretend to be 'neutral'. They can avoid some of the normative weaknesses and theoretical inconsistencies of a secular pedagogy and school system built on the ideal of 'neutrality'. Religious schools can and should be places where normative issues are openly discussed and thus are prevented from implicitly and secretly influencing students in the form of a 'hidden curriculum'. This again will contribute to the students' freedom of religion and belief. But is such an educational concept of religious schools compatible with the religiously neutral secular state that is in charge of public education? This is a question that belongs in the legal context and will be addressed in the next thesis.

Thesis 4

The fourth thesis proposes that from a legal perspective, religious schools can refer to the fact that the concept of 'neutrality of the state' leaves room for the integration of worldview-related values and for various forms of cooperation between state and religious communities.

The ideal of the 'religious neutrality of the state' has been hotly debated in a number of western countries over recent years. Often these discussions have had to do with religion-related conflicts in the area of public-school education, such as crucifixes in classrooms, Muslim teachers wearing headscarves, or the reference to God in the American 'Pledge of Alliance' that is recited at many American public schools in their daily morning ritual. In the following, I will concentrate on the German context with some sideways-glances at the situation in the USA, a country with a stricter constitutional and legal separation of religion and state than Germany or Britain. As German law professor Stefan Huster points out, one important distinction made in social-philosophical and juridical discourse is that between the state's neutrality concerning *justifications* and neutrality concerning *effects*. The former implies that actions of the state must not be justified by referring to the truth, or higher quality, of a religious faith or worldview. The state must not identify with or privilege a certain religion or worldview (Huster, 2004: 6–8). However, even very neutral-looking state legislation may in effect come in conflict with certain religious beliefs. For instance, sports education and education about sexuality at public schools are guided by educational goals which seem in no way biased by religious or worldview beliefs. Yet, conservative Muslims may have problems and regard this kind of education as incompatible with their religious values. Thus the state can only guarantee neutrality concerning justification and not neutrality concerning effects. It is not possible to establish a public order that will suit all religious and worldview groups to the same extent. However, all these groups may legitimately engage in the political dispute about the further development of public order – and they may promote the awareness that the state's neutrality is not as neutral as it appears but is, of course, based upon certain worldview and value traditions.

This is a point that has been prominent and contested in the American context as well. The discussion here concentrates on the 'Establishment Clause' of the First Amendment to the USA Constitution ('Congress shall make no law respecting an establishment of religion ...' Amendment I, 1791). It has been argued by some that, *in effect*, constitutional liberalism has turned 'militantly secular' (Fish, 2007; see Amesbury, 2009: 204), excluding religion from the public sphere, or tolerating only a 'domesticated religion' (Hauerwas, 1991: 70) – especially in the context of public education.

Another distinction can illuminate the problem even more clearly: the distinction between positive and negative neutrality of the state. Within the legal framework of religious neutrality, the state may subscribe to a strict and complete separation of state and religion, to a 'wall of separation' in the sense of laïcité and thus enforce an exclusion of religion from

the public sphere (= negative neutrality). Or the state may aim at benevo-
lently integrating the diverse religious and worldview groups into public
institutions and thus seek co-operation with them (= positive neutrality).
American Ethics professor Richard Amesbury speaks of two models of
state neutrality: on the one hand 'strict separationism' and on the other
hand an inclusive model, 'according to which all religions are afforded an
equal opportunity to participate in the public sphere' (Amesbury, 2009:
205). USA Law scholar Michael McConnell calls the former view the
'secular state' model and the latter the 'religiously pluralistic state' model
(Amesbury, 2009: 205). The German Constitution (the 'Grundgesetz' GG)
– which does not explicitly mention the principle of religious neutrality of
the state – clearly favours the latter concept, although it leaves scope for
political dispute and democratic decisions to determine which way to go
(Huster, 2004: 19; Weth, 1997: 424f.). This has been repeatedly underlined
by the German Constitutional Court in several of its decisions on school-
related issues. For instance, in their decision on the dispute about crucifixes
in Bavarian classrooms – which the court criticized – the constitutional
judges offered a general explication about the relationship of the state and
religious or worldview related aspects. It reads:

> [The state is not obliged] in fulfillment of its educational duty, as given by the basic
> right to education laid down in Art. 7,1 GG, to renounce completely any references
> to religions or world views. Even a state that comprehensively guarantees the freedom
> of religion and belief and thus commits itself to religious and ideological neutrality
> cannot strip off all culturally transmitted and historically rooted moral beliefs and
> attitudes on which the cohesion of society rests and on which the fulfillment of its
> own duties depends. The Christian faith and the Christian churches – however their
> heritage may be judged today – have in this respect had an outstanding impact. The
> state cannot be indifferent to these intellectual traditions, experiences of meaning
> and codes of conduct. This goes in particular for the school, in which primarily
> the cultural foundations of society are handed down and renewed. Moreover, the
> state, which obliges parents to send their children into a public school, is allowed
> to take regard of those parents who wish for a religiously informed education. The
> Grundgesetz [the German Constitution] has acknowledged this by allowing for
> state-run worldview or confessional schools (in Art. 7,5), by providing for Religious
> Education to be an ordinary school subject (Art. 7,3) and furthermore by leaving room
> for active practice of religious beliefs [...]. (Bundesverfassungsgericht [Constitutional
> Court], 1995, translation: M. P.)

In this passage the judges base their arguments mainly on *two pillars*, which are both significant for religious schools. The first pillar, which becomes relevant toward the end of the text, is the *positive dimension of the right of freedom of religion and belief* used by those parents who wish for a religiously informed education. Religious schools as well as (confessional) Religious Education at all public schools can be perceived as a consequence of this basic human right. It reaches its limits when it infringes on its negative dimension, the right of not being forced, obliged or unwillingly subjected to religious practice or influences. It is in correspondence to this negative dimension of the right of freedom of religion and belief that the court ruled that a Bavarian state regulation demanding of public schools to have crucifixes on the walls in every classroom was unconstitutional. And it is also in line with this dimension that students can be exempted from confessional Religious Education at German public schools. In a number of court decisions as well as in scholarly dispute it has been emphasized that in principle the negative and positive freedom of religion and belief have to be balanced, and schools have to seek a way of enabling such a balance (see also de Wall, 2006). For the USA context, the counterpart or 'companion' of the Establishment Clause is the 'Free Exercise Clause', which in the second part of the first sentence in the First Amendment provides that Congress shall make no law 'prohibiting the free exercise' of religion. In consequence, Amesbury sees the public debate in the USA arrive at a conclusion similar to the above advanced view of balancing positive and negative freedom of religion: 'Neutrality cannot be achieved by excluding religious values in favor of secularist values. It is achieved only when all such points of view are afforded a hearing'. (Amesbury, 2009: 206).

The second pillar of argumentation is the distinction between, as it were, *cult* and *culture*, between *Christianity as a religion* and *Christianity as a cultural force*. It is remarkable how positively the contribution of Christianity to the foundations of the modern democratic state and to its public education is valued here by the court. However, according to the court's explication, this does not mean that the state identifies with Christianity *as a religion*; it can only acknowledge that state and society rest on the *cultural heritage* rooted in Christian traditions. Legal expert and theologian Rudolf Weth aptly argues that it is not the specifically Christian characteristics that are in view here, but exactly those aspects of Christianity that have been generalized and have found wide approval beyond the borders of the Christian churches. Such aspects can be categorized under the notion of 'Civil Christianity' ('gesellschaftliches Christentum': Rössler, 1986) or, even wider, of 'Civil Religion' (Bellah, 1967). Of course, what is considered to belong to the realm of 'Civil Christianity' or 'Civil Religion' will be a matter of negotiation and communication within the whole of society, in which the churches are only one voice among others. There is one criticism that can be voiced against the way the argument is advanced by the Constitutional Court: the court only refers to the traditional and historical aspect of Christianity, it does not refer to the question of how compatible a religion and its specific culture currently are with the fundamental values of the democratic, human-rights-based state. However, in my opinion, this is definitely also a question toward which the state cannot be indifferent, as is mirrored in the American debate on liberal political theory. Despite controversial issues, there seems to be a wide consensus here that the state 'cannot remain neutral' when it comes to fundamental values such as freedom and equality (Amesbury, 2009: 210); it therefore cannot retain equal distance toward religious sects that renounce or endanger these values and religions that promote them.

Religious schools, I believe, can and should be based on both pillars of argumentation. First, even as private schools, they should make every effort to find a good balance between the positive and negative dimension of the right of freedom of religion and belief. Although private religious schools have a greater degree of freedom to allow for a specific religious perspective on education, they should also respect the negative freedom of religion and belief of all their students and avoid any pressure on them to participate in religious practice as well as any attempts to manipulate them in their religious attitudes. Second, I suggest that 'Civil Christianity' can be a good starting point in the endeavours to develop a Christian profile of Christian schools and disclose the valuable heritage of Christianity to the students as well as to the teachers. Starting with 'Civil Christianity' would also be a way that combines communitarian and liberal perspectives in the above sketched-out sense. It can also be recommended to look at empirical findings as a basis on which Christian and Non-Christian teachers at

Christian schools are likely to agree (more on this below). Such a school profile will be based on Christian faith but be open to non-believers among the students and among the teachers – and in this way respect the right of freedom of religion and belief. The challenges to religious schools that have up to now been outlined mainly from an 'outsider perspective' chiefly need to be addressed from an 'insider perspective', which means from a theological perspective. This will be outlined in thesis five.

Thesis 5

The fifth thesis proposes that from a (Christian) theological perspective, the central task regarding religious schools can be described as a multi-dimensional translation within the framework of a public theology. The language game and rationality of a specific religion must be translated into educational as well as secular languages and rationalities without giving up the representation of its identity.

Public education can and should be regarded as a subject-matter of a public theology. The notion of 'public theology' that was initially introduced into theological discussion by theologians from various countries and denominations (Ronald Thiemann, Max Stackhouse, Don Browning, David Tracy in the USA; Duncan Forrester and Will Storrar in the UK; John de Gruchy and Dirkie Smit in South Africa; Wolfgang Huber and Jürgen Moltmann in Germany; see Bedford-Strohm, 2008: 344) has recently crystallized into an internationally propagated paradigm and cross-cultural network (Global Network of Public Theology, http://www.csu.edu.au/special/accc/about/gnpt/). Public theology is broadly defined as 'reflexion on questions of public relevance in the light of theological traditions' (Huber, 2008: 2; Bedford-Strohm, 2008: 345; see also Bedford-Strohm, 2009). In a wider sense, all theological contributions of socio-ethical scope can be summarized under the label of 'public theology'. Public theology's most characteristic feature is that it aims at benefitting religious persons as well as non-religious persons and society as a whole. Public theology reacts to the rising need for orientation in modern civil societies. It acknowledges that in pluralistic western societies Christianity is no longer generally accepted as an unquestioned authority in ethical issues, yet suggests that exactly in this situation the potentials for ethical orientation from the Christian tradition should and can be voiced anew. In order to do so, public theology aims at making its interpretations of religious traditions as understandable as possible in the context of general discourse. This implies a kind of *translation* of the traditional religious language into a language that can be understood by secular people as well as by people from other religions. Public theologians need a kind of bilingual competence to communicate in the religious language game of their particular tradition, to communicate in the common secular language game of public reason and to translate between the two.[2]

Accordingly, questions of public education in general – for instance matters of social justice regarding educational opportunities – belong to the area of public theology, but also and particularly the issues of religious schools. In the realm of public education, most religious schools principally claim to benefit all students, regardless of their own religious or non-religious views, even though they may – especially as private schools – concentrate on students with a certain religious background.

In this context, processes of translation and transformation play an important role which in the following will be exemplified by reference to *Christian* schools. Christian schools claim to be guided in their educational work by Christian principles or values. In order to honour this commitment, the language game of Christian faith, with its typically Christian rationality,

---

2   This also implies engaging in a constant negotiating process about the scope and substance of 'public reason'. The secular language of public reason is in no way static and permanent, but rather an alterable product of historical developments. This is why in a theological view the task cannot only be to translate religious language into the secular language of public reason but also to try to enlarge and correct such notions of public reason that seem too narrow or one-sided – as has been done by German theologians such as Johannes Fischer (2002) or Peter Dabrock (2000, 2010). See also Pirner, 2012b.

has to be translated into educational rationality, that is, it must be shown what particular aspects of the Christian faith can mean in the field of public education. For instance, the Christian view that all humans are sinners, in the sense of imperfect and fallible human beings, may be translated into an educational concept and a school culture in which teachers and students are accepted on principle despite their mistakes and shortcomings. Such a translation may have two different meanings for the Christians and the non-Christians among the teachers at a Christian school. For the Christians it may be a way of putting their faith into practice in a specific field of their life. For the non-Christians, the anthropological view and/or the consequence drawn may be acceptable without the need for the religious principle, but is one that is compatible with their own worldviews, and thus a guide to their educational practice.

That this can happen in Christian schools is supported by empirical evidence. In a quantitative empirical study we did among the 6,000 educational staff of the 'Christliche Jugenddorfwerk' (CJD), a big Christian educational institution in Germany, it turned out that a high proportion of the non-believers among them felt that some ideas from Christian faith were helpful orientation points for them in their educational work (Pirner, 2008, 2012a). Obviously, only a few of them were able to identify with a 'Christian pedagogy' without seeing themselves as believing Christians.

These empirical findings can draw our attention to another aspect. Translation in this example is not a one-way process of theologians unfolding assertions of Christian faith in their meaning for education, but people from the CJD educational staff translated Christian principles *for themselves* into their educational thinking and practice. Such translation processes appear to be of an interactive nature. This insight is also mirrored by recent theories of translation in which translation is principally conceptualized as an intercultural and interactive process (Bachmann-Medick, 2010; Bassnett, 1990). In such interactive translation processes, it is ultimately the addressees who complete the process of translation and thus decide whether or not successful translation takes place. Moreover, it is possible for them to learn the language of Christian faith in a way that enables them to translate on their own some of its aspects into the language of educational theory and practice.

Understanding translation as an interactive and intercultural phenomenon can also mean starting with the secular (or educational) side and, consequently, seeing the Christian religion and its tradition in a new light. A good example of this is in the development of the international human rights, which only after their secular triumphal march through the centuries were recognized by the churches as being largely rooted in basic convictions of the Christian faith and therefore as being appropriate secular translations for them (Joas, 2010; Bielefeldt, 1998, 2009). In the educational field, teachers may discover that an already existing (secular) educational concept is compatible with basic Christian propositions and indeed sheds a new light on them, so that this educational concept may offer itself as an appropriate way of 'translating' those Christian propositions into educational rationality.

These examples indicate that theology, and Christianity as a whole, can profit considerably from addressing the field of public education. In a wording that I consider to be particularly fortuitous, an official paper of the Evangelical Church in Germany (EKD) calls the area of public education a big chance for the church, because in it 'the abilities of the Christian faith within society to communicate, to promote tolerance, and to engage in dialogue are put to the test' (Kirchenamt der EKD, 2009: 61f.; translation: M. P.). This argument also points to the task that a public theology has with regard to the churches and religious communities: it should promote the understanding amongst believers that public responsibility is an integral and necessary part of the Christians' mission in this world (see, for example, Polke, 2008).

The task of theology with regard to Christian schools can now be specified as being two-fold: theology can and should, on the one hand, offer a representation of the Christian faith[3] in the literal sense of the word a *re-presentation*: it should keep the Christian tradition present and make it understandable in its richness and potential in the context of the present

---

3   I owe thanks to my Erlangen colleague Andreas Nehring for drawing my attention to the significance of the notion of representation in the area of religious studies and theology.

world, which includes making it connectable with present thought and experience so that people can relate to it and translate it into their diverse lifeworlds – this is generally conceptualized as the core task of Systematic Theology. On the other hand, theology should engage in dialogical processes that allows it to offer translations of aspects of Christian faith into diverse other rationalities, for instance into ethical, political, or educational rationalities – this can be regarded as a specific subtask of theological (social) ethics and public theology. *Representation* and *translation* can thus be understood as the two basic assignments of theology with regard to the public sphere in general.

One further important aspect needs to be addressed in this context. In line with the argument above, the renowned agnostic philosopher Jürgen Habermas, in his impressive speech on receiving the Peace Prize of the German Publishers and Booksellers Association (Habermas, 2001), pointed out that propositions of the Christian faith can also have an important meaning for the 'religiously unmusical' like himself (p. 30). As one example among others, he refers to the biblical narrative that man was created in the image of God as one root and interpretation of the value of human dignity. What is more, he argues that through such translations from the religious language into secular languages important areas of meaning may get lost. 'Secular languages that simply eliminate what was once meant leave behind only irritation. Something was lost when sin became guilt' (p. 24). In contrast to Hegel, whose project was the assimilation of religion into philosophical thinking, Habermas aims at such a kind of secularizing translation of religion that acknowledges its exceeding potential of meaning and humanity: 'Giving due consideration to the religious origin of its moral foundations, the liberal state should consider the possibility that in the face of completely new challenges the "culture of common sense" (Hegel) may not be able to catch up with the articulation level of its own history of origins' (pp. 22–23). While with Hegel, religion can be overcome and become superfluous as soon as its valuables are all translated into secular philosophical language, Habermas clearly advocates the ongoing importance of religion in society. Following this line of argument, theology may – together with Habermas and other non-theologians – look for modes of translation that keep the 'added value' of the translated original present in the translation, or, to put it differently, modes of translation in which the representational dimension does not entirely get lost.

To be sure, from a theological perspective the translation of Christian religion into other rationalities will always bear the risk of a self-seculari- zation of Christianity. Already, the transformation of the living Christian religion into theological reflection has an alienating effect – religion does not equal religious rationality or theology. This goes even more for the translation of Christian religion into secular rationalities. It is true, this secularizing effect can, in principle, be theologically accepted as participat- ing in God's incarnation into the world. And it is also true that Christian concepts such as charity can only gain general acceptance when they can be disentangled from the Christian tradition – and perhaps be reconnected to secular or other religious worldviews (a point Bielefeldt makes for human rights: Bielefeldt, 2009). Yet, what Habermas states for a secularizing trans- lation of the Christian tradition from 'outside' also applies for an 'insider', that is, a theological perspective: In some very liberal currents of theology such translation processes seem to imply such a high degree of adjustment to the 'Zeitgeist' (the predominant trends of thinking), that they in effect almost dissolve Christian faith into ethics or a secular ideology. It is this form of translation and self-secularization that Protestant church leader Wolfgang Huber (1999), as well as Pope Benedict, have, in my opinion rightly, criticized recently.

Let us apply the distinction between different ways of translating Christian propositions to our own example from above. Non-Christian teachers, we found, may be able to relate to the Christian notion of human beings as sinners without accepting the religious background of them. They can, it seems, do so with two possible consequences. First, they may find it plausible to view all humans as imperfect and fallible and – in a Hegelian way – forget about or marginalize the religious source of this insight, especially if the school and Christian teacher colleagues do not make much effort to communicate the religious background of such views. Second, the non-Christian teachers may – in a Habermasian way – find the Christian anthropology plausible, appreciate its theological connota- tions and positively expect that the Christian tradition has more to offer of such valuable insights even for those who are not believing Christians.

This will probably be supported by a school culture in which the religious sources of a good school programme are explicitly communicated; the significance of the school culture in this context is supported by empirical evidence. Research among teachers at Protestant private schools in Germany indicates that on the one hand, there are indeed types of these schools of high quality, but whose teachers find it difficult to talk about religious issues and link them with educational issues. On the other hand, there are schools whose teachers communicate well about religious issues and relate them to their educational task, but sometimes in an all too simplifying or inappropriate way (Holl, 2010).

Both findings, together with the deliberations above, can be seen as stimulations to promote translation and linking processes between religious rationality and educational rationality in religious schools that do justice to either side. For this task, Christian schools need the support of a Christian theology that takes up the challenge and opportunity of representing, as well as translating, the Christian tradition into the public sphere. By doing so, it will serve the case of religious schools in a way that can be specified by adopting the well-known distinction from British religious education theory between learning religion (in the sense of religious nurture), learning about religion (in the sense of getting information and understanding) and learning from religion (in the sense of receiving personal benefits from dealing with a religion). By offering representations and translations of Christian faith, theology can help to invite people to learn more about and get personally involved in Christianity and the Christian faith (= learn religion), but also help to allow them to benefit from Christianity without giving up their own secular or different religious views (= learning from religion). This seems the best path to follow in religious schools, one which conforms with both the positive and negative dimension of the right of freedom of religion and belief.

References

Amendment I. (1791). *Bill of Rights.* Retrieved March 13, 2012, from http://www. archives.gov/exhibits/charters/bill_of_rights_transcript.html

Amesbury, R. (2009). Religious neutrality and the secular state: The politics of God's absence? In I. U. Dalferth (Ed.), *The presence and absence of God.* Tübingen, Germany: Mohr Siebeck.

ap Siôn, T., Francis, L. J. and Baker, S. (2007), Experiencing education in the new Christian schools in the United Kingdom: Listening to the male graduates. *Journal of Beliefs and Values, 28*(1), 1–15.

Astley, J. (1994). *The philosophy of Christian Religious Education.* Birmingham, AL: Religious Education Press.

Bachmann-Medick, D. (2010). *Cultural turns. Neuorientierungen in den kulturwissenschaften* (4th edn). Reinbek bei Hamburg: Rowohlt.

Bassnett, S. (1990). The translation turn in cultural studies. In S. Bassnett & A. Lefevere (Eds), *Translation, History, and Culture* (pp. 123–140). London: Pinter.

Bedford-Strohm, H. (2008). Öffentliche theologie in der zivilgesellschaft. In I. Gabriel (Ed.), *Politik und theologie in Europa* (pp. 340–365). Ostfildern: Schwabenverlag.

Bedford-Strohm, H. (2009). Vorrang für die armen. Öffentliche theologie als befreiungstheologie für eine demokratische gesellschaft. In F. Nüssel (Ed.), *Theologische ethik der gegenwart. Ein überblick über zentrale ansätze und themen* (pp. 167–182). Tübingen: Mohr Siebeck.

Bellah, R. N. (1967). American civil religion, *Dædalus. Journal of the American Academy of Arts and Sciences, 96*(1), 1–21.

Bielefeldt, H. (1998). *Philosophie der menschenrechte. Grundlagen eines weltweiten freiheitsethos.* Darmstadt: Wissenschaftliche Buchgesellschaft.

Bielefeldt, H. (2009). Historical and philosophical foundations of human rights. In M. Scheinin & C. Krause (Eds), *International Protection of Human Rights: A Textbook* (pp. 3–18). Turku, Finland: Abo Akademi University.

Bundesverfassungsgericht. (1995). Urteil BVerfG 1 BvR 1087/91 vom 16.5.1995 (Kruzifix-Urteil). Retrieved March 8, 2012, from http://www.servat.unibe.ch/dfr/bv093001.html#Rn002. Critically checked with Weth, 1997: 424.

Dabrock, P. (2000). *Antwortender glaube und vernunft. Zum ansatz evangelischer fundamentaltheologie.* Stuttgart: Kohlhammer.

Dabrock, P. (2010). Leibliche Vernunft. Zu einer Grundkategorie Fundamental-theologischer Bioethik und ihrer Auswirkung auf die Speziesismus-debatte. In

P. Dabrock, R. Denkhaus, & S. Schaede (Eds), *Gattung Mensch. Interdisziplinäre Perspektiven* (pp. 227–262).Tübingen: Mohr Siebeck.

de Wall, H. (2006). 'Religion im Schulleben' – Rechtliche Aspekte. In B. Schröder (Ed.), *Religion im Schulleben. Christliche Präsenz nicht Allein im Religionsunterricht* (pp. 51–64). Neukirchen-Vluyn: Neukirchener.

Dressler, B. (2006). *Unterscheidungen. Religion und bildung.* Leipzig: Evangelische Verlagsanstalt.

Fischer, J. (2002). Zur Frage der 'übersetzbarkeit' Religiöser Unterscheidungen in eine Säkulare Perspektive. *Freiburger Zeitschrift für Philosophie und Theologie, 49:* 1(2), 214–235.

Fish, S. (2007, September 2). Liberalism and secularism: One and the same. *Think Again (New York Times).*

Habermas, J. (1984). *The theory of communicative action: Vol. 1: Reason and the rationalization of society.* Boston, MA: Beacon Press.

Habermas, J. (1987). *The philosophical discourse of modernity. Twelve lectures.* Cambridge, MA: The MIT Press.

Habermas, J. (1992). The unity of reason in the diversity of its voices. In J. Habermas, *Post-metaphysical thinking. Philosophical essays* (pp. 115–148). Cambridge, MA: MIT Press.

Habermas, J. (2009). *Zwischen Naturalismus und Religion. Philosophische Aufsätze.* Frankfurt am Main: Suhrkamp.

Habermas, J. (2001). *Glauben und Wissen. Friedenspreis des Deutschen Buchhandels.* Frankfurt a.M.: Suhrkamp. (Unauthorized and not in all parts successful English translation, retrieved March 8, 2012, from http://www.nettime.org/Lists-Archives/nettime-l-0111/msg00100.html)

Hauerwas, S. (1991). *After Christendom: How the Church is to behave if freedom, justice, and a Christian nation are bad ideas.* Nashville, TN: Abingdon Press.

Hirst, P. H. (1972). Christian education: A contradiction in terms? *Learning for Living, 11*(4), 7–8.

Hirst, P. H. (1974). *Moral education in a secular society.* London: University of London Press.

Hirst, P. H. (1993). Education, knowledge and practices. In R. Barrow & P. White (Eds), *Beyond liberal education. Essays in honour of Paul H. Hirst* (pp. 184–199). London: Routledge.

Hofmann, M. (Ed.). (2006). *Pädagogische Modernisierung. Säkularität und Sakralität in der Modernen Pädagogik.* Bern: Haupt.

Holl, A. (2010). *Orientierungen von Lehrerinnen und Lehrern an Schulen in Evangelischer Trägerschaft. Eine Qualitativ-Rekonstruktive Studie.* Unpublished dissertation, Universität Erlangen-Nürnberg.

Hollm, J., & Pirner, M. L. (2010). The boundary is the best place for acquiring knowledge. Religionsdidaktik und Englischdidaktik im Dialog. In M. L. Pirner & A. Schulte (Eds), *Religionsdidaktik im Dialog – Religionsunterricht in Kooperation* (pp. 73–100). Jena: IKS Garamond.

Huber, W. (1999). *Kirche in der Zeitenwende. Gesellschaftlicher Wandel und Erneuerung der Kirche.* Gütersloh: Gütersloher Verlagshaus.

Huber, W. (2008). Ökumene der Profile. Vortrag zur Eröffnung der Dietrich-Bonhoeffer-Forschungsstelle für öffentliche Theologie am 29 Januar 2008 in der Universität Bamberg. Retrieved March 8, 2012, from http://www.uni-bamberg.de/fileadmin/uni/fakultaeten/ppp_lehrstuehle/evangelische_theologie_1/pdf_Dateien/Vortrag_WHuber_Oekumene_der_Profile_080129.pdf

Huster, S. (2004). *Der Grundsatz der Religiös-Weltanschaulichen Neutralität des Staates – Gehalt und Grenzen* (Schriftenreihe der Juristischen Gesellschaft zu Berlin, H. 176). Berlin: de Gruyter.

I'Anson, J. (2010). RE: pedagogy – after neutrality. *British Journal of Religious Education, 32*(2), 105–118.

Joas, H. (2001). *The genesis of values.* Chicago: University of Chicago Press.

Joas, H. (2008). Value generalization – Limitations and possibilities of a communication about values. *Journal for Business, Economics & Ethics, 9*(1), 88–96.

Joas, H. (2010, December 22). Der Mensch Muss uns Heilig Sein. *Die Zeit, 49–50.*

Kirchenamt der EKD (Ed.). (2009). *Kirche und Bildung. Herausforderungen, Grundsätze und Perspektiven Evangelischer Bildungsverantwortung und Kirchlichen Bildungs Handelns.* Eine Orientierungshilfe des Rates der EKD. Gütersloh: Gütersloher Verlagshaus.

merkur-online. (2010, May 6). Nach Kirchenaustritt: Schülerin (17) darf bleiben. *merkur-online.de.* Retrieved March 8, 2012, from http://www.merkur-online.de/nachrichten/bayern-lby/nach-kirchenaustritt-schueler-17-darf-bleiben-lby-750199.html

Nipkow, K. E. (1998). *Bildung in einer Pluralen Welt: Vol. 2: Religionspädagogik im Pluralismus.* Gütersloh: Gütersloher Verlagshaus.

Nord, W. A. (1995). *Religion & American education. Rethinking a national dilemma.* Chapel Hill, NC: The University of North Carolina Press.

Oelkers, J. (Ed.). (2003). *Das Verdrängte Erbe. Pädagogik im Kontext von Religion und Theologie.* Weinheim: Beltz.

Parsons, T. (1971). *The system of modern societies.* Englewood Cliffs, NJ: Prentice-Hall.

Pigott, R. (2008, September 15). First Hindu faith school opening. *BBC News.* Retrieved March 8, 2012, from http://news.bbc.co.uk/2/hi/uk_news/7615539.stm

Pirner, M. L. (2008). *Christliche Pädagogik. Grundsatzüberlegungen, Empirische Befunde und Konzeptionelle Leitlinien.* Stuttgart: Kohlhammer.

Pirner, M. L. (2012a, in press). Christian Pedagogy? A research report on the Christian profile of an educational institution in Germany. *British Journal of Religious Education.*

Pirner, M. L. (2012b, in press). Übersetzung. Zur bedeutung einer fundamental-theologischen kategorie für kirchliche bildungsverantwortung. In G. Meier (Ed.), *Festschrift für Hartmut Rupp.* Stuttgart: Calwer Verlag.

Pirner, M. L., & Schulte, A. (Eds). (2010). *Religionsdidaktik im dialog – Religionsunterricht in kooperation.* Jena: IKS Garamond.

Polke, C. (2008). Die religiös-weltanschauliche neutralität des Staates. Ein kapitel politische ethik des Christentums. *Neue Zeitschrift für Systematische Theologie und Religionsphilosophie, 50*(2), 158–177.

Rawls, J. (1971). *A theory of justice.* Cambridge, MA: Harvard University Press.

Rawls, J. (1993). *Political liberalism.* New York: Columbia University Press.

Rawls, J. (1999). *Collected papers.* In S. Freeman (Ed.). Cambridge: Harvard University Press.

Romain, J. (2009, December 16). The JFS ruling is a victory for Jews. *The Guardian.* Retrieved March 8, 2012, from http://www.guardian.co.uk/commentisfree/belief/2009/dec/16/jfs-supreme-court-ruling

Rössler, D. (1986). *Grundriss der praktischen theologie.* Berlin: de Gruyter.

Schoberth, W. (2002). Pluralismus und die freiheit evangelischer ethik. In W. & I. Schoberth (Eds), *Kirche – Ethik – Öffentlichkeit* (pp. 249–264). Münster: Lit.

Shaull, R. (2007). Foreword. In P. Freire [1970], *Pedagogy of the oppressed* (pp. 29–34). New York: Continuum.

Taylor, C. (1985). *Philosophy and the human sciences: Vol. 2.* Cambridge: Cambridge University Press.

Teachers call for faith schools to be abolished in the interest of community relations. (2008, March 24). *Daily Mail.* Retrieved March 8, 2012, from http://www.dailymail.co.uk/news/article-543378/Teachers-faith-schools-abolished-community-relations.html

Welsch, W. (1995). *Vernunft. Die Zeitgenössische Vernunftkritik und das Konzept der Transversalen Vernunft.* Frankfurt am Main: Suhrkamp.

Welsch, W. (1998). Rationality and reason today. In D. R. Gordon & J. Niznik (Eds), *Criticism and defense of rationality in contemporary philosophy* (pp. 17–31). Amsterdam: Rodopi.

Weth, R. (1997). Erinnern an Gottes reich. Positive religionsfreiheit der Kirche und weltanschauliche neutralität des Staates in der zivilgesellschaft. In C. Daling-

Sander et al. (Eds), *Herausgeforderte Kirche. Anstöße – Wege – Perspektiven* (pp. 419–439). Wuppertal: Foedus.

Ziebertz, H-G., & Schmidt, G, R. (Eds). (2006). *Religion in der Allgemeinen Pädagogik. Von der Religion als Grundlegung bis zu ihrer Bestreitung.* Gütersloh: Gütersloher Verlagshaus.

PART III

Empirical Perspectives

RENÉ FERGUSON

11 Communities of Practice: Encountering the Unexpected in Narratives of Religious Diversity

Abstract

The contents of this chapter form part of a wider study in which I investigated how participation by teachers in a learning community, a community of practice, would contribute toward improving their professional knowledge base for Religion Education as a focus area of Citizenship Education. The chapter tells a story of how qualitative research may produce the unexpected. Forty-five kilometres west of Johannesburg, South Africa, a small mining town lies tucked away. The Group Areas Act in which people of different 'races' were forced to live separately during the apartheid era is still in evidence, seventeen years after liberation. Four people, a researcher and three secondary school teachers who live, or lived, in these former segregated areas, encountered one another in this out-of-the-way town, in a participatory action research project designed to investigate options for teacher-learning about religion, religious diversity and democratic citizenship education. What was the nature of the unexpected? Various narratives arose out of dialogue with these teachers and subsequent reflections on their personal histories and experiences of religion and belief, and how these contribute toward understanding regional differences in religious expression, tradition and belief, experiences which are largely undocumented. The narratives presented within this chapter explore how situated knowledge unearthed by participants through engagement in a community of practice provide examples of experiences and interpretations of religion and religious diversity which are valuable resources for Citizenship/Religion Education.

Introduction

The right to the freedom of religion or belief is clearly stipulated in the Bill of Rights in the Constitution of the Republic of South Africa, 1996 (2011, (15) (1)). The recognition of this right and the freedom that it affords citizens since democratization in 1994 presented my own empirical research (2007–2008) with significant possibilities (Ferguson, 2011). In the qualitative phase of the study I investigated how participation by teachers in a learning community, a community of practice (Lave & Wenger, 1991; Wenger, 1998; Wenger, McDermott & Snyder, 2002), would contribute toward teacher development for democratic Citizenship Education, in which knowing about diversity of religion or belief and cultures is a key component. Since 1994, *Religious* Education has transformed significantly and has been renamed *Religion* Education (Department of Education, 2003a). This term is used in the national curriculum statements and the National Policy on Religion and Education (Department of Education, 2003a, 2003b: 9) to refer to a subject area in which learning and teaching about religions, beliefs and worldviews is central. Hence, Religion Education is not a stand-alone subject but is taught as an aspect of Citizenship Education within a learning area or subject titled Life Orientation.

The way in which teachers could respond to Religion Education as a Citizenship Education topic was the issue that inspired the wider study. The wider study was designed using mixed methods, viz. a cross-sectional survey (quantitative) followed by a qualitative phase, operationalized as participatory action research (Creswell, 2003; Creswell & Plano Clark, 2007; Kemmis & McTaggart, 2000). The findings of the survey informed the stages of the action research, which was conducted over a period of eight months in 2008 (*cf.* Ferguson, 2011). During these eight months, I worked closely with three secondary school teachers in a community of practice, focusing specifically on the Citizenship and Religion Education components of the Life Orientation curriculum. The community of practice comprised the three participant teachers directly, their colleagues in their respective schools indirectly, and I, the researcher. The 'unexpected' alluded to in the title of this chapter refers to the narratives that emerged in the data obtained from focus group interviews and discussions conducted with the participants, classroom observations and one-to-one semi-structured interviews. These narratives provided valuable insights into the activities of various social groups and thus also contributed to the domain of interest (Wenger, 1998: 73; Ferguson, 2011: 86) of this Citizenship/Religion Education community of practice.

This chapter consists of a network of narratives: 'my narrative' as researcher, a 'shared narrative' and the participants' narratives constructed from the qualitative data. 'Narrative' could refer to oral or written accounts of personal experiences or events; or to the legends, myths, or fables tied into the worldviews and cosmologies of different societies. In the context of this chapter, the former definition is most relevant. Hence, it is the oral accounts of the participants' knowledge and experiences of discrimination and segregation, of how discrimination and segregation have given rise to various new religions and African Independent Churches (AIC),[1] and how the participants' day-to-day experiences are coloured by the beliefs, activities and practices of adherents of such movements. With particular application to research data, Punch (2009: 190) suggests that research data often occurs 'naturally in story form'. He points out that even when the researcher has not explicitly 'solicited data in story form', participants may give narrative responses to an interviewer's questions (p. 190). 'Storied accounts' are ways of responding to questions of meaning (Gubrium & Holstein, 2009: 42; Clandinin & Connelly, 2000). Hence, telling stories in response to questions posed by interviewers enables interviewees to make sense of experiences and personal histories in relation to the social context (Elliot, 2005: 10; *cf.* Roux, 2009: 116). From a social justice perspective, Iris Young (2000: 70ff) maintained that narrative in public discourse becomes the means for people to 'give voice to' different kinds of experiences that might otherwise go unheard.

---

1   For an overview of types and terms of reference for the AICs, *cf.* Anderson (2001).

Background – the 'shared narrative'

To begin, it is necessary to discuss something of the 'shared narrative' shaped by the socio-political circumstances of apartheid and post-apartheid South Africa. The landmark event for all South Africans was the first democratic election in 1994. This election meant liberation from a social-political system that had entrenched segregation according to racial specifications as an ideology, the legacy of which is still evident to this day in what was known as the Group Areas Act,[2] the laws that assigned different 'races' to different residential areas in cities and towns. Consequently, democracy would mean dismantling this political ideology that had positioned 'white-ness' being superior to 'blackness', and a particular form of Calvinistic Christianity being superior to all other forms of religion or worldview (Malherbe, 1977). This type of Calvinistic Christianity had informed the indoctrinating machinery of the apartheid state dictating where we could live (the Group Areas Act); who we could love and marry (the Mixed Marriages Act; laws against homosexuality); where we could go to school (segregated education); where we could set up business; which beaches we could swim at (separate amenities); and who we could befriend (Group Areas Act). The education system was one dimension of social life in which segregation was severe, and where we directly experienced the state ideology of Christian-National Education (CNE).[3] Religious education in schools,

2   *Group Areas Act* refers to the Act of 1950 designed by the Government of the time in South Africa to restrict black, coloured and Indian people to their own residential areas. Forced removals to enforce this policy started in 1955 and continued until 1985. This Act was repealed in June 1991 (See http://www.saha.org.za/news/2010/April/ freedom_from_oppression_50_years_since_the_group_areas_act.htm, retrieved March 13, 2012.).

3   *Christian-National Education*: the ideology propagated by the Nationalist Government in South Africa from 1948 to the early 1990s. It was a particularly narrow interpre-tation of Calvinistic Christianity which propagated white superiority and racial segregation. This policy marginalized and discriminated against the inclusion of all other religions in the school subject, Religious Instruction, later to be named Bible Education (Summers, 1996: 1, 2).

white and black, was shaped by CNE. The exception was the moral-cum-cultural subject called Right Living, taught in Indian schools, designed to accommodate Islam, Hinduism and Christianity, the religions practised amongst Indian people in South Africa (Tate, 1995: 15).

It is significant to note that although CNE was deeply entrenched in all social systems, the apartheid government did not necessarily launch any overt attacks to oppress religions other than Christianity. A conscience clause was included in national curriculum documents allowing adherents of religions or denominations that did not aspire to Trinitarian Christianity the freedom to withdraw from Religious Education classes. This opportunity was extended to Jewish learners, Jehovah's Witnesses, learners who belonged to the New Apostolic Church, Latter Day Saints or any other denominations who did not aspire to Trinitarian Christianity.

Having said this, however, the marginalizing effects of racial discrimination either overtly or covertly contributed to religious discrimination for anyone who was designated 'non-white'. For example, the Church of the Nazarites, a uniquely South African religious movement whose founder was the prophet Isaiah Shembe (Oosthuizen, 1968; Vilakazi, 1986), can be observed worshipping in the outdoors on Saturdays (the Sabbath) in circles of white stones in various parts of the Gauteng and KwaZulu-Natal provinces. The Nazarites also practise adult baptism by total immersion in the outdoors in dams and rivers. A colleague who is a member of the Church of the Nazarites and my main informant and dialogue partner (I shall refer to him as Jabu), explained that services take place in this way because in the early days of the church's existence (1920s and 1930s), the South African police at the time destroyed the buildings that they erected to serve as places of worship. I learned through another source that the same treatment was handed to Rastafari and members of other African Independent church movements, such as the small Zionist/Apostolic and Pentecostal congregations, also highly visible in urban areas in South Africa (Anderson, 2001; Kiernan, 1995; Oosthuizen, Kitshoff & Dube, 1994; Chidester, 1992). Gatherings of black people for whatever reason were regarded with suspicion by the apartheid state and disbanded, often violently. To this day, the Nazarites and members of the Zionist/Apostolic congregations worship outdoors, the Nazarites in their circles of white stones, and the Zionists under trees in fields and parks, on river banks or on beaches for the purposes of baptism. Many Zionist congregations in urban areas also tend to hire rooms in office blocks or halls and class-rooms in schools to conduct their church meetings. According to Jabu, the destruction of Nazarite structures apparently remains a part of the oral traditions of the Nazarites, a central theme in the sermons conducted by the leaders in the Shembe lineage, with explanations of why services take place in circles of stones told with legendary proportion.

Another feature for which the members of the Independent Churches are well known is their wearing of uniforms or special items of clothing. Members wear their uniforms to church gatherings only and the churches to which the members are affiliated are easily recognized by the colours of the uniforms. For example, the Nazarites wear white flowing garments, the women of the Zionist Christian Church (ZCC) wear blouses and skirts in yellow and bottle green while the men wear khaki with distinctly shaped peaked caps. The members of the small Zionist/Apostolic Pentecostal-type churches are associated with their bright blue and/or green and white clothing. The clothing is worn with great pride and contributes to the sense of belonging and identity of members with these particular churches. In the absence of formal structures (chapels, temples) the uniforms also contribute to the sense of being in the presence of God in the form of the Holy Spirit (Dube, 1994). Donning their church clothes symbolizes the separation of the sacred from the profane. When members dress in their church colours, they enter Zion, the place where the Holy Spirit is present (Dube, 1994).

The demise of the apartheid system was followed by a period of radi-cal reform to deracialize South African society. So began the process of restructuring a new national curriculum shaped by the values of the new Constitution, including the right to the freedom of religion or belief (Constitution, 2011 (15) (1)). Religious Education was one of the subjects that received a radical overhaul. Against the background of CNE, this reconceptualizing of religion in education was complex in that it was inte-grated with democratic Citizenship Education (Department of Education, 2003a: 11; Chidester, 2003). The goals of Citizenship Education are outlined in the national curriculum in this description of the responsible citizen:

> In a transforming and democratic society, personal and individual needs have to be placed in a social context to encourage acceptance of diversity and to foster commitment to the values and principles espoused in the Constitution. Discrimination on the basis of race, religion, culture, gender, age, ability and language as well as issues of xenophobia are addressed ... It is important for learners to be politically literate ... to know and understand democratic processes ... Knowledge of diverse religions will contribute to the development of responsible citizenship and social justice. (Department of Education, 2003a: 11)

The problem as I perceive it to be is linked to the fact that this entry in the national curriculum describes the ideal *learner* and his/her development as a citizen by the end of the Twelfth Grade. The national curriculum envisages teachers being 'key contributors to the transformation of education in South Africa' (Department of Education, 2003a: 5), the mediators of their learners' understanding of 'democratic processes' and how learners acquire knowledge about diverse religions. Hence, learners need to rely on the assumed professional competences of their teachers in order to demonstrate the explicit knowledge, skills and values associated with the ideals of Citizenship Education as envisaged in the national curriculum. In fact, the wording and contents of the national curriculum demand that teachers acquire the content knowledge and pedagogical skills to bring learning about diversity to effect (*cf.* Shulman, 1999: 65).

My narrative

As a consequence of the above, my research was conceptualized to explore options for teacher development for Religion Education taking the complexities of the shared narrative into account.

The findings of the survey confirmed that a 'one-size-fits-all' approach to Religion Education as outlined in the national curriculum and other learning and teaching support materials is problematic (*cf.* Ferguson, 2011: 153). To elaborate, a fixed list of six or seven religions as presented in the national curriculum is problematic on the grounds that uninformed teachers run the risk of presenting these religions in reified terms, as if there is no diversity within, or no other religions or beliefs to study, except those in the list or matrix (Department of Education, 2003a: 25; *cf.* Jackson, 1997). In the South African context, new movements, such as the various Zionist congregations, the Nazarites, and others including Wicca/Paganism and Rastafari, various Neo-Hindu movements (Kumar, 2000; Diesel & Maxwell, 1993) as well as those who do not follow any institutionalized religion, stand a fair chance of being ignored or misrepresented by teachers who have not been formally exposed to the methods and content of Religion Studies (Kumar, 2006). I agree with Jarvis (2009) that religious freedom may not be fully comprehended by teachers who do not have a background in religious diversity and democratic education, because they are the products of CNE, or because they have explicit beliefs that prevent them from recognizing the equal value of the beliefs of others (*cf.* Roux, 2007; Chidester, 2006; Ferguson & Roux, 2004; Roux, 1998).

Hence, I maintain that teacher development in professional communities is a more viable option for teachers to develop a professional knowledge base for Citizenship/Religion Education than the large-scale transmission-type approaches that have dominated in-service programmes in South Africa from 1995 to the present. As Westheimer (2008: 766) has suggested, teacher-learning for democratic participation and understanding ought to occur discursively in professional communities in such a way as to contribute to teachers' capacity to engage in the workings of a democratic society (*cf.* Howard & Aleman, 2008). Although the literature on teacher-learning in professional communities is extensive (*cf.* Hoban, 2002; Zellermayer & Munthe, 2007; Westheimer, 2008; Miller, 2009), I focused on Wenger's (1998) communities of practice concept for the emphasis he places on 'practice', 'negotiation of meaning' and 'learning through participation' (Wenger, 1998: 5, 55; Ferguson, 2011: 84). When I conceptualized communities of practice for my own research, I envisaged that teacher-learning about the complexities of democracy, diversity and inclusivity could be maximized if teachers participated more personally or directly in negotiating, generating and acquiring the content knowledge for Citizenship/Religion Education than if they were subjected to a vertical transmission of knowledge by department of education in-service training facilitators (Ferguson, 2011: 62). My theorizing the community of practice concept for teacher-learning for diversity extended what Wenger (1998) refers to as the 'internal dynamics' (p. 73) of communities of practice, to refer specifically to Religion Education in a democratic Citizenship Education framework (Ferguson, 2011: 86). The three dimensions that characterize the internal dynamics of a community of practice are: a shared domain of interest or the subject of shared enquiry (Wenger, 1998: 73); mutual engagement or the dialogical interaction between members of the community of practice (p. 77); and the shared repertoire (p. 82), discourses or resources that are available or become available to the community of practice over time, including concepts, metaphors, symbols, narratives and objects, amongst others.

Furthermore, with regard to the diversity of religions or beliefs, the *'situatedness'* of communities of practice means that participants could draw on the religions, denominations, cultures, sub-cultures and experiences evident in their particular neighbourhoods or school communities to create the domain of interest and shared repertoire for investigation in the classroom (Cochran-Smith, 2004: 69; Nieto, 2000: 139).

The site of my fieldwork was a small mining town 45 kilometres west of Johannesburg. The legacy of the Group Areas Act which was designed to enforce the segregation of different ethnic groups is still evident (at the time of writing this, seventeen years into democracy). The qualitative data obtained from the action research phase conducted at this site indicated that teacher-learning in a community of practice is more meaningful to the study of religion and religious diversity than merely capitulating to the reified list of six or seven religions in the national curriculum and other learning materials. The teacher participants made valuable contributions to the domain of interest as they drew attention to the particular denominations, religions and traditional practices in their communities, which had to an extent become invisible as a result of the legacy of segregation.

The teachers' biographies with their personal histories and experiences of ('mainline') Protestant Christianity, ZCC, Zionist/Apostolic congregations, the Nazareth Baptist Church (and various others), not forgetting traditional African beliefs (*cf.* the 'shared' and 'personal' narratives), contributed significantly to generating the domain of interest and the shared repertoire for this particular community of practice (Wenger, 1998: 214; Ferguson, 2011: 192, 202; *cf.* Ter Avest & Bakker, 2009: 14). Their narratives were reminders that movements of people to different residential areas have taken place across South Africa, meaning that Zionist Christianity and African traditional practices have infiltrated what were formerly white suburbs. The Independent churches have increasingly become a more obvious and acceptable presence in former white suburbs in urban areas. For example, numerous Zionist/Apostolic congregations have become partners with the municipal authorities in an area in north-western Johannesburg known as the Melville *Koppies*[4] (*cf.* Skelton, 2009). These churches conduct their services on Sunday afternoons in the *koppies* which are part of a greenbelt in Johannesburg. The churches contribute to the conservation of these *koppies* and to crime reduction in the area, and in return benefit by being able to conduct their services openly and undisturbed by the surrounding communities. My own observations have led me to conclude that this space becomes symbolic of freedom and power for the Zionists, holy ground, reminiscent of Mt Sinai and Mt Zion, biblical symbols associated with the presence of the Divine. The authorities allowed the various congregations to throw down circles of concrete at various sites all over the *koppies* to prevent the destruction of the vegetation. Before you enter any of the concrete circles, you should take off your shoes, for you *are* standing on holy ground.

Participant narratives – 'Our narrative'

From the analysis of the various data sets, I have constructed three more narratives, the narratives of the participants. These are collective narratives since, during the data collection process, the narratives of other teachers, learners and family members became inextricably interwoven with the

---

4   *Koppie* is the Afrikaans word for 'small hill'.

individual narratives, giving rise to a new one – 'our narrative'. These narratives can only be fully understood against the background of the shared narrative. What did the narratives of each participant tell that was significant to the internal dynamics of the community of practice?

The narratives as these have been created within the framework of this research are a compilation of observations, experiences and personal histories identified in the data. They are by no means complete accounts of the encounters in the field, or an attempt to impose on the participants in the research, but simply an attempt to pay tribute to religious diversity as it is experienced in particular ways in different neighbourhoods and to recognize these as valuable contributions to the domain of interest and shared repertoire. Hence, these accounts have been constructed from the narratives that could be identified in the raw data. The names of the participants are pseudonyms, used to preserve their anonymity.

Narrative: Phumzile

Phumzile is a Setswana[5] speaking man in his forties. He speaks fluent English and holds a Bachelor of Education degree. Phumzile admitted to being a 'lapsed Seventh Day Adventist' (*cf.* Ferguson, 2011: 177). He continues to live in the area in this mining town which had been designated for black people under apartheid, commonly referred to as a 'township', because he owns property there. All the learners in the school at which he teaches are resident in this township. The learners are mainly Setswana speaking, with some isiXhosa and isiZulu speakers. This information implies that there are different cultural practices associated with the different language and ethnic groups resident in the township. Phumzile had no formal training in Religion Education (diversity of religions and beliefs) or Religious Education (Christian).

---

5   Setswana is a South African language, one of the eleven languages recognized as being an official language. IsiXhosa, isiZulu and Afrikaans are three of the other official languages spoken in South Africa.

Phumzile continuously provided snippets of information in our various discussions together which illuminated the religious and cultural make-up of his context. Religious diversity means something different in his neighbourhood than in some of the other areas not too far away (*cf.* Rochelle's narrative). We established early on that to slavishly follow the list of religions in the national curriculum was not that meaningful as a starting point in a township school such as this one. Christianity prevails in the form of different denominations, including the 'mainline' Christian churches (including Methodist, Roman Catholic and Seventh Day Adventist) and various Zionist Churches as described earlier in the chapter. Phumzile mentioned that different church groups use the school premises on weekends for church services. He provided me with school records which indicated that these were Zionist/Apostolic congregations. In addition, I observed that the school's watchman was a member of the Zionist Christian Church.[6] I was able to draw this conclusion because members of the Zionist Christian Church wear a badge comprising a piece of green felt with a silver star on their left breast as a symbol of their membership. Phumzile explained that the Zionist Christian Church is strongly represented in the community. The watchman is in fact a prophet in the Zionist Christian Church and people often come to the school so that he can pray for them to be healed. Faith healing through prayer and the laying on of hands by prophets, facilitated by the power of the Holy Spirit, is a central tenet of the Zionist Christian Church and Zionist Apostolic churches (Dube, 1994; Anderson, 1991).

Phumzile frequently mentioned that the learners in township schools needed materials about the differences and relationship between religion and culture, since the syncretism of Christian beliefs and traditional African beliefs and practices is common. Phumzile was acutely aware that his learners did not perceive traditional African beliefs and practices as being 'religion'. He mentioned that his learners regard Christianity and

6   The Zionist Christian Church is one of the largest Independent Churches in Southern Africa. Zionist Christian Church members can be identified from the badge that they wear on the left breast. Small Zionist congregants can be identified from their church uniforms worn on Sundays – the colours, white, blue and green being the most common.

Islam as 'religion', and traditional beliefs and practices as 'culture' (Ferguson, 2011: 225).

During my observation of a Twelfth Grade class, one of the learners (a male of about eighteen years) told his peers that he had changed religions – from the Zionist Christian Church to Islam. This was a shock to Phumzile, who explained that the youth's uncle is a high-ranking leader of the Zionist Christian Church in the community. I intervened and asked the youth to explain why he had done so. He said that he had become bored with Christianity and liked the way 'the Muslims do things, like praying to Allah'. When the lesson ended, I again asked the learner why he had been attracted to Islam. His response was, 'It keeps us away from crime' (Ferguson, 2011: 224).

Narrative: Tlaletso

Tlaletso is a Setswana speaking women in her fifties. She speaks fairly good English, fluent Afrikaans and various other South African languages, including isiZulu. She had obtained a four-year diploma in education and a Bible School diploma which included one module on 'World Religions'. The school where Tlaletso teaches is situated about 45 km north of where Phumzile's school is situated, but is still a part of the same official school district, hence her participation in the community of practice. This school is a country boarding school, situated amongst the farms and nature reserves that characterize the region. The school was formerly an exclusively white Afrikaans-medium school. It is dual-medium now (Afrikaans and English) and multicultural. Tlaletso willingly teaches Religion Education and explained that she always drives home the values of 'acceptance' and 'tolerance' of difference in her classes (Ferguson, 2011: 177, 190).

Tlaletso is a devout Christian. She serves as a pastor in her church and is highly respected as a church leader in the district. She is deeply committed to bringing women together from different African church denominations for services and prayer meetings. She is proud that she accommodates women from various churches, whether they are Methodists

or Zionists: 'All are welcome. Even the *izangoma*[7] are accommodated!'
(Ferguson, 2011: 205).

The final-stage interview with Tlaletso in the cycles of action research
added significantly to the depth of her narrative (Ferguson, 2011: 228).
The interview was conducted at her home. Tlaletso had brought her aged
mother-in-law to spend the afternoon and so the interview was interspersed
with chats with her. As it turned out, the old woman had been part of the
forced removals with the enforcement of the Group Areas Act. This woman
had lived in an area called Western Native Townships in the mid-1950s.
The old woman remembered the time she lived there with fondness and
spoke of a time when people from different 'races' had lived and social-
ized side by side.

I asked the old woman if she could remember the year in which these
forced removals had taken place. She could not – saying she was too old to
remember. Tlaletso intervened, relating how she had been only a day old
(as told to her by her own mother) when the forced removals had taken
place. She recalled that she too was born in Western Native Townships – in
1955 – so these removals took place in August 1955. Tlaletso's mother had
told her how she had wrapped Tlaletso in blankets to protect her from the
wintery weather. The families who lived in Western Native Townships were
relocated to an area called Meadowlands, now a part of Soweto.

Narrative: Rochelle

Rochelle is in her forties. Her ethnic designation is Coloured. Her school is
situated in what formerly would have been designated a 'Coloured' township. Her home language is English, but she also speaks fluent Afrikaans.
She obtained a Higher Diploma in Education at a college of education and
a diploma in ministry at a Bible College. Her courses included counselling,

---

7   *Izangoma* is the plural form of the isiZulu word *isangoma*, meaning *diviner*. The
     izangoma in traditional African religions are able to communicate with family
     ancestors.

youth ministry and World Religions. Rochelle is a Christian in the Reformed tradition and an active member of her church community. Christianity dominates in the area, judging by the number of different churches that I observed (Ferguson, 2011: 176). Rochelle commented at one point: 'We don't have such a big diversity of religions. We have Christianity, that's more than 80 per cent. We have a few children following Islam, and very few learners who are African traditional.'

The Indian neighbourhood in which Islam is prominent is based on the other side of the town. It boasts a small Islamic university, visible from the main road into the town. Most Muslim children would more than likely attend school in this section of the town, although the demise of the Group Areas Act means that parents have a choice as to where their children may attend school.

In the final-stage interview in the cycles of action research, Rochelle spoke of how her Christian faith inspires her to work with the young people in her community, many of whom live in dire poverty. We had discussed the meaning of tolerance frequently over the months and what it would mean for her as a deeply committed, evangelical Christian. In spite of being conscious of promoting tolerance as a value of Religion Education, she commented at one point in the interview that she had been concerned that one of her learners had converted to Islam (Ferguson, 2011: 236). Her comment indicated that articulating the desire to be tolerant and making the mental shift to accept the choices that people make regarding their beliefs, is not always that simple or clear cut (*cf.* Nieto, 2000: 340). Rochelle tells:

> Some of the learners are changing their religion because of what they can get out of it. Like I said, the community is very under privileged ... then there's this hand that just sticks out, making provision for them giving them food packages and things like that so they would change and follow a different belief system, but it is not out of a desire to do so. It's because they are tired of their lack of having. I had a group of learners, Grade Eleven, and this one boy I knew him, Grade Eight, Grade Nine, Grade Ten. He was Christian and now Grade Eleven he says he must leave at twelve (o'clock) because he must go to pray. And then during the fasting period I saw he had on his [topee]. This was new and then I said to him, when did all this happen? And then I realised they are just tired of not having.

The significance and value of the 'personal narratives'

The meaning of the 'personal narratives' lies in their connection to the 'shared narrative' and 'my narrative' as researcher. When I set out, I did not approach the research with narrative in mind. It was only after I spent some time in the field, simultaneously transcribing and analysing the data, that the narratives emerged. Keeping the narratives intact meant that they contributed significantly to constructing the domain of interest of the Citizenship/Religion Education community of practice. Moreover, the dilemmas that the teachers encountered in the classroom and in the neighbouring community pertaining to religious and cultural diversity, particularly where these differed from or conflicted with their own frames of reference, provided opportunities for negotiation, dialogically, reflectively and meaningfully, all integral to engagement in a community of practice (Wenger, 1998: 73; cf. Mezirow, 1991: 207; Bohman, 1996: 24; Ferguson, 2011: 77, 90).

The narratives are evidence that freedom, not only of religion and belief but also freedom of association (Constitution, 2011 (18)) and freedom of movement (Constitution, 2011 (21) (3)), made the engagement between the participants and I (a white person), possible. The narratives emerged partly as a consequence of the history of racial segregation, partly as a reflection of the 'situatedness' (Young, 2000) of the different school communities and mostly because of freedom. What emerges as significant for the Citizenship/Religion Education community of practice is the recognition of religious and cultural phenomena that were formerly marginalized as being worthy of investigation for generating the domain of interest (Taylor, 1994; Young, 2000). Moreover, the narratives indicate that the particular knowledge and experiences that teachers and their learners already possess, relevant to their particular contexts, may need prompting to unearth such knowledge and experiences for further investigation or study. The shared narrative illuminates what potentially remains to be discovered about the social, historical and economic influences on the formation of religious communities in South Africa and on the choices that young people are making regarding their beliefs (*cf.* Phumzile and Rochelle's narratives, young people converting to Islam; *cf.* Ferguson, 2011). Moreover, the narratives indicate that much is to be gained from the oral transmission of personal histories and experiences, since so much of these cannot be located in a written text (*cf.* Jabu's story, 'my narrative'). This reality draws attention to how attuned or conscious teachers of this rich domain of interest need to be to generate meaningful 'practice' to ensure that inter-religious and cross-cultural learning occur, way beyond the confines of reified representations of religions in some of the learning and teaching materials (Jackson, 1997; Buchardt, 2007).

Conclusion

Whilst there is evidence that the personal narratives of teachers and their social contexts could contribute significantly to the domain of interest, the personal narratives also hint at misrecognition or even non-recognition or *in*tolerance by teachers of the choices that people are entitled to make within a framework of religious freedom (Taylor, 1994; Young, 1997). The shared narrative as background and the narratives of researchers in this field emphasize that a 'politics of recognition' (Taylor, 1994: 106–107) needs to be fore-grounded as teachers participate in creating the domain of interest for Citizenship/Religion Education.

The Group Areas Act did not only affect the activities of African Churches and other Black African religious movements. There is also evidence in the larger cities in South Africa of how the enforcement of the Group Areas Act resulted in Indian and Coloured people having to abandon their places of worship as the areas in which these were constructed were re-zoned for whites. Examples of these include the Melrose Shree Siva Subramaniar Temple in northern Johannesburg and various Hindu temples in Durban, Pretoria and Port Elizabeth. Hindu temples bear witness to the arrival of Indians in South Africa to work as indentured labourers in the sugar-cane fields in KwaZulu-Natal. The labourers brought with them their north and south Indian architectural styles and symbols evident in temple building (Kumar, 2000; Diesel and Maxwell, 1993). The historical significance and the relevance of the architectural styles of many of the temples remain unknown because knowledge about them is not always easily available. It is possible that information may be locked away from the public eye in private journals or in the oral histories of communities. With regard to two Hindu temples, one in Johannesburg and the other in Pretoria, I learned from a pundit in the case of the former, and a devotee in the case of the latter, that court orders were brought against municipalities by devotees to prevent the destruction of the one and the construction of a road right through the middle of the grounds of the other. How did I come to learn this? Through direct engagement with members of the respective Hindu communities. One could conclude, therefore, that the value of drawing on 'personal narratives' of religion, culture and traditions may only be realized when teachers are willing to venture from the confines of a reified curriculum or limited explanations of religious and cultural diversity in text books, through engagement with one another, in professional learning communities, and with adherents or devotees of religious and cultural communities.

There is in fact no conclusion to this narrative, since the 'unexpected' should be continuously sought in the idea of the shared narrative and the personal narratives of Citizenship/Religion Education researchers and practitioners. There can be no doubt that such narratives are generative of the domain of interest and shared repertoire, providing rich, fascinating and relevant material for further investigation and exploration in the community of practice.

Acknowledgements

I wish to acknowledge the contribution made to the chapter by my colleague and dialogue partner, Mr Jabulani Nkosi, who is a member of the Church of the Nazarites. Jabu's knowledge of the history of Isaiah Shembe and the Nazarites as an insider has been invaluable to the development of my understanding of the rituals and practices of the Nazarites.

References

Anderson, A. (1991). *Moya. The Holy Spirit in an African context*. Pretoria: University of South Africa.

Anderson, A. (2001). *African reformation. African initiated Christianity in the 20th century*. Trenton: Africa World Press, Inc.

Bohman, J. (1996). *Public deliberation: Pluralism, complexity and democracy*. Cambridge, MA: MIT Press.

Buchardt, M. (2007). Teachers – and knowledge and identity technologies around 'religion'. Discursive and other social practices in the religious education classroom. In C. Bakker & H. G. Heimbrock (Eds), *Researching RE teachers. RE teachers as researchers* (pp. 17–36). Munster: Waxmann.

Chidester, D. (1992). *Religions of South Africa*. London: Routledge.

Chidester, D. (2003). Religion education in South Africa: teaching and learning about religion, religions and religious diversity. *British Journal of Religious Education*, 25(4), 261–278.

Chidester, D. (2006). Religion Education and the transformational state in South Africa. *Social Analysis, 50*(3), 61–83.

Clandinin, D. J., & Connelly, F. M. (2000). *Narrative inquiry. Experience and story in qualitative research*. San Francisco: Jossey-Bass.

Cochran-Smith, M. (2004). *Walking the road. Race, diversity and social justice in teacher education*. New York: Teachers College Press.

Constitution of the Republic of South Africa, 1996. (2011, September 27, date last modified). *South African Government Information*. Retrieved March 8, 2012, from http://www.info.gov.za/documents/constitution/1996/96cons2.htm

Creswell, J. W. (2003). *Research Design. Qualitative, Quantitative and Mixed Methods Approaches* (2nd edn). Thousand Oaks, CA: Sage Publications.

Creswell, J. W., & Plano Clark, V. L. (2007). *Designing and conducting mixed methods Research*. Thousand Oaks, CA: Sage Publications.

Department of Education. (2003a). *National Curriculum Statement (Grades 10–12)*. Pretoria: Department of Education.

Department of Education. (2003b). *National Policy on Religion and Education*. Pretoria: Department of Education.

Diesel, A., & Maxwell, P. (1993). *Hinduism in Natal. A brief guide*. Pietermaritzburg: University of Natal Press.

Dube, S. W. D. (1994). Hierophanies: Hermeneutic paradigm for understanding Zionist ritual. In G. C. Oosthuizen, M. C. Kitshoff, & S. W. D. Dube (Eds), *Afro-Christianity at the grassroots. Its dynamic and strategies* (pp. 105–110). Leiden: E. J. Brill.

Elliot, J. (2005). *Using narrative in social research. Qualitative and quantitative approaches*. London: Sage Publications.

Ferguson, R. (2011). *Teacher development for religious and cultural diversity in citizenship education: a community of practice approach*. Unpublished PhD dissertation, University of Stellenbosch.

Ferguson, R., & Roux, C. D. (2004). Teaching and learning about religions in schools: responses from a participation action research project. *Journal for the Study of Religion, 17*(2): 5–23.

Gubrium, J. F., & Holstein, J. A. (2009). *Analysing narrative reality*. Thousand Oaks, CA: Sage Publications.

Hoban, G. F. (2002). *Teacher learning for educational change*. Buckingham: Open University Press.

Howard, T. C., & Aleman, G. R. (2008). Teacher capacity for diverse learners. What do teachers need to know? In M. Cochran-Smith, S. Feiman-Nemser, & D. J. McIntyre (Eds), *Handbook of research on teacher education. Enduring questions in changing contexts* (3rd edn) (pp. 157–174). New York: Routledge, Taylor & Francis Group and the Association of Teacher Educators.

Jackson, R. (1997). *Religious education: An interpretive approach*. Great Britain: Hodder & Stoughton.

Jarvis, J. (2009). The voice of the religion education teacher in the context of religious diversity. *Alternation. Journal of the Centre for the Study of Southern African Literature and Languages*, Special Edition, 3, 138–156.

Kemmis, S., & McTaggart, R. (2000). Participatory action research. In N. K. Denzin & Y. S. Lincoln (Eds), *Handbook of qualitative research* (2nd edn) (pp. 567–605). Thousand Oaks, CA: Sage Publications.

Kiernan, J. (1995). The African Independent Churches. In M. Prozesky & J. De Gruchy (Eds), *Living Faiths in South Africa* (pp. 116–128). Cape Town: David Philip.

Kumar, P. P. (2000). *Hindus in South Africa. Their traditions and beliefs.* Durban: The University of Durban-Westville.

Kumar, P. P. (2006). Religious pluralism and religion education in South Africa. *Method and Theory in the Study of Religion, 18*, 273–293.

Lave, J., & Wenger, E. (1991). *Situated learning. Legitimate peripheral participation.* Cambridge: University of Cambridge Press.

Malherbe, E. G. (1977). *Education in South Africa: Vol. 2 (1923–1975).* Cape Town: Juta & Co. Ltd.

Mezirow, J. (1991). *Transformative dimensions of adult learning.* San Francisco: Jossey-Bass Publishers.

Miller, J. (2009). Raising humanities' teachers' understanding of their pupils' religious and cultural backgrounds. In J. Ipgrave, R. Jackson, & K. O'Grady (Eds), *Religious education research through a community of practice. Action research and the interpretive approach* (pp. 130–147). Münster: Waxmann.

Nieto, S. (2000). *Affirming diversity. The sociopolitical context of multicultural education.* (3rd edn). New York: Longman.

Oosthuizen, G. C. (1968). Isaiah Shembe and the Zulu world view. *History of Religions, 8*(1), 1–30.

Oosthuizen, G. C., Kitshoff, M. C., & Dube, S. W. D. (Eds). (1994). *Afro-Christianity at the grassroots. Its dynamic and strategies.* Leiden: E. J. Brill.

Punch, K. F. (2009). *Introduction to research methods in education.* London: Sage Publications.

Roux, C. (1998). Paradigm shift in teaching religion. *Journal for the Study of Religion, 11*(2), 125–138.

Roux, C. (2007). Interreligious learning. Teachers' abilities and didactic challenges. In D. Pollefeyt (Ed.), *Interreligious learning* (pp. 103–127). Leuven: Leuven University Press.

Roux, C. (2009). Religion Education as praxis: voices and narratives on teaching and learning experiences. *Alternation. Journal of the Centre for the Study of Southern African Literature and Languages.* Special Edition, 3, 112–137.

Shulman, L. S. (1999). Knowledge and teaching: foundations of the new reform. In J. Leach & B. Moon (Eds), *Learners and Pedagogy* (pp. 61–77). London: Paul Chapman Publishing.

Skelton, C. (2009). *Spiritual circles: rituals and the performance of identities in the Zionist Christian Church.* Unpublished Master of Arts thesis, University of the Witwatersrand, Johannesburg.

Summers, H. C. (1996). Religious Education: the problem in South Africa. In H. C. Summers & R. R. Waddington (Eds), *Religious Education for Transformation* (pp. 1–18). Pretoria: Kagiso Tertiary.

Tate, K. (1995). Religious education in South Africa: Past, Present and Future. In D. Rossouw (Ed.), *At the Crossroads. Perspectives on Religious education and Biblical Studies in a new education system* (pp. 1–23). Hatfield: Acacia.

Taylor, C. (1994). The politics of recognition. In A. Gutmann (Ed.), *Multiculturalism: Examining the politics of recognition* (pp. 105–138). Princeton, NJ: Princeton University Press.

Ter Avest, I., & Bakker, C. (2009). The voice of the teacher(s) – Researching biography and pedagogical strategies. In A. Van Der Want, C. Bakker, I. Ter Avest, & J. Everington (Eds), *Teachers responding to religious diversity in Europe. Researching biography and pedagogy* (pp. 13–27). Munster: Waxmann.

Vilakazi, A. (1986). *Shembe: The revitalization of African Society.* Johannesburg: Skotaville.

Wenger, E. (1998). *Communities of practice. Learning, meaning and identity.* Cambridge: Cambridge University Press.

Wenger, E., McDermott, R., & Snyder, W. M. (2002). *Cultivating communities of practice. A guide to managing knowledge.* Boston: Harvard Business School Press.

Westheimer, J. (2008). Learning among colleagues. Teacher community and the shared enterprise of education. In M. Cochran-Smith, S. Feiman-Nemser, & D. J. McIntyre (Eds), *Handbook of research on teacher education. Enduring questions in changing contexts* (3rd edn) (pp. 756–783). New York: Routledge, Taylor & Francis Group and the Association of Teacher Educators.

Young, I. M. (1997). Difference as a resource for democratic communication. In J. Bohman & W. Rehg (Eds), *Deliberative Democracy* (pp. 383–406). Cambridge, MA: MIT Press.

Young, I. M. (2000). *Inclusion and democracy.* London: Oxford University Press.

Zellermayer, M., & Munthe, E. (2007). Teachers learning in communities. In M. Zellermayer & E. Munthe (Eds), *Teachers learning in communities. International perspectives* (pp. 1–6). Rotterdam: Sense Publishers.

KEVIN O'GRADY

12 Freedom of Belief for English Religious Education Pupils: Some Findings from the Warwick REDCo Community of Practice

Abstract

The Warwick REDCo community of practice was a key part of the English strand of Religion in Education: A contributor to dialogue or a factor of conflict in transforming societies of European countries? (REDCo), a three-year European Commission-funded project (2006–2009). The community of practice was a team of nine researchers collaborating on action research into five aspects of Religious Education: pupil motivation, assessment, gender issues, teacher education and teaching gifted and talented pupils. As with the wider REDCo project, the interpretive approach to Religious Education formed the theoretical background to its work. The community of practice's findings were wide-ranging. However, this chapter focuses on the experience of secondary-age Religious Education pupils and how they might exercise freedom of belief during lessons. A view of freedom of belief for Religious Education pupils is developed, as dialogical rather than romantic, and subject to a pedagogy that takes account of reflexive elements in learning. The desired pedagogy clashes with the performativity culture dominant in current UK education. However, this poses a dilemma: should Religious Education resist and become marginal, or adapt and become unrecognizable?

Context

The first broad context for this chapter is the REDCo research project. REDCo (Religion in Education. A contribution to Dialogue or a factor of Conflict in transforming societies of European Countries?) was a three-year (March 2006–March 2009) European Commission financed project, aiming to understand the challenges faced by religious education in European countries, exploring possibilities for dialogue between different religious traditions without ignoring potential problems (Weisse, 2007: 12). Since the project's conclusion, and with the appearance of a substantial publications output within the Waxmann series *Religious Diversity and Education in Europe*, REDCo has been received as a major contributor to debates about the handling of religion within public education, one reviewer suggesting that:

> When distance permits some retrospective evaluation of the whole series, one suspects that it will be seen as a very significant process in the development of academic thought on the place of religion in contemporary educational practice in Europe. (Richardson, 2010: 331)

Only a brief sketch of REDCo as a whole can be made here. The findings ranged across historical and contextual material for religion and education (Jackson, Miedema, Weisse, & Willaime, 2007); school pupils' experiences of religion and education (Knauth, Jozsa, Bertram-Troost, & Ipgrave, 2008; Valk, Bertram-Troost, Friederici, & Béraud, 2009); Islam in education (Alvarez Veinguer, Dietz, Josza, & Knauth, 2010); teachers' responses to religious diversity (Van der Want, Bakker, ter Avest, & Everington, 2009); and classroom interaction (ter Avest, Josza, Knauth, Rosón, & Skeie, 2009). As a part of the introduction to this chapter, the most relevant results are those concerning the perspectives of the several hundred teenagers who reported their experiences of religion and education through the qualitative and quantitative studies undertaken. These findings were summarized helpfully by Robert Jackson in the text of the presentation of the REDCo project to the European Parliament on 3 December 2008 (Jackson, 2008: 35; original italics):

- Students wish for peaceful coexistence across differences, and believe this to be possible.
- For students, peaceful coexistence depends on knowledge about each other's religions and worldviews and sharing common interests/doing things together.
- Students who learn about religious diversity in school are *more willing* to have conversations about religions/beliefs with students of other backgrounds than those who do not.
- Students wish to avoid conflict: some of the religiously committed students feel vulnerable.
- Students want learning to take place in a safe classroom environment where there are agreed procedures for expression and discussion.
- *Most* students would like school to be a place for learning *about* different religions/worldviews, rather than for instruction *into* a particular religion/worldview.

A related REDCo finding underlined by Wolfram Weisse, in an earlier part of the same presentation, is the crucial role of the school in supporting these aspirations of young people. For many teenagers the school will be the only forum for dialogue about religion or encounter with those who are different. Religious Education teachers may feel pressure at this point. As the chapter progresses, this feeling will get worse. Still, part of the appeal of the REDCo project is its reach from the European policy arena to the micro-world of the individual classroom and back.

The second broad context for the chapter is, naturally, the 2010 International Seminar on Religious Education and Values in Ottawa, and its theme of freedom of religion and belief. The two contexts are related because another strength of REDCo was the evident transferability of its data from the original conceptual framework of dialogue and conflict to others arising from Religious Education, in this case, that of young people's freedom of belief. Already in Jackson's summary of findings (above) we see the potential for a nuanced understanding of what freedom of belief in the Religious Education classroom might mean in practice, and what challenges have to be met so as to promote it.

In general, the practice of re-interrogating an established dataset through a different analytical lens is an interesting one that can be most productive. It might be recommended to educational researchers, who wish to probe the multi-layered richness of, for instance, young people's accounts of classroom life. In an earlier publication, for example, I went back to a group interview transcript originally used to investigate factors in pupil motivation in Religious Education (O'Grady, 2007: 224–227) and re-analysed it to bring out points about how to cope with dialogue and conflict in the Religious Education classroom (O'Grady, 2009a). The argument was that conflict has to be investigated rather than concealed; that though this presents teachers with a daunting task, conflicts should be identified in line with pupils' readiness to handle them; managed through a climate of mutual respect; used to create dialogues and stopped from spiralling out of control; within a framework of general human concern that is inclusive of young people of any or no particular faith background (O'Grady, 2009a: 58). As we will see, these claims also relate closely to the definition of freedom of belief to be advanced in this chapter.

As its title indicates, and in order to develop the anticipated discussion from the initial premise, this chapter focuses down on one amongst REDCo's several linked studies. The Warwick REDCo community of practice, in which nine researchers conducted action research studies investigating the use of the interpretive approach to Religious Education in secondary schools, teacher education and continuing professional development, was a key part of the English strand of REDCo (Ipgrave, Jackson, & O'Grady, 2009; O'Grady, 2010). This chapter is a further re-interpretation of a selection of the community of practice's data. Its flow is: to show how the concept of freedom of belief is adaptable to the work of the Warwick REDCo community of practice, though not originally explicit in it; to elucidate a concept of freedom of belief in Religious Education; and to illustrate that concept through the community of practice's four secondary school-based studies. The argument is that freedom of belief should be understood not in a romantic way – it does not arise naturally – or as simply the removal of constraint, but as dialogical. Religious Education could either promote or prevent freedom of belief, depending on the philosophy and methods.

For, unfortunately, there is a mismatch between current UK school culture and the desired philosophy and methods. Whereas current UK school culture is characterized by extremely high performativity, we will see that the desired philosophy and methods for Religious Education emphasize truth and therefore dialogue. The concept of performativity is usually linked with the work of Jean-Francois Lyotard (1979). For Lyotard, as an aspect of the postmodern condition exists a social economy in which utility is privileged over truth, success over justice and information over knowledge. The consequences for schools are a battery of tests, targets, league tables and other narrowly-defined and measurable outcomes. In a balanced educational regimen the assessment of pupils' learning serves the learning. In current UK school culture the relationship is reversed. Teachers and their managers spend much time on how to get pupils to meet their targets and how to secure favourable inspection judgements. Subject content is rarely mentioned and whether the targets are the right ones never debated, never mind whether 'meeting targets' is a sufficiently broad or humane educational model. Abstractions such as the percentages of pupils meeting examination targets are paramount, and one wonders whether concepts such as education and curriculum are dying out.

This mismatch ought to give teachers of Religious Education a dilemma, though the current performativity culture is hegemonic and therefore some, perhaps many or most of them, will face the consequences of the mismatch whilst being unaware of the nature of the dilemma. I will return to this problem in the conclusion, offering no solution to it but pointing to some hopeful signs. In the meantime, it will be necessary to move to a closer discussion of Religious Education and freedom of belief.

Religious education and freedom of belief

Freedom of belief may not have been a guiding concept for REDCo, nor for the Warwick REDCo community of practice, but it was after all implicit in our premises. The interpretive approach has three key concepts: all have a bearing on freedom of belief. First, religious believers have the right to have their beliefs represented fairly in Religious Education. Second, the subject's students should be free to give attention to their own beliefs whilst interpreting those of others. Third, they should be helped to reflect back over what they have learned, making a critical commentary on both this content and the methods used (for example, Jackson, 1997, 2004).

Action research too has a democratic basis. The form of action research that influenced the community of practice originated in attempts to increase the motivation of secondary school Religious Education students by listening to what they said about their lessons and then adapting pedagogy on that basis (for example, O'Grady, 2003, 2005, 2006).

In both Robert Jackson's interpretive approach and my action research pedagogy, freedom of belief develops in an educative community. It has as much to do with safeguarding others' freedom as with safeguarding one's own. The Warwick REDCo community of practice did not originate this view of freedom in education or in Religious Education. In the thought of the nineteenth-century Danish historian, educator, politician, priest, hymnist and translator N. F. S. Grundtvig, if I am free when my neighbour is not, then my freedom is my burden (see, for example, Bugge, 1994: 277). John Hull has conceptualized true authority in Religious Education as mediated and dialectical: freedom is a matter of self-criticism and enquiry (Hull, 1996).

Freedom of belief is not the 'freedom' to believe or say whatever occurs to you, or to repeat your prejudices. Young people enjoy freedom when they have the responsibility and skill to participate in dialogues with others who are perhaps very different from them. This concept of freedom is very close to those of responsibility, citizenship, self-awareness and personal growth.

What is the relation of this 'educational' concept of freedom of belief to 'political' concepts of freedom of belief such as those enshrined in human rights declarations? There are different ways to approach the issue of freedom of belief, complicated enough without considering, say, whether human rights is a 'western construct'. So this chapter has a narrower remit: once overall freedom of belief is enshrined in law, how do we ensure that Religious Education pupils develop it in the *educational* sense defined in the last few paragraphs? My contention is that the secondary school studies of the Warwick REDCo community of practice help us to answer that question and it is to those studies that I now turn.

Freedom of belief in the secondary school studies of the REDCo project

Four studies of secondary Religious Education were undertaken. These were Nigel Fancourt's study of assessment (Fancourt, 2009), Gemma O'Dell's of gender (O'Dell, 2009), my own of motivation (O'Grady, 2009b), and Amy Whittall's of teaching the gifted and talented (Whittall, 2009). Throughout, there are implicit examples of adolescent pupils learning to appreciate freedom of belief through Religious Education. The purpose of this section is to draw those examples out, so as to make clearer the meaning of freedom of belief in the Religious Education classroom.

Fancourt explored the inter-relationship between the interpretive approach and assessment (one area of pedagogy not originally considered). Jackson mentions assessment, recommending that pupils re-assess their understanding of their own ways of life and make a running critique of the interpretive process, but offers no assessment practices. Drawing on Fancourt's attempt to fill the gap, I will now suggest that the chance to reflect on how one's own attitudes and values have been affected by religious studies is a necessary condition for freedom of belief within Religious Education, because pupils cannot have conscious freedom of belief if they do not understand how their beliefs have developed or changed.

Fancourt shows that 'traditional' (mark or grade) forms of assessment can be inimical to such reflexivity, but also illustrates discussion-based or 'dialogical' assessment practices that engage his pupils in evaluation of how their own beliefs and values are developing. They become more open to others' viewpoints and to the possibility of different interpretations of religious truth. Whilst the notion of a test on Hinduism prejudices 'Alan' against Hindus, who will know more and do better, 'Charlie' reports that a class discussion about what and how much had been learned over a topic helps him to relate to others' points of view (Fancourt, 2009: 88, 92).

Gemma O'Dell set out to enrich learning about religious identity by concurrently enabling reflection on gender identity. O'Dell investigated boys' perceptions of Religious Education as a 'feminine' subject. What might improve if boys were encouraged to see their own 'masculine' identities as diverse, and open to reconstruction? Adapting Jackson's representation concept, O'Dell suggests that this move can enable boys to appreciate the heterogeneous character of religious traditions. Those most able to conceptualize religious traditions as represented at individual, membership group and wider tradition levels are those most open to conceptualizing their personal identities in a flexible way.

O'Dell remarks that Religious Education's notion of tradition should expand to include students' personal influences. This call for Religious Education to include a phenomenology of pupils' life worlds is not new but O'Dell's data are strikingly original. In relation to freedom of belief, O'Dell's argument would be that young people should investigate any possible inner constraints on their ability to engage sympathetically and critically with others' traditions. Once the grip of such constraints weakens, that is, when they are consciously recognized, the potential for new insight is increased. Once 'James' realizes the extent to which the media shape his view of Islam, he is 'embarrassed' (O'Dell, 2009: 67).

My own classroom-based action research studies, together with the interpretive approach, were foundational to the community of practice project. A second part of my PhD field study was re-focused as a community of practice case, the data once more re-interpreted through the REDCo conceptual framework of dialogue and conflict (O'Grady, 2009b). Here, a group of pupils studied interfaith relations, peace and reconciliation. My aims were to increase their opportunities for dialogues (with other pupils and with different religious traditions), to investigate what dialogues meant to the pupils, and why they were important. Pupils preferred dialogues on concrete situations, such as the relationships between different groups around them in Sheffield. Dialogues mattered for two reasons: pragmatically, they helped to generate ideas; philosophically, they extended the range of ideas to be encountered. Whilst showing awareness of suffering, conflict and war, the pupils also viewed the plurality of religious and cultural belonging in and around their class as an opportunity:

> HP: My friend ... he's only a Buddhist because his sister died ... he thinks his sister's going to have afterlife and he wants it. I believe in the afterlife as well and he's talked to me about it ... I wouldn't know about this sort of stuff unless he'd told me, because it's not as if you've just read it in a book. You take it all in, it's better when someone's talking to you. (O'Grady, 2009b: 52)

Amy Whittall's concern was the needs of gifted and talented pupils (Whittall, 2009). She built on findings that, too often, Religious Education can be academically unchallenging. Yet Whittall identified several strategies within the interpretive approach (gaining representative knowledge and understanding, building bridges between one's own life and the lives of others and reflecting on that process, analysing different influences and views, making links between beliefs and historical and cultural settings) as useful in promoting higher-order thinking. Of interest in Whittall's study is the use of direct dialogue between Muslim and non-Muslim pupils, and how the Muslim pupils took some responsibility over the representation of Islam, involving themselves in the planning of learning tasks: for example, they organized a process in which all the pupils wrote down questions about Islam, which they then answered in a whole class discussion (Whittall, 2009: 76). In Whittall's study, it is the enhancement of critical skill and agency that allows pupils to move back and forth between different questions, ideas and beliefs. Some of them simultaneously develop a heightened sense of social justice in relation to religious diversity as can be seen in the following anonymous pupil quotation (Whittall, 2009: 78):

> The most important thing in Christianity is love ... the very word Islam means peace. Over the course of this study I have started to think about what it would be like if I was brought up as a Muslim instead of a Christian, how I would feel and how I would react. What life might be like and the hardship of living under these accusations. Muslims don't deserve this treatment and I think they are unbelievably powerful people to live so seemingly calmly in this kind of environment.

Within the Warwick REDCo community of practice, data from the action research studies were analysed in a three-level scheme. At the first level, as shown in the four examples given above, individual study data would receive ethnographic content analysis, interview transcripts being read repeatedly until themes emerged, then again to test for the presence of the themes. At the second level, emergent themes would be traced across different individual studies (for example, Ipgrave & Jackson, 2009). At the third level, themes that had been found to be common across individual studies would be discussed alongside those that had appeared in other REDCo national studies or across the project as a whole (for example, Skeie, 2009).

If we look across the four secondary studies summarized above, in a 'second-level' way, it is clear that each study illustrates the reflexive nature of learning in Religious Education. A common theme is that once pupils are helped to become more aware of their own background conditions and assumptions, their freedom to engage with the beliefs of others increases. They themselves have increased freedom of belief because they are less constrained by affective forces that have previously narrowed their range from within. This does not happen in a free or uncontrolled way; rather, it is the gradual outcome of a theorized, planned pedagogical process.

The other common aspects are pupil voice and iterativity (iterativity is a term in action research that signifies the cyclic activity of establishing and acting upon field data). Pupils' confidence grows because their teachers are researchers committed in the first place to listening to them. The teacher-researchers then take this further, allowing pupil views to shape pedagogy. Because pupils have more agency than usual, their freedom to express their own beliefs increases and (again) this increases their inclination to engage with those of others, itself a form of freedom of belief.

Action research, Religious Education, freedom of belief and performativity

Whether as research or as pedagogy, action research is not neutral, but laden with values. In terms of Religious Education, the subject includes in its self-understanding the principle that young people should be helped to develop spiritually and morally, but this is inconceivable unless they themselves have a say in the process – and if teachers do not take account of what young people say, they will soon lose interest in saying it. When Hans-Gunter Heimbrock asks how, according to the logic of research, action research and pedagogy can be combined with one another, my response must be that it is the value-laden nature of action research that makes such a combination possible (Heimbrock, unpublished conference paper). I do not argue that the combination is neat, nor free from tensions (O'Grady, 2011). It was suggested earlier in this chapter that the need to address religious conflict in the classroom offers a daunting task to the Religious Education teacher. Now, the idea that teachers have to take on board pupils' comments on lessons – including whether lessons are spiritually and morally enriching – may be taken as further evidence that we have a highly demanding, complex professional role. For Heimbrock, however, the 'irritation' that we may feel is 'fruitful' and he asks how teachers may push pupils further and further into the arena of competing truth-claims through action research dialogues.

This is a crucially important question. If we have found a pedagogy that safeguards and enables pupils' freedom of belief, we will want to know how to develop and improve it. In principle, we should do so by documenting and disseminating case studies of the pedagogy in various settings. That was the rationale for the Warwick REDCo community of practice and continues to be an aim for its individual members. In more developed action research studies, when the action research pedagogy is applied in several cycles over extended periods, pupils' trust and commitment grow and they become ready to take on increasingly complex material (O'Grady, 2007).

The problem is not that we do not know how to develop the appropriate Religious Education pedagogy; it is that the current performativity-based school culture militates against such development. In fact, this claim has recently begun to attract empirical evidence. It is deliciously ironic that one evidence base is provided by the Office for Standards in Education (Ofsted). In Ofsted's 2010 report on the quality of Religious Education in secondary schools, *Making Sense of Religion*, the complaint is made that for fourteen- to sixteen-year-olds, the subject is reduced to training to pass an examination. They are trained by their teachers to produce formulaic answers to unchallenging questions when instead they should be engaged in an enquiry into the complex nature of religion in the twenty-first century.

A second source is the project 'Does RE Work?' (Conroy, unpublished conference paper; Lundie, 2010). This project is a large-scale, multi-modal study of the processes of Religious Education curriculum formation in twenty-four schools: what are the meanings and intentions of Religious Education in the school settings, as enacted by teachers and impacting on pupils? At the time of writing, the project's conclusions are provisional but some timely warnings recur. Though religion is strange to young people, Religious Education is not, because examination boards and text book writers collude to smooth out the awkward elements, reducing Religious Education to the production of pre-set responses to trivial questions. There is an increasing emphasis on training pupils to pass examinations, which strips Religious Education of its intrinsic value and results in much pointless rote-learning. Assertions that Religious Education improves young people's thinking skills are threadbare: in practice, opportunities for dissent or criticism are severely limited. Though there are exceptions, Religious Education does not really work.

Conclusion

There are some paradoxes in the material I have presented, not least, that one is taught and learns to exercise freedom rather than being free 'freely' or outside institutional influence or constraint. However, I repeat, mine is not a romantic concept of freedom. Freedom of belief within Religious Education depends on a form of pedagogy and is in other ways contingent; currently it is subject to direct threats.

Religious Education should have an educational impact on pupils' freedom of belief, meaning, it should enable personal growth through increasing awareness of the world and their place within it. Distinctively, Religious Education does this in relation to plurality of beliefs, not by relativizing young people's commitments, but by widening their repertoire, enabling them to respond more and more intelligently to the world and asking them to think about their personal bases for doing so.

In the four Warwick REDCo community of practice studies described, pupils are liberated through opportunities to discuss, debate, explore, investigate and reflect. There is a focus on intrinsic meaning, which raises the question: is this form of education best done without target-driven pressures? That leads to the second question: What is the impact of the performativity culture on freedom of belief? It is to push such a basic but unmeasurable educational concern right out to the margins.

Thence, the penultimate question: Should we oppose the performativity culture, protecting Religious Education's integrity – or absorb it, to protect against the subject's marginalization? This is the dilemma. In the present UK education context, if Religious Education does not absorb the targets-and-outcomes culture we will be marginalized. That would be a *tragic* plot. The protagonist would move away from integration toward isolation. On the other hand, if Religious Education does fully absorb the targets-and-outcomes culture we will lose our integrity. That would be a *comic* plot. The protagonist would move away from isolation toward integration (but once integrated would be unrecognizable).

Apparently, the present situation is that some of us are tolerating the comic option whilst others do not know that we are in a comic situation.

What is hopeful is that Religious Education's bizarre predicament is finally coming out into the open, though Religious Education researchers still do not give sufficient attention to school political factors. Many have been unaware of the real extent of the distorting influence of the performativity culture on the subject's character. For now, it is not an easy time to be a Religious Education teacher, but that invites the ultimate question: was it ever?

Acknowledgements

I have a considerable number of people to thank for help, in various ways, with the production of this chapter. Principally, thanks are due to my colleagues in the Warwick REDCo community of practice: Judith Everington, Nigel Fancourt, Julia Ipgrave, Robert Jackson, Joyce Miller, Gemma O'Dell, Amy Whittall and Linda Whitworth; to Geir Skeie, for his critical friendship; to Wolfram Weisse, for his inspirational leadership of the REDCo project; to Hans-Gunter Heimbrock, for his detailed and thoughtful response to an earlier version of the paper; to the Westhill Trust, for the financial support given to the Warwick REDCo community of practice; and to St Gabriel's Trust, for enabling my participation in the Ottawa ISREV conference and for ongoing support of my research over the last decade.

References

Alvarez Veinguer, A., Dietz, G., Josza, D. P., & Knauth, T. (Eds). (2010). *Islam in education in European countries – Pedagogical concepts and empirical findings.* Münster: Waxmann.

Bugge, K. E. (1994). The school for life. The basic ideas of Grundtvig's educational thinking. In A. Allchin, D. Jasper, J. H. Schørring, & K. Stevenson (Eds), *Heritage and prophecy: Grundtvig and the English-speaking world* (pp. 271–282). Norwich: Canterbury Press.

Conroy, J. (2010, July). *Does religious education work?* Paper presented at Session XVII of the International Seminar on Religious Education and Values, Saint Paul University, Ottawa, Canada.

Fancourt, N. (2009). Reflexive assessment: The interpretive approach and classroom assessment. In J. Ipgrave, R. Jackson, & K. O'Grady (Eds), *Religious Education research through a community of practice: Action research and the interpretive approach* (pp. 84–99). Münster: Waxmann.

Heimbrock, H. G. (2010, July). *A Response to: Freedom of belief for English religious education pupils: some findings from the Warwick REDCo community of practice.* Paper presented at Session XVII of the International Seminar on Religious Education and Values, Saint Paul University, Ottawa, Canada.

Hull, J. (1996). Freedom and authority in Religious Education. In B. Gates (Ed.), *Freedom and authority in religions and Religious Education* (pp. 97–111). London: Cassell.

Ipgrave, J., & Jackson, R. (2009). Reflecting on the interpretive approach. Issues and responses. In J. Ipgrave, R. Jackson, & K. O'Grady (Eds), *Religious Education research through a community of practice: Action research and the interpretive approach* (pp. 151–168). Münster: Waxmann.

Ipgrave, J., Jackson, R., & O'Grady, K. (Eds). (2009). *Religious Education research through a community of practice: Action research and the interpretive approach.* Münster: Waxmann.

Jackson, R. (1997). *Religious Education: An interpretive approach.* London: Hodder and Stoughton.

Jackson, R. (2004). *Rethinking Religious Education and plurality: Issues in diversity and pedagogy.* London: Routledge Falmer.

Jackson, R. (2008). The contribution of teaching about religions and beliefs to education for democratic citizenship in Europe and beyond: Consequences of the REDCo-project. In W. Weisse, R. Jackson, C. Rudelt, & J-P. Willaime (Eds), *Religion in education – a contribution to dialogue or a factor of conflict? The REDCo-project: Presentation in the European Parliament* (pp. 30–37). Retrieved March 8, 2012, from http://www5.quvion.net/cosmea/core/corebase/mediabase/awr/redco/research_findings/REDCo_Brussels_Doc_2.pdf

Jackson, R., Miedema, S., Weisse, W., & Willaime, J-P. (Eds). (2007). *Religion and education in Europe: Developments, contexts and debates.* Münster: Waxmann.

Knauth, T., Jozsa, D. P., Bertram-Troost, G., & Ipgrave, J. (Eds). (2008). *Encountering religious pluralism in school and society: A qualitative study of teenage perspectives in Europe*. Münster: Waxmann.

Lundie, D. (2010). 'Does RE work?' An analysis of the aims, practices and models of effectiveness of religious education in the UK. *British Journal of Religious Education, 32*(2), 163–170.

Lyotard, J. F. (1979). *The Postmodern Condition*. Manchester: Manchester University Press.

O'Dell, G. (2009). Action research into teaching about religious diversity: Pedagogical and gender issues in the application of the interpretive approach. In J. Ipgrave, R. Jackson, & K. O'Grady (Eds), *Religious education research through a community of practice: Action research and the interpretive approach* (pp. 56–71). Münster: Waxmann.

Ofsted. (2010). *Making sense of religion*. London: Ofsted.

O'Grady, K. (2003). Motivation in religious education: A collaborative investigation with year eight students. *British Journal of Religious Education, 25*(3), 214–225.

O'Grady, K. (2005). Pedagogy, dialogue and truth: Intercultural education in the Religious Education classroom. In R. Jackson & U. McKenna (Eds), *Intercultural education and religious plurality* (pp. 25–33). Oslo Coalition Occasional Papers 1. Oslo: Oslo Coalition on Freedom of Religion or Belief.

O'Grady, K. (2006). The development of beliefs and values in early adolescence: A case study through religious education pedagogy. *International Journal of Children's Spirituality, 11*(3), 315–327.

O'Grady, K. (2007). *Motivation in secondary Religious Education*. Unpublished PhD thesis, University of Warwick.

O'Grady, K. (2009a). Brainwashing? An example of dialogue and conflict from Religious Education in England. In I. ter Avest, D. Josza, T. Knauth, J. Rosón, & G. Skeie (Eds), *Dialogue and conflict on Religion: Studies of classroom interaction in European countries* (pp. 41–61). Münster: Waxmann.

O'Grady, K. (2009b). 'There is a bit of peace in England': Dialogue and conflict between teenage religious education pupils in Sheffield. In J. Ipgrave, R. Jackson, & K. O'Grady (Eds), *Religious Education research through a community of practice: Action research and the interpretive approach* (pp. 45–55). Münster: Waxmann.

O'Grady, K. (2010). Researching Religious Education pedagogy through an action research community of practice. *British Journal of Religious Education, 32*(2), 119–132.

O'Grady, K. (2011). Is action research a contradiction in terms? Do communities of practice mean the end of educational research as we know it? Some remarks based on one recent example of religious education research. *International Journal of Educational Action Research, 19*(2), 189–200.

Richardson, N. (2010). Book review: *Religious Education research through a community of practice: Action research and the interpretive approach*, edited by Julia Ipgrave, Robert Jackson, & Kevin O'Grady. *British Journal of Religious Education, 32*(3), 331–334.

Skeie, G. (2009). A community of dialogue and conflict? Discussion of community of practice findings in a wider European context. In J. Ipgrave, R. Jackson, & K. O'Grady (Eds), *Religious Education research through a community of practice: Action research and the interpretive approach* (pp. 216–234). Münster: Waxmann.

ter Avest, I., Josza, D. P., Knauth, T., Rosón, J., & Skeie, G. (Eds). (2009). *Dialogue and conflict on religion: Studies of classroom interaction in European countries.* Münster: Waxmann.

Valk, P., Bertram-Troost, G., Friederici, M., & Béraud, C. (Eds). (2009). *Teenagers' perspectives on the role of religion in their lives, schools and societies: A European quantitative study.* Münster: Waxmann.

Van der Want, A., Bakker, C., ter Avest, I., & Everington, J. (Eds). (2009). *Teachers responding to religious diversity in Europe.* Münster: Waxmann.

Weisse, W. (2007). The European research project on religion and education 'REDCo': An introduction. In R. Jackson, S. Miedema, W. Weisse, & J-P. Willaime (Eds), *Religion and education in Europe: Developments, contexts and debates* (pp. 9–25). Münster: Waxmann.

Whittall, A. (2009). Developing appropriate principles and strategies for the teaching of gifted students of religious education. In J. Ipgrave, R. Jackson, & K. O'Grady (Eds), *Religious education research through a community of practice: Action research and the interpretive approach* (pp. 72–83). Münster: Waxmann.

JAN GRAJCZONEK

13 Acknowledging Religious Diversity and Empowering Young Children's Agency and Voice in the Religion Classroom

Abstract

Young children are often denied a voice concerning their thoughts and beliefs regarding religion, particularly in single-faith schools where they are presumed to be, and taught as, believers or members of that particular religion. Contemporary early childhood theory and practice advocates young children's agency and voice. It rejects the notion of the 'universal child', that is, every child as being the same. Children today come from diverse backgrounds and their socio-cultural contexts shape their views and perspectives on all kinds of issues including religious beliefs and practices. This chapter reports on part of a qualitative study conducted in an early years Australian Catholic primary school, wherein all children were constructed through the teacher's classroom interaction, as if they were members of the local faith community. The specific analytic tools of Conversation Analysis and Membership Categorization Analysis afford key insights into how young children are constructed as all belonging to, and sharing, the same religious beliefs.

Introduction

Classroom talk is central to teaching and learning and in constructing children as students (Austin, Dwyer, & Freebody, 2003; Austin, Freebody, & Dwyer, 2001). In the religion classroom it also has the ambiguous potential of constructing young children in specific ways that can both dismiss and deny their individual religious beliefs and practices. This potential exists in single-faith Church-related schools where students are presumed to be, and taught as, believers of that particular faith. Contemporary early childhood theory and practice advocate young children's agency and voice rejecting the notion of the 'universal child', that is, every child as being the same (Arthur, Beecher, Death, Dockett, & Farmer, 2005; Dahlberg, Moss, & Pence, 2007). Children today come from diverse backgrounds; their socio-cultural contexts shape their views and perspectives on all kinds of issues, including religious beliefs and views. Those children who come from religious backgrounds different from the dominant religion of their school can be silenced and denied a voice regarding their religious beliefs and questions about religious content.

This chapter reports on research conducted in early years classrooms in Australian Catholic primary schools, research that investigated the nature of teachers' classroom interaction during their religion classes.

Key themes

The research builds on three bodies of knowledge regarding: the contemporary view of childhood; recognition of children's religious diversity; and the central role of classroom interaction.

The contemporary view of childhood

A critical element and starting point in the teaching and learning process for all teachers is to have a deep and insightful knowledge and understanding of how childhood and children are currently viewed and constructed. Until more recent times, developmental psychology has had significant influence on our understandings of childhood. The starting point for such theory has been with the *universal* child, that is, the *one* child who represents *all* children and develops through a series of stages including physical, cognitive, social and moral. These theories have been advanced by such theorists as Piaget, Kohlberg and Erickson (Arthur et al., 2005). Developmental psychology has also influenced theories regarding the religious development of children, such as proposed by Fowler (1981). However, contemporary views of early childhood challenge this view of universal childhood, suggesting that *the child* in the singular form cannot be representative of *all children*, as each child's experiences of childhood is unique and distinct to a variety of contexts including their social, cultural, political and religious contexts. Further, Dahlberg, Moss, and Pence (2007) argue that such constructions produce a 'poor' image of a child, one which 'is weak and passive, incapable and under-developed, dependent and isolated' rather than a child who is 'rich in potential, strong, powerful, competent and most al all, connected to adults and other children' (Malaguzzi, 1993, cited in Dahlberg, Moss, & Pence, 2007: 48). A contemporary view of childhood accords children as involved and active participants, rather than as passive recipients waiting to be shaped and moulded in particular ways.

Reconceptualized constructions of childhood are emerging from a number of more recent theories and phenomena (Arthur et al., 2005; Soto and Swadener, 2002). Theories that have had significant influence on the reconceptualized views of childhood include: socio-cultural theory (Vygotsky, 1967), which advocates the social nature of learning; bio-ecological theory (Bronfenbrenner, 2005), which emphasizes the many contexts children inhabit, all of which influence their learning; the new sociology of childhood (James & James, 2004; Mayall, 2002), which focuses on the child as an individual and values each child's *being* and *current* experiences of his/her childhood; poststructuralism influenced by the work of Foucault

(1972), which rejects the many theories of structures into which children are placed in order to explain their development, advocating that children should have agency in constructing their own lives; and postmodernity, which argues that the world is complex and ambiguous, and can only be understand at the local level (MacNaughton, 2003). The reconceptualized view of childhood criticizes the universal child construct for its emphasis on progression rather than valuing the present for what it is. In other words, when the focus of childhood as a stage in the life course is on becoming, maturing, wanting, needing and so on, childhood is constructed as a journey toward adulthood, that is, children are constructed as *becoming* rather than *being* (Qvortrup, 1994). It is as if the stage of childhood is not significant in its own right; it is simply a means to an end.

Childhood, then, is not a universal stage experienced in the same way by all children. *The child* is not representative of *all children* who seemingly are passive recipients rather than active agents. A contemporary, reconceptualized view of childhood is understood to be a social construct shaped and influenced by many historical, political, cultural and economic contexts (James & James, 2004; Skelton, 2007). Such criticism has implications for early childhood education in the religion classroom of Church-related schools where, as this chapter will reveal, young children can be constructed as all belonging to the one religious tradition. Early childhood teachers in these schools recognize the diversity of childhoods, and their general classroom practice reflects this deep knowledge and understanding of contemporary views of childhood. However, when it comes to the religion classroom, the same acknowledgement of diversity is not as evident.

Religious diversity

A significant aspect of the reconceptualization of childhood is the focus on the child as agent and participant (Mayall, 2002; Skelton, 2007). Skelton and others connect this focus on participation with the introduction of the *Convention on the Rights of the Child* (CRC) (United Nations, 1989) ratified by the General Assembly of the United Nations on 20 November 1989. Whilst the *CRC* maintained the two previous 'P's (provision and protection) of the 1959 *Declaration of the Rights of the Child*, it introduced a third 'P', participation, which emphasizes participation of children in decisions that affect their own lives (Skelton, 2007: 167). This emphasis on children's participation rights includes their right to participate in their own religious traditions and the right for these religious beliefs to be respected, as explicitly stated in Articles 1, 14 and 29 in the *Convention on the Rights of the Child* (United Nations, 1989). Article 1 requires that children's religious rights be respected without discrimination; Article 14.1 requires that 'State Parties shall respect the right of the child to freedom of thought, conscience and religion' (Article 14, para. 1); and Article 29 concerns the role of education in ensuring that it be directed to the 'development of respect for human rights and fundamental freedoms' (Article 29, para 1.[b]), and further, that the preparation of the child as a responsible citizen, is done 'in the spirit of understanding, peace, tolerance, equality of sexes, and friendship among all peoples, ethnic, national and religious groups and persons of indigenous origin' (Article 29.1.[d]).

The Catholic Church also advocates children's religious freedom. In the document *The Religious Dimension of Education in a Catholic School* (Congregation for Catholic Education, 1988: para. 6), the place of students who are not Catholics in Catholic schools is explicitly outlined:

> Not all students in Catholic schools are members of the Catholic Church; not all are Catholic ... The religious freedom of the personal conscience of individual students and their families must be respected, and this freedom is explicitly recognized by the Church. On the other hand, a Catholic school cannot relinquish its own freedom to proclaim the Gospel and to offer a formation based on the values to be found in a Christian education; this is its right and its duty. To proclaim or to offer is not to impose, however; the latter suggests a moral violence which is strictly forbidden, both by the Gospel and by Church law.

Three key points are to be drawn from this paragraph: first, students who are not Catholics are welcome in Catholic schools; second, their own religious freedom and personal conscience, in other words their religious beliefs, principles and practices, are to be respected; and third, the Catholic religion is not to be imposed on them. It is to be noted here that the words 'proclaim the Gospel' is evangelization, not indoctrination or imposition of religious beliefs and practices. It is important that Catholic schools' administrators, teachers and all connected to the schools are fully cognizant of this particular paragraph and its implications for both the religion curriculum and religious life of the school.

It is clear, then, that both the United Nations and the Catholic Church recognize and uphold children's rights to religious freedom. Furthermore, education in both the public and Catholic arenas plays two significant roles. First, it is to ensure that all children's religious rights be respected without discrimination, and second it is to ensure that children themselves be taught to respect the religious freedom of others.

Classroom interaction

Talk is the key mode of delivery in all classrooms. 'Talk is a tool that shapes classroom thinking. It is the major resource that teachers draw upon to shape any episode into a learning experience. It is the main mechanism by which the curriculum is delivered and negotiated' (Edwards-Groves, 2003: 15). Lessons are accomplished in and through classroom talk and teachers can learn much about classroom practice by studying classroom interaction (Freebody, 2003). This argument is emphasized by Mehan (1979: 6): 'Because educational facts are constituted in interaction, we need to study interaction in educational contexts.' Significant insights regarding the nature and construction of classroom practice have been made by investigating classroom talk. Such insights include how lessons are structured (Mehan, 1978, 1979), how students learn and show what they have learnt in terms of content knowledge (Edwards & Westgate, 1994), and how students learn to become students (Austin et al., 2003; Austin & Freebody, 2001). If teachers come to understand and appreciate the fundamental nature of their classroom interaction with students, they will gain significant insights, not only into their own teaching but also into how they construct their students and for what they hold them accountable.

Method

Procedure

The following presents one aspect of a study that investigated teachers' classroom interaction in their religion lessons (Grajczonek, 2006). It reveals how young children are constructed *in* and *through* classroom talk, as first belonging to the same religious tradition, and second, held accountable for their religious practices rather than for what they learnt in the lesson. The classroom interaction was recorded during a religious education lesson in an Australian Catholic preschool. This class was comprised of one teacher and approximately twenty-five four- and five-year-old students and was held on the first day following the ten-day Easter vacation. The students and the teacher were sitting in a circle and in the centre was a prayer cloth. The focus of the lesson was the religious symbols of Easter. During the lesson, as the teacher introduced each symbol of Easter, she placed it into the middle of the circle. These symbols included a small loaf of bread, a goblet of wine, a cross, an egg and a chicken. To the side of this circle was an incubator which had been brought into the preschool so that students could observe the hatching of eggs over the following weeks.

Analysis

The recorded classroom talk was transcribed using transcript notation based on Atkinson and Heritage's (1984: ix–xvi) notation (see Appendix). An initial analysis was made using Conversation Analysis (CA) which locates meaning in talk-in-interaction (Freebody, 2003; Heritage, 2004). CA is an analytic tool employed within Ethnomethodology (EM) (Garfinkel, 1967, 1984). EM is an interpretive methodology that seeks to interpret members' everyday activities *in situ* and *in vivo*, that is, in the place of the event as it is happening. By analysing teachers' questions, emphases, lexical choices, responses to students' answers, as well as the students' subsequent replies, other interruptions and such like, the constitutive nature of the classroom teaching of religion can be revealed. CA reveals what is done *in* and *through* the talk (Schegloff & Sacks, 1973) and affords key insights into the realities of how institutions are invoked. Heritage (1984: 290) argued that it is only in locally produced sequences of talk that 'these institutions are ultimately and accountably talked into being'. In other words, we can gain key insights, not only into the institution of the classroom but also into how classroom talk actually constitutes the institution of the classroom.

Together with CA, a second Ethnomethodological method, Member Categorization Analysis (MCA) was applied. MCA affords further insights into how knowledge is organized in interaction and texts (ten Have, 2004) in terms of Categories and the Category Bound Activities which include characteristics, attributes, rights, obligations and so on (Baker, 2004; Freebody, 2003), assigned to those Categories by speakers and writers (Sacks, 1992). By analyzing sequences of talk in terms of the specific category students and their assigned Category Bound Activities raised in teachers' classroom talk, a closer examination of how students are constructed is facilitated (Freebody, 2003).

A further key aspect of MCA is to note how Categories (in this case, students) are cohorted. Classroom talk establishes various groupings or cohorts who participate in the talk within a classroom (Freebody, 2003: 109; Sacks, Schegloff, & Jefferson, 1974: 712–713). During classroom inter-action, teachers establish three different cohorts:

- students constructed as individuals, indicated by their name or the singular use of the pronouns 'you' and 'your';
- all students constructed collectively as a single cohort that excludes the teacher, indicated by the plural form of 'you' and 'your'; and
- one that places all students, the teacher and the school as a single cohort, indicated by the pronouns 'we', 'us' and 'our' (Austin et al., 2003; Freebody, 2003; Freebody and Herschell, 2000). (Please note the explanations for the symbols used throughout these excerpts are available in the appendix.)

In other words, then, by placing all students into the same cohort through the use of the plural form of 'you' and assigning certain attributes or characteristics to this cohort, such as including all of them in the activity of 'praying at home', the teacher constructs all students as being religious in a particular way. In this construction, students' individual or actual ways of being religious or otherwise may be dismissed.

Analysis and findings

The first interactional excerpt of interest occurred at the beginning of the lesson after the teacher had placed bread, wine and a cross into the centre of the circle. This excerpt occurs at turn 19 of the interaction just as the teacher explained that the class was going to learn to make the sign of the cross during the school term. At this point the teacher placed an egg and a baby chicken into the circle.

Table 1: *Interactional sequence 1: Turns 19–28*

19.	Teacher:	= to ↑pra::ctise making the si:gn of the cross. So you can follow the numbers to ↑pra::ctise making the sign of the cross. So we can add the cross to our prayer circle. It's a very important symbol for our church. And I've got two (teacher places an egg and a baby chicken into the middle of the circle onto the prayer cloth.) °↑Wh::y do you think I would put (0.3) an egg and a BABY ↑CHICKEN into our pra:yer ci:rcle? ↑Yasmin?
20.	Yasmin:	New life?
21.	Teacher:	Because (0.1) they (0.1) rem:ind us of ↓n::ew (0.2) li::fe. (0.3) ↑Why >new life?< Why are we talking about (0.1) new life?
22.	Student:	Because they ( )
		[
23.	Teacher:	Cindy
24.	Cindy:	Because um ( )
25.	Teacher:	↑Who had new life?
26.	Student:	Jesus.
27.	Teacher:	And did you think of that on Easter Sunday ↓morning?
28.	Students:	Yeah.

In terms of the construction of students as all belonging to the same religion, the first indication of this occurred in the second part of turn 19 (Table 1) when the teacher explained:

19. Teacher: So we can add the cross to our prayer circle. It's a very important symbol for our church.

Note the word used by the teacher to qualify church was '*our* church'. At turn 19 by inserting the personal pronoun 'our' in front of 'church', the teacher has established a cohort that includes all students, herself as the teacher and the school as one single cohort belonging to the institution of the Catholic Church. This particular construction of the cohort does not recognize individual children's religious affiliations and beliefs. This was shown by the teacher's lexical choice 'our', the use of which constructed her and all students as agreeing with the presumption that all share the same religious beliefs, that is, Catholic and that the cross is a significant religious symbol for all of them. The use of the lexical choice 'our' in this particular example indicates that the teacher is speaking not only on behalf of the institution of the Catholic Church (Drew & Heritage, 1992) but also on behalf of the students who, as members of the school, are implied members together with herself of the wider institution of the Catholic Church.

Table 2: *Interactional sequence 2: Turns 27–29*

27.	Teacher:	And did you <u>think</u> of <u>that</u> on Easter Sunday ↓morning?
28.	Students:	Yeah.
29.	Teacher:	↑Because (0.1) preschoolers (0.1) on Easter Sunday morning remember that Easter Bunny – he's such a clever thing that Easter Bunny – >I better not put that chicken in there, hey?< He might walk away. I'll put him back in here. (Teacher places chicken back into incubator.) Preschoolers (0.2) when you got those eggs on Easter Sunday ↓morning (0.3) °it wa:s to rem::ind you of <u>Jesus' new life</u>°.

The second instance of a similar construction occurred at turns 27 and 29, as shown in Table 2.

In this construction, the teacher through her lexical choice of 'you' has established all students collectively as a single cohort, which excludes herself as the teacher. By implication she is suggesting that she herself did think about Jesus' new life on Easter Sunday morning and further, through her emphasis on the two words 'think' and 'that' at turn 27, that the students also should have thought about Jesus' new life on Easter Sunday morning. With this question, students were held accountable for their own personal thoughts and attitudes in their homes, rather than being held accountable for an educational aim, knowing that Easter is a time when Christians think about Jesus' new life.

The teacher again emphasized this point at turn 29 when she repeated, 'Preschoolers (0.2) when you got those eggs on Easter Sunday ↓morning (0.3) °it wa:s to rem::ind you of Jesus' new life°'. Three key points are made available in this final sentence: first, the pause after the word 'preschoolers' indicates that an emphasis was placed on the children's roles in this matter; second, the stretching of the words 'was' and 'remind' emphasized the role the eggs played; and third, the underlining of the words 'Jesus' new life' which were said with greater emphasis than other words indicates what students should have been thinking about. All students, then, are required *in* and *through* this talk to regard Easter as a religious time when they should have thought about Jesus' new life, as the teacher herself did.

The lesson continued with the teacher reading a Gospel passage and then concluded with prayer. The usual practice for class prayer in this setting is that students may opt not to pray and indicate this by tapping the shoulder of the person next to them. It is to be remembered that this lesson took place on the first day at school after the ten-day Easter vacation, which might have been the reason why very few students chose to say a prayer, a point on which the teacher commented as shown in Table 3.

Table 3: *Interactional sequence 3: Turns 72–74*

72.	Teacher:	°You've probably just forgotten how to pray. Did you remember to pray over Easter time <u>too</u>?°
73.	Students:	Na. Yes. No.
74.	Teacher:	Did you remember that? ↑It's not just at this time we pray.

In this small interaction, we note the establishment of two specific cohorts, one that did not include the teacher (as indicated by her lexical choice 'you') and the second in which the teacher did include herself (as indicated by 'we'). In her first statement at turn 72 the teacher suggested that students had not prayed during this prayer time because they had forgotten how to pray because of the Easter break:

> 72. Teacher: °You've probably just forgotten how to pray.

She then, at turn 74, immediately added:

> 74. Teacher: Did you remember to pray over Easter time <u>too</u>? °

Further, in asking students if they remembered to pray over Easter time, and placing the emphasis on the word 'too' (indicated by the underlining), she has held students accountable for their religious practices at home. By implication she has also held children's families accountable.

The second cohort, which includes all students and herself as one cohort, is established by the teacher in the second part of turn 74 with her lexical choice of 'we':

> 74. Teacher: Did you remember that? ↑<u>It's not just at this time we pray.</u>

As members of this one cohort, the teacher indicated that they should not only pray in class, but also pray at home. Again, the use of the lexical choice 'we' indicated that everyone was presumed to belong to the institution of the Catholic Church, and as such should adhere to the religious practice of praying at home.

Another point worth noting in the above sequence at turns 72 to 74 concerns for what students were held accountable in the lesson. In this concluding section of the lesson, students' religious literacy was not the subject of interrogation. At no point during the conclusion of this lesson was a revision of the religious symbols associated with Easter made to synthesize and reinforce key teaching points. Students were not asked as part of the lesson's conclusion about the symbols and their meanings. Rather, they had been interrogated and held accountable for their personal faith lives and religious practices which, in this case, included praying at home as well as at school.

Discussion

In this religion lesson, children were constructed *in* and *through* the teacher's interaction as all belonging to the Catholic faith, and further, were held accountable for the ways in which it was perceived that they should be living out that faith at home. In the first instance, it was the teacher's use of cohorting language that dismissed and indeed denied children's agency and voice regarding their personal religious beliefs and practices in the lesson. Students were placed into two distinct cohorts. The first cohort, indicated by the lexical choice of 'you', included all of them as belonging to the Catholic religion but not living out the religious practices required by that religion. In these particular constructions it was implied that the teacher was part of the same religion, but unlike the students, did follow the religious practices, which included thinking about Jesus' new life on Easter Sunday and remembering to pray over Easter. In these constructions the teacher used homiletic language rather than academic language more appropriate to the classroom (Moran, 1989, 1997).

The second cohort, indicated by the lexical choices of 'our church' and 'we pray', constructed children together with the teacher and everyone in the school as all belonging to the Catholic religion. When used in such ways, cohorting language is described as *presumptive* language, meaning that presumptions have been made regarding students' faith or religious lives (Crawford & Rossiter, 1988; Doulin et al., 1987). Using such language does not acknowledge students' individual religious affiliations, beliefs and practices, including those who have no religious affiliations. It not only denies their individual religious beliefs or otherwise, but it also discriminates on the basis of religious tolerance and seeks to impose a particular religious belief. Such actions directly disregard the directives of both the

Convention of the Rights of the Child (United Nations, 1989: Articles 1, 14 & 29) and *The Religious Dimension of Education in a Catholic School* (Congregation for Catholic Education, 1988: para. 6).

In these constructions, the young children in this class have been constructed as all being Catholic. Such constructions disregard the contemporary view of childhood. The students have been constructed as *becoming* rather than *being* (Qvortrup, 1994; Soto & Swadener, 2002) and both their socio-cultural (Vygotsky, 1967) and bio-ecological contexts (Bronfenbrenner, 2005) have been dismissed. Throughout the classroom interaction these young children had no opportunity to exercise agency (Dahlberg et al., 2007; Macfarlane & Cartmel, 2008; Malaguzzi, 1993; Mayall, 2002; Soto & Swadener, 2002) concerning their own religious beliefs or otherwise, nor had the opportunity to voice any resistance to how they had been judged in terms of their religious practices outside of school.

Conclusion

Classroom talk is central to classroom practice. However, it can achieve much more in terms of the ways young children are constructed and for what they are held accountable. Whilst it is acceptable classroom practice to cohort students in referring to experiences or activities that have been shared by everyone including the teacher, and to hold the student cohort accountable for the knowledge and understanding of the content of the lesson, it is not acceptable to cohort students in ways that imply they all share the same religious beliefs and practices. Nor is it acceptable that students be categorized as members of the one same religion as the school's affiliation, and then be required to adhere to those particular religious beliefs and practices. It is important that teachers become aware of the significant role their classroom interaction occupies in the religion classroom. The nature of this talk can potentially deny or silence student agency and voice. Teachers understand and are conscious of their own roles in respecting children's rights, which includes their rights to religious freedom. However, as revealed in this small study, they may not be as conscious of the key role their classroom talk plays in this matter. It is essential that teachers are not only conscious of students' religious diversity, but also conscious of the nature of their classroom talk which might deny or dismiss students' religious beliefs.

References

Arthur, L., Beecher, B., Death, E., Dockett, S., & Farmer, S. (2005). *Programming and planning in the early childhood settings* (6th edn). Southbank: Thomson.

Atkinson, J. M., & Heritage, J. (1984). Transcript notation. In J. M. Atkinson & J. Heritage (Eds), *Structures of social action: Studies in conversation analysis* (pp. ix–xvi). Cambridge: Press Syndicate of University of Cambridge.

Austin, H., Dwyer, B., & Freebody, P. (2003). *Schooling the child: The making of students in classrooms.* London: RoutledgeFarmer.

Austin, H., & Freebody, P. (2001). Assembling and assessing the 'child-student': The 'child' as a criterion of assessment. *Journal of Curriculum Studies, 33*(5), 535–550.

Austin, H., Freebody, P., & Dwyer, B. (2001). Methodological issues in analysing talk and text: The case of childhood in and for school. In A. McHoul & M. Rapley (Eds), *How to analyse talk in institutional settings: A casebook of methods* (pp. 183–195). London: Continuum.

Baker, C. (2004). Membership categorization and interview accounts. In D. Silverman (Ed.), *Qualitative research: Theory, method and practice* (pp. 162–176). London: Sage.

Bronfenbrenner, U. (Ed.). (2005). *Making human beings human: Bioecological perspectives on human development.* Thousand Oaks, CA: Sage Publications.

Congregation for Catholic Education. (1988). *The religious dimension of education in a Catholic school.* Homebush: St Paul Publications.

Crawford, M., & Rossiter, G. (1988). *Missionaries to a teenage culture: Religious education in a time of rapid change.* Sydney: Christian Brothers Province Resource Group.

Dahlberg, G., Moss, P., & Pence, A. (2007). *Beyond quality in early childhood education and care: Languages of evaluation* (2nd edn). London: Routledge.

Doulin, P., Kelly, G., Lawson, E., Monro, J., Monro, T., Mavor, I., et al. (1987). *Religious education teaching approaches.* Brisbane: Curriculum Services Branch, Department of Education, Queensland.

Drew, P., & Heritage, J. (1992). Analyzing talk at work: An introduction. In P. Drew & J. Heritage (Eds), *Talk at work: Interaction in institutional settings* (pp. 3–65). Melbourne: Cambridge University Press.

Edwards, A. D., & Westgate, D. P. G. (1994). *Investigating classroom talk.* London: The Falmer Press.

Edwards-Groves, C. (2003). *On task: Focused literacy learning.* Newtown: Primary English Teaching Association.

Foucault, M. (1972). *The archaeology of knowledge.* London: Tavistock.

Fowler, J. (1981). *Stages of faith: The psychology of human development and the quest for meaning.* Blackburn: Dove Communications.

Freebody, P. (2003). *Qualitative research in education: Interaction and practice.* London: SAGE Publications.

Freebody, P., & Herschell, P. (2000). The interactive assembly of social identity: The case of latitude in classroom talk. *International Journal of Inclusive Education, 4*(1), 43–61.

Garfinkel, H. (1967). *Studies in ethnomethodology.* Englewood Cliffs, NJ: Prentice Hall.

Garfinkel, H. (1984). *Studies in ethnomethodology.* Cambridge: Polity Press.

Grajczonek, J. (2006). *'Wot's in a string o' words?': An ethnomethodological study investigating the approach to, and construction of, the classroom religion program in the Catholic preschool.* Unpublished EdD, Griffith University, Brisbane.

Heritage, J. (1984). *Garfinkel and ethnomethodology.* Cambridge: Polity Press.

Heritage, J. (2004). Conversation analysis and institutional talk: Analyzing data. In D. Silverman (Ed.), *Qualitative research: Theory, method and practice* (pp. 222–245). (2nd edn). London: Sage.

James, A., & James, A. L. (2004). *Constructing childhood: Theory, policy and social practice.* Basingstoke: Palgrave MacMillan.

Macfarlane, K., & Cartmel, J. (2008). Playgrounds of learning: Valuing competence and agency in birth to three-year-olds. *Australian Journal of Early Childhood, 33*(2), 41–47.

MacNaughton, G. (2003). *Shaping early childhood: Learners, curriculum and context.* Buckingham: Open University Press.

Malaguzzi, L. (1993). For an education based on relationships. *Young Children, 49*(1), 9–12.

Mayall, B. (2002). *Towards a sociology for childhood: Thinking from children's lives.* Buckingham: Open University Press.

Mehan, H. (1978). Structuring school structure. *Harvard Educational Review, 48*(1), 32–64.

Mehan, H. (1979). *Learning lessons: Social organization in the classroom.* London: Harvard University Press.

Moran, G. (1989). *Religious education as a second language.* Birmingham, AL: Religious Education Press.

Moran, G. (1997). *Showing how: The act of teaching.* Valley Forge, PA: Trinity Press International.

Qvortrup, J. (1994). *Childhood matters: Social theory, practice, and politics.* Aldershot: Avebury.

Sacks, H. (1992). *Lectures on conversation: Volumes I & II.* G. Jefferson (Ed.). Oxford: Blackwell Publishers.

Sacks, H., Schegloff, E. A., & Jefferson, G. (1974). A simplest systematics for the organization of turn-taking for conversation. *Language, 50*(4), 696–735.

Schegloff, E. A., & Sacks, H. (1973). Opening up closings. *Semiotica, 7*, 289–327.

Skelton, T. (2007). Children, young people, UNICEF and participation. *Children's Geographies, 5*(1–2), 165–181.

Soto, L. D., & Swadener, B. B. (2002). Toward liberatory early childhood theory, research and praxis: Decolonizing a field. *Contemporary Issues in Early Childhood, 3*(1), 38–66.

ten Have, P. (2004). *Understanding qualitative research and ethnomethodology.* London: Sage Publications.

United Nations. (1989). Convention on the Rights of the Child. Retrieved March 8, 2012, from http://www2.ohchr.org/english/law/pdf/crc.pdf

Vygotsky, L. (1967). *Mind in society: The development of higher psychological processes.* Cambridge, MA: Harvard University Press.

Appendix: Transcription Notation

The transcript notation used in this study is based on Atkinson and Heritage (1984: ix–xvi). Following is an explanation of the symbols used to notate the classroom interaction in the lesson.

[[	Simultaneous utterances – Double left-hand brackets indicate where utterances start simultaneously.
[	Overlapping utterances – Single left-hand brackets are used to show when overlapping utterances do not start simultaneously at the point where an ongoing utterance is joined by another.
]	Overlapping utterances cease shown by single right-hand bracket.
=	Contiguous utterances indicated by equal signs indicate where there is no interval between adjacent utterances, the second being latched immediately to the first (without overlapping it).
(0.0)	Intervals within utterances indicated by numerals in brackets timed in tenths of a second.
co::lons	Colons indicate an extension of the sound or syllable it follows. More colons prolong the stretch.
↑↓	Upward and downward pointing arrows indicate rising and falling shifts in intonation.
Underlining	Underlining indicates emphasis
CAPITALS	Capital letters indicate an utterance, or part thereof, that is spoken much louder than the surrounding talk.
° °	Degree signs indicate a passage of talk that is quieter than the surrounding talk.
( )	Single parentheses indicate that what is enclosed is in doubt. If they are empty, no hearing could be achieved for the talk.
> <	Greater than and less than signs enclose talk that is noticeably faster than the surrounding talk.

Notes on Contributors

JEFF ASTLEY is Honorary Professorial Fellow in Practical Theology and Christian Education at Durham University, UK, and an Anglican priest. For over thirty years he has been the Director of the ecumenical North of England Institute for Christian Education. He is the author or editor of over thirty-five books on Christian education, practical theology or religious faith, including *The Philosophy of Christian Religious Education*, *Theological Perspectives on Christian Formation*, *Ordinary Theology*, *Exploring God-Talk*, the *SCM Studyguide to Christian Doctrine* and *Teaching Religion, Teaching Truth* (also published with Peter Lang).

LORNA M. A. BOWMAN, EdD (Columbia University) is Professor of Religious Studies and former Academic Dean, Brescia University College at The University of Western Ontario, London, Ontario, Canada. She is past president of the Association of Professors & Researchers in Religious Education and of the Religious Education Association. Her research interests include the history of women, religion and education and Catholic education in Canada including an educational biography of Gerald Emmett Carter in the Christian Educators of the 20th Century Project.

MARIO O. D'SOUZA, CSB, is a Roman Catholic priest and a member of the Congregation of St Basil. He is Dean of Theology at the University of St Michael's College, Toronto, where he also holds the Basilian Fathers Chair in Religion and Education. He is an associate member of the School of Graduate Studies of the University of Toronto and cross-appointed to the School of Theory and Policy Studies at the Ontario Institute for Studies in Education. He has earned degrees from University College, Dublin; the University of Calgary; the University of Toronto; the University of St Michael's College; and Boston College. He teaches in the area of religion and education. His primary area of research is the philosophy of education. Other research areas include the philosophy of Jacques Maritain and Bernard Lonergan, Catholic educational theory, person and personalism, pluralism and religious identity, and hermeneutics and education.

PETRO DU PREEZ is an Associate Professor at the North West University (Potchefstroom) in South Africa. She obtained her PhD from the University of Stellenbosch in 2008. Her research foci include curriculum studies and human rights for diverse education environments. Petro's research involvement includes national and international projects and publications. She has delivered several papers and published widely on the topics of human rights in education for multicultural and multi-religious environments.

DR RENÉ FERGUSON is a full time lecturer and researcher in the School of Education at the University of the Witwatersrand in Johannesburg, South Africa. She teaches religion education, human rights and democratic citizenship education to primary, secondary and post-graduate certificate teacher education students. Her research interests focus on pre-service and in-service teacher development for diversity, democracy and human rights education, as well as on the place of African Independent Churches and African Traditional religions in religion education classroom practice in the South African context.

LESLIE J. FRANCIS is Professor of Religions and Education within the University of Warwick Religions and Education Research Unit, UK, and Canon Theologian of Bangor Cathedral, Wales. He obtained his PhD from the University of Cambridge in 1976. His published works have been recognized by three higher doctorates: ScD from Cambridge in 1997, DD from Oxford in 2001 and DLitt from University of Wales, Bangor in 2007. His research in Religious Education has been shaped by creative links with practical and empirical theology and with the individual differences approach to psychology.

DR ROB FREATHY is Director of Taught Programmes for the College of Social Sciences and International Studies and Director of Education for the Graduate School of Education at the University of Exeter. His research interests include Religious Education, education for citizenship, the historiography of twentieth-century education and the application of historical methods in educational research. He is the Book Reviews Editor of *History of Education* and a member of the History of Education Society (UK) Executive Committee. He has published articles in *History of Education*, *History of Education Researcher*, *Oxford Review of Education*, *Religious Education* (USA), *British Journal of Religious Education* and *Journal of Beliefs and Values*.

BRIAN GATES, Emeritus Professor of Religious and Moral Education at the University of Cumbria, studied at the universities of Oxford, Cambridge and Yale, principally in the fields of Theology, Social Ethics and Education. His subsequent doctoral research on children's religious and moral development was at Lancaster University. He was Principal Lecturer in Religion at University of London, Goldsmiths College, before becoming Head of Department of Religion and Ethics at St Martin's College Lancaster (later the University of Cumbria). From 1973 he has been closely associated with the Religious Education Council of England & Wales, latterly as chair. He has been a member of the Journal of Moral Education Editorial Board since 1985, Chair of the Board and Trust (1999–2006) and is an ongoing Trustee. His publications include *Transforming Religious Education: Beliefs and values under scrutiny* and 'Religion as cuckoo or crucible: Beliefs and believing as vital for citizenship and citizenship education', in the Special Issue of the *Journal of Moral Education 35*(4), which he edited.

PETA GOLDBURG is Professor of Religious Education and Head of the School of Religious Education at Australian Catholic University. She is national president of the Australian Association of Religious Education and recently was appointed to the advisory panel for Civics and Citizenship for the Australian Curriculum, Assessment and Reporting Authority (ACARA). Peta's area of research is focused on Jewish-Christian relations and religion and film.

DR JAN GRAJCZONEK is a senior lecturer in the National School of Religious Education at the Australian Catholic University. She has published several books and scholarly articles in the area of early childhood Religious Education in pre-school and school settings. Her specific areas of research explore the image and construction of the child and childhood in the ever-increasing pluralist contexts of religiously affiliated child care centres and schools and the consequences these might have for the religion program. She also has a great interest in the role of children's literature in Religious Education.

DZINTRA ILIŠKO is an Associate Professor and Head of the Institute of Sustainable Education which is at Daugvapils University, Latvia. She is the head of the Institute of Sustainable Education. Her research interests are education for sustainable development, teachers as researchers, and inclusive Religious Education. She is a member of a number of international networks, including the International Seminar on Religious Education and Values (ISREV), European Society of Women in Theological Research (ESWTR) and the Baltic and Black Sea Consortium in Educational Research (BBCC).

KARIN NORDSTRÖM is Senior Lecturer in Religious Studies at the School of Education and Communication, Jönköping University. She has a PhD from Lund University. Her thesis, which was defended 2009, is an ethical study of autonomy and moral education, dealing with pedagogic and philosophic aspects of autonomy as a goal of moral education. She is also involved in an EU research project on ethical questions related to individualized health promotion.

KEVIN O'GRADY studied at the universities of Lancaster (BA Religious Studies 1985, PGCE Religious Education [St Martin's College Lancaster] 1986) and Warwick (MA distinction Religious Education 2002, PhD 2007). He has over twenty-five years' experience of leading Religious Education in secondary schools. His research interests are Religious Education pedagogy; action research; Religious Education and adolescents' needs; Religious Education, creativity and the arts; Religious Education, intercultural education and citizenship education. Kevin was a member of the EC-funded project Religion in Education: A contributor to dialogue or a factor of conflict in transforming societies of European countries? (REDCo, 2006–2009) and acted as a research co-ordinator for the Warwick REDCo community of practice, a collegial group that used action research to investigate the uses of the interpretive approach in different settings. He is an Associate Fellow of the Warwick Religions and Education Research Unit.

DR STEPHEN PARKER is Head of Postgraduate Studies and Research Degrees Coordinator at the Institute of Education, University of Worcester, UK. His research interests include the cultural, political and ideological history of Religious Education, Religious Education in the broadcast media, the lives of Religious Education teachers and the effects of Religious Education on students' values and worldviews. He is a Fellow of the Royal Historical Society, a member of the History of Education Society (UK) Executive Committee, and Book Reviews Editor for the *Journal of Beliefs & Values*. He has published articles in the *Journal of Beliefs & Values*, *History of Education*, *British Journal of Religious Education* and *Midland History*.

DR MANFRED L. PIRNER is Ordinary Professor of Religious Education at the Friedrich-Alexander-University in Erlangen-Nuremberg, Germany. His research interests include popular culture and Christian theology, Religious Education and media education, theology of education, religious schools, inter-religious learning, and human rights education. He is co-editor of *Theo-Web. Academic Journal of Religious Education* (www.theo-web.de) and chairman of the German Academic Society of Religious Education. He has published numerous books and articles in a wide range of topics related to Religious Education, some of them in English (see http://www. manfred-pirner.de).

JULIAN STERN is General Secretary of ISREV and Professor of Education and Religion, and Dean of the Faculty of Education & Theology, at York St John University (http://www.yorksj.ac.uk), having previously worked as a schoolteacher and as an academic in the Institute of Education, London, the Open University, Brunel University, and the University of Hull. He has published widely on Religious Education, spirituality, and general education issues.

Index of Names

Index of Subjects

Tables are indicated by page numbers in **bold**.

Religion, Education and Values

Debates about religion, education and values are more central to contemporary society than ever before. The challenges posed by the interaction between these different spheres will continue to increase as the effects of globalization and cultural pluralization impact on educational settings. Our radically changed and rapidly changing environment poses critical questions about how we should educate individuals to live in increasingly diverse societies.

Books in this series offer the most recent research, from a variety of disciplinary perspectives, on the interface between religion, education and values around the world. The series covers such themes as the history of religious education, the philosophies and psychologies of religious and values education, and the application of social science research methods to the study of young people's values and world-views.

Books within the series are subject to peer review and include single and co-authored monographs and edited collections. Proposals should be sent to any or all of the series editors:

Dr Stephen Parker (s.parker@worc.ac.uk)
The Rev'd Canon Professor Leslie J. Francis (Leslie.Francis@warwick.ac.uk)
Dr Rob Freathy (r.j.k.freathy@ex.ac.uk)
Dr Mandy Robbins (mandy.robbins@glyndwr.ac.uk)

Vol. 2   Stephen Parker, Rob Freathy and Leslie J. Francis (eds):
Religious Education and Freedom of Religion and Belief.
286 pages. 2012. ISBN 978-3-0343-0754-3